THE VANISHING CONGRESS

NORTH AMERICAN INTERNATIONAL
Publishers of Quality Books from Around the World

P.O. Box 28278 Central Station Washington, D.C. 20005

The Vanishing Congress

WHERE HAS ALL THE POWER GONE?

By David J. Muchow

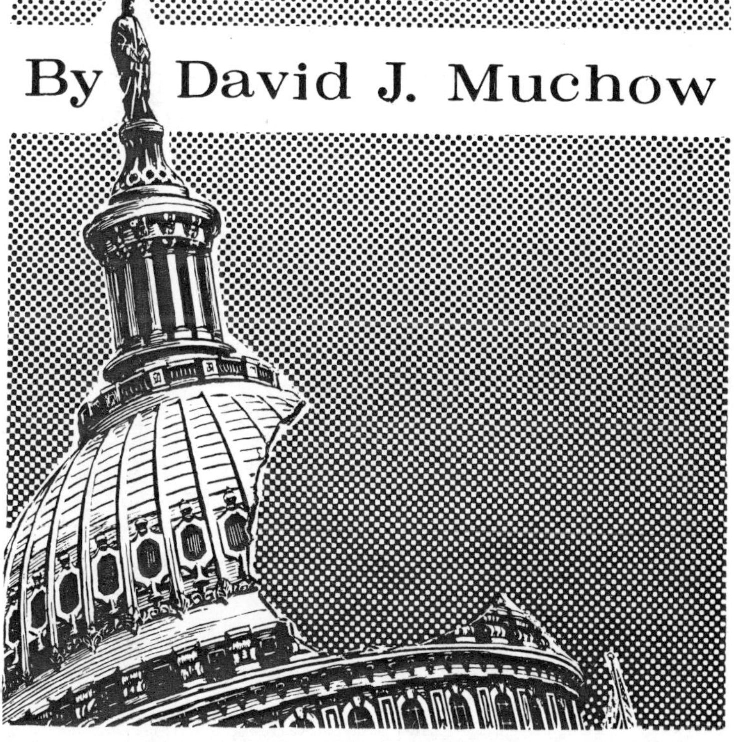

Acknowledgments

Many people deserve thanks for their help with this book. Certainly my dear wife, Marilee and my daughter Heather must come first. They very patiently put up with me while I worked on it.

Mr. R. Elmo Hood of Winter Haven, Florida, and Congressman James A. Haley who made it possible for me to come to Washington, D.C. many years ago deserve special thanks. And I owe thanks to Judy Wilcox and Sandy Metcalf who so ably assisted with translating my scribbles into typed drafts.

International Standard Book Number 0–88265–005–X
Library of Congress Card Number 76–39610
Printed in the United States of America

DEDICATED

To
My Mother

Table of Contents

PART TWO: How the President Moves Legislation

PART THREE: The Constitutional Basis

DIRECTORY OF CHARTS AND EXHIBITS

CHARTS:

EXHIBITS:

PART ONE: Almost Everything You Wished To Know About The Sources of Legislation But Didn't Know Whom To Ask

You show your badge to the White House policeman, nod, and walk down the imposing corridor in the ornate old Executive Office Building, a massive gloomy gray Victorian-era structure just across a private street from the White House. You turn the corner at the end of the hall, and there, on the ground floor, is The Room: one floor above the bowling alley, one floor beneath the President's hideaway office. You go in, and you are glad to find that there is someone in that room at all times. There ought to be.

Over against one wall you see it: a small table with a curved wooden strip on top. There's a clamp to hold the fountain pen—just an ordinary pen, but not quite. It's the Presidential auto-pen. It can sign the President's name to anything and it can write off almost anyone, including senators and congressmen. If you're a senator trying to bust your pet bill out of the clutches of the Administration, you know what that pen can do.

Over the years, political scientists and others have concentrated on the congressional side of legislation. But since the time of Franklin D. Roosevelt, there has been far greater interest in the legislative process that takes place within the Executive Branch.

Numerous political science texts describe how a bill moves through Congress. But few, if any, have looked at the legislative process within the Executive Branch in any detailed fashion. This book, however, attempts to do just that. It highlights some of the more important aspects of the President's legislative powers. It includes a look at the sources of these powers in the Constitution, in statutes and in other places. And it seeks to describe, step-by-step, how legislation is handled in the Executive Branch—from the various agencies to the President's Oval Office.

But this is not just the story of legally and purposefully used power; it is also the story of powers assembled without specific intention or plan. In some cases Congress gave the President powers he did not seek. In other cases, the President seized powers and got away with it. Over the years, the President's legislative powers have grown so strong his legislative initiatives are daily facts of life.In the early days of this century, Woodrow Wilson wrote about "Congressional Government." Today, with the Vietnam, Cambodian and Watergate abuses of power a very recent memory, many can be heard decrying Presidential Government. The pendulum swings; the goal of this book is to show where we are now—not by the theoretical organizational and flow charts of political science, but by an examination of how things actually work.

The Constitution says that "All legislative Powers herein granted shall be vested in a Congress of the United States..." These are the first words in the Constitution after the Preamble, and they are important words. With them, the Founding Fathers clearly put the Congress in charge of legislation. But things have changed.

Today, the President's legislative powers have grown so vast that we can only touch on the surface of them, even in a book-length study. Clearly the President has seized a major role from Congress as the Nation's chief legislator: there may well be more Executive Branch employees directly or indirectly working on legislation than there are employees (with all their various duties) of both houses of Congress combined. Sometimes it appears that the President's "legislative powers" are legally unbounded, and are limited only by what the President "can't get away with" politically. Alternately, it may seem that the ways in which these powers can be exercised are limited only by the limits of imagination. Indeed, much of the President's power over legislation is actually exercised in secret, making an analysis of these powers doubly difficult. But it is worth the effort.

"The Founders of this Nation entrusted the lawmaking power to the Congress alone in both good and bad times. It would do no good to recall the historical events, the fears of power and the hopes for freedom that lay behind their choice." —Mr. Justice Black in *Youngstown Sheet and Tube Co. v. Sawyer,* 343 U.S. 579, 589 (1952).

The Legislative process does different things to different people. Take for example the former Chairman of the House of Representatives' Rules Committee, Rep. Howard W. Smith of Virginia. They called him "Judge" from his earlier days as a judge. He used to get so fed up with President John F. Kennedy's liberal bills, such as for the Peace Corps and civil rights, that he'd send his staff home, lock the doors to the Rules Committee on the third floor of the Capitol, and go home to Virginia "to paint his barn." At least that's what he said he was doing. He'd "paint his barn" and "paint his barn" until "them liberals gave up." Whether he really did any painting doesn't matter. But what he did to legislation will be long remembered.

One day, after weeks of fierce debate on the Civil Rights Bill of 1965, Judge Smith walked slowly from the Rules Committee room to the elevator outside the House Press Gallery. Smith seemed more bent over than usual, and his advanced age showed with every step as he shuffled down the dim and deserted hall. Just a few hours before, the corridor had been filled with bright lights and T.V. cameras when the Civil Rights Bill had been voted out of the Rules Committee for consideration by the entire House of Representatives. The Committee had defied its chairman, and so Judge Smith had lost the biggest poltical battle of his life.

"Come here, son," he said to the young elevator operator. "I want to show you something." The startled elevator operator replied "Yes, Judge," and followed the congressman into the Rules Committee chambers, past the green felt-topped Committee table and beneath the massive chandelier that dominated the room. "Come back into my private office," said the "Judge" as he went through another door. "See that," he said, pointing a trembling finger toward a magnificently framed document on the wall in his office. The elevator operator moved closer to see it. "That," said the "Judge," in the softest, most sorrowful voice imaginable, "is the Bill of Rights; we tore it up today."

Judge Smith moved slowly and deliberately toward the document as though acting out the final scene in a tragedy. He clutched the gilded frame, and with a slight jerk dislodged it from the nail that held the frame on the wall. Holding it tenderly with both hands, the old congressman looked at it awhile, then exceedingly gently lowered it to the floor and turned it around so that it faced the wall. "That" he said, "is the end of the Bill of Rights."

The "Judge" then simply walked from the room, leaving the bewildered elevator operator alone in the room. He stood there for a long time, then also left and walked to his elevator. He drove the elevator directly to the basement, shut it off, and walked in the dark the two blocks to his boarding house. Remembering that night still sends a chill through his mind.

A. The Jungle Journey of Legislation

Every facet and stage of the legislative process has its tales of battles bitterly fought. The movement of legislation from idea to reality has sometimes been called "legislation by hurdle." That isn't far from the truth. To become law, a proposal must pass a mind-numbing number of potential barriers. One wrong move by those desiring it and the proposed legislation can die while rival bills triumph.

So perhaps a more accurate metaphor for the legislative process is a jungle journey at night. You may well know where you wish to go, but you can never be entirely certain whether you are on the right path, and of what dangers lie ahead. And just when you think you've reached a calm part of the legislative stream, you may find yourself running headlong into rapids filled with rocks that tear your proposed legislation into shreds.

The legislative jungle trail is narrow, twisted, and filled with surprises. A snake you never saw can drop on you from a tree and strangle your proposal. The ground can shift, and the quicksand of a thousand promises can swallow it up. And along the way, the provisions you had packed for a long journey, such as campaign contributions, can become rancid when exposed to the light of day.

In this jungle journey, perhaps no person or agency plays a more important role than the OMB—the Office of Management and Budget in the Executive Office of the President. In fact, the OMB might be considered the tour director for the legislative jungle trip, though some would consider OMB the snake. Your view of OMB is likely to depend greatly on where you view it from—the White House staff, agencies of the Executive Branch, or Congress:

> "One must remember that the Bureau of the Budget [now called the Office of Management and Budget] is concerned only with the humbler and routine business of government. Unlike cabinet officers, it is concerned with no questions of policy, save that of economy and efficiency." —Former Budget Director Charles Dawes[1]

> "How in the world can you ever get a bill out of OMB? They won't even let you look at their phone book to see who's handling the legislation." —Overheard in the Capitol.

> "I'd rather deal with the Politburo [the ruling body of the U.S.S.R.] than with the OMB." —Unnamed Congressman.[2]

Two examples should make clear one of the types of power OMB wields:

The Department of Defense eagerly drew up proposed legislation to permit its military helicopters to be utilized to rush traffic victims to hospitals. But when Congress held hearings on the proposal, it reversed itself and its testimony was in opposition to the proposal.

The National Oceanic and Atmospheric Administration (NOAA) prepared testimony to be given before a congressional committee asking for authority over the proposed deep water ports for tankers. But NOAA never made it to the Hill (Congress) to give that testimony.[3]

Similarly, a proposal originating in the Department of Housing and Urban Development (HUD) seeking cash subsidies to provide better housing for the poor met with resistance within OMB and never received the blessing of the White House.

Obviously each of these proposals was blocked by the exercise of policy judgment, which may or may not have been correct. Significantly, the judgment was exercised primarily at OMB, during what is often termed the "legislative clearance process." This process is the mechanism through which the President, working through the OMB, controls the movement of legislative proposals within the Executive Branch as well as to the Congress. During this process, proposals are developed, coordinated, and finally communicated to Congress. In OMB's own language, it "performs legislative coordination and clearance functions to:

> "(a) assist the President in developing his position on legislation,
>
> "(b) make known the Administration's position on ... legislation for the guidance of the agencies and the information of Congress,
>
> "(c) assure appropriate consideration of the views of all affected agencies, and
>
> "(d) assist the President with respect to his action on enrolled bills [those officially passed by Congress]."[4]

Generally, OMB works out of public sight; if the exercise of its powers forces an agency to reverse its position, it is left to the embarrassed agency to try to explain away its sudden change of position to Congress or the press. Not infrequently department and agency chiefs must testify before Congress in opposition to bills they actually favor, or plead for bills they would rather oppose. OMB's power to make "puppets" even of the heads of agencies and departments is one of the major reasons for its lack of popularity among high-level federal bureaucrats.

Although the OMB sometimes works relatively directly and openly (as when it lobbies at Congress in behalf of the "President's" budget—which it helped prepare), its continuing task of legislative clearance remains little-known. This process begins, in general, long before the usually acknowledged"beginning" of legislation: it's introduction in Congress.

In 1974, the Office of Management and Budget received 3,318 agency views on pending legislation, and sent on (or "cleared," as they call it) 2,235 of these to Congress. The OMB also received 317 drafts of proposed bills from federal agencies; 145 of these were "cleared" and sent to Congress, while an additional 10 draft bills were originated at OMB itself. OMB also gave reports to the President on all 502 bills passed by Congress that year.[5]

Under the rules laid down by OMB to carry out its legislative clearance duties, no agency may send proposed legislation to the Congress or testify in regard to proposed legislation without OMB's prior approval. And when Congress passes legislation, the OMB advises the President whether he should approve it or veto it. In short, legislative clearance is the mechanism the President uses to control legislative proposals within the Executive Branch and to attempt to control the legislative process in Congress.

Legislative clearance is not the only tool the President uses to control legislation. But it is central to all of his other tools. Part One of this book deals with legislative clearance, while Part Two examines other means and aspects of the President's powers in regard to legislation. These include such Constitutionally granted powers as the veto, treaty making and Executive Privilege, plus such statutory tools as the budget and impoundment powers, as well as Executive Orders, Proclamations, persuasion, and patronage.

B.The Apparent and Real Sources of Legislation

Ever since you were a child in grade school you knew that legislation "began" when it was introduced into Congress or some other legislative body. Now you know that the world is more complex and you are right.

The "public" (apparent) source of legislation is usually one or more members of Congress announcing their submission of a bill for the consideration of the other members. The "real" source may be of any number of types, but most commonly these "real" sources are the Congressional staff (or even basically the Congressman himself, which would equate "real" and "public" sources), the Executive Branch, as well as a third category we will term for the moment simply "other sources." Let's look at the Congressional sources first.

C. Congressional Sources of Legislation

1) Legislators

First, there is the somewhat rare case of the congressman or senator who thinks up an idea on his own and introduces legislation to carry it out. In this case, the private and public sources are the same. It is said that Senator Hubert Humphrey's Peace Corps idea and bill falls into this class. But not many legislators have time to walk into a dark closet like Descartes, and wait for a good idea. And when constituents, lobbyists and others are constantly banging the legislator's door down with ideas for legislation they desire, it isn't difficult to see why so few bills introduced fall into this first category.

CHART ONE:

MAJOR SOURCES OF FEDERAL LEGISLATION

1. CONGRESSIONAL SOURCES:

→Members of Congress
→Congressional Staff
→Constituents
→Lobbies

2. EXECUTIVE BRANCH SOURCES:

→Departments and Agencies
Annual Legislative Program
Special Requests
→Office of Management & Budget
and other Executive Offices
→The White House
State of the Union Address
Budget Message
Annual Economic Report
Special Messages

3. OTHER SOURCES:

→Judicial Branch
→The Public

(2) The Congressional Staff

Though legislators themselves don't usually think up their bills, their staffs frequently do. That's what they're paid for. What percentage of bills begin this way is impossible to say, because no one apparently has ever done a study of the real sources of legislation. But clearly legislative staffs, particularly those who are attached to congressional committees, come up with many legislative ideas which are then approved by their bosses and become bills. Committee staffs in turn get their ideas from many sources, but one of the most likely is through testimony arising out of congressional investigative hearings. Often such hearings are held when House or Senate members know there is a scandal that could generate favorable publicity for them with the voters back home. The type of remedy to cure or prevent a repetition of the situation may be completely unknown. But those testifying may not only document the abuses present; they may also suggest remedial legislation. The committee staff, working closely with the legislators, can take this information and turn it into a bill that may use the publicity generated by the hearings to keep the legislation moving through Congress.

Sometimes it works the other way around. The congressman may begin by choosing the issues he believes he should become identified with in order to get re-elected. He then looks for a forum in which to raise these issues. Sometimes it is the committee or subcommittee on which he sits. If so, he is in luck. If he chairs that committee or subcommittee, he is doubly fortunate.

If he is not a member of an appropriate committee he might get a colleague who chairs one to arrange a day or so of hearings on the issue. The congressman then testifies before that committee and pushes his legislation. His personal staff may have drafted a bill before he appears, in which case it is made a part of the hearing transcript. Or he may call for legislation of a general nature without being so specific as to alienate voters who might find fault in the details. Thus a substantial amount of legislation stems from congressional committee action.

Sometimes during oversight hearings (into how legislation is functioning), the agency operating under the legislation will propose changes or radically new legislation. The real source for legislation in this case is the agency itself. There is another type of situation in which agencies also get involved in writing legislation for "the Hill." Under OMB guidelines, agencies may provide a "drafting service" for congressmen. They may thus help the Congress draft legislation as a technical service, but they may not comment on its merits without OMB approval.

(3) Constituents and the General Public

(a) Private Bills

Another source of legislation originating in the Legislative Branch is the legislators' constituents. These may be individuals or private interests, and they may or may not be represented by lobbyists. Individuals often write their congressman or senator asking for special legislative favors. Perhaps the immigration laws won't allow a relative to come to this country. If so, the constituent may wish the congressman to introduce a "private relief bill" to allow the named individual to enter the United States despite what other laws may say. These other laws are referred to as "public laws" because they apply to the public as a whole rather than to individuals. Another citizen may wish to recover damages against the United States because of an injury caused by some agency of the United States government for which legal remedies in the courts have been inadequate. An example would be a case in which the brakes on an Army truck failed, and the truck injured a person or his property. Generally the injured person would go first to court. But if he or she loses there, he or she can still appeal to his congressman or senator and ask for a private relief bill granting the payment requested. The success of such private bills is generally directly related to the legislator's power and his connections. Because no one except the individual injured and the congressman usually cares about the outcome of the legislation, it is up to the particular congressman to get the bill through the appropriate committee and the Congress on his own. Such private relief bills usually are not favored, however and are easily bogged down because of more pressing business. It is partly because a congressman needs help from his colleagues to get such legislation through the Congress that the famous Hill saying "To get along, go along," [to succeed, agree] keeps its currency.

Sometimes, a bill or a clause in a bill which helps only one or two individuals and is actually a private relief bill will be introduced in language disguising it as a public bill. Many amendments to the Federal Income Tax Code have been introduced in this way, and some have become law. Such bills may be discussed on the record at committee hearings or on the floor of the House or Senate without any hint that they are private relief bills affecting just one or a few influential people. One tax bill considered by the House Ways and Means Committee in 1975, for instance, might have appeared to be a small amendment of a general nature. In reality, however, it would have given Texas millionaire Ross Perot and only a very few others several million dollars worth of tax benefits.

(b) Public Bills

Public bills constitute the bulk of congressional concern. Often congressmen and senators are asked to introduce legislation to aid special interests; they may wish virtually anything: to build a post office, obtain exemptions from or cancellations of air or water polution controls, or change the tax structure to encourage residents to buy more houses. Regardless of what legislation is requested, it usually arrives at the legislator's office in one of two forms. The first is in a phone call or visit from constituents (members of his District) or members of the general public seeking to obtain the aid of the congressman. The second is from lobbyists, and is discussed below.

The visiting constituents may have a bill already drafted for him to introduce, or it may be a mere idea, and they may have already generated local interest through newspaper publicity or resolutions by various organizations in the district. Such potential face-to-face meetings are hard for congressmen to avoid, particularly if the constituents speak for a substantial interest. But once the meeting is over, the congressman can breathe easier, because the folks at home often are satisfied if the congressman merely introduces legislation and tells them he is pushing it. In fact, he may tell his colleagues he's introducing the legislation merely to get his constituents off his back, and may secretly even urge his colleagues to kill the proposed legislation. Gun control legislation reputedly has frequently been the subject of such dealings: constituents are made happy by official support given to a bill, while lobbyists are partly appeased by their knowledge of the congressman's actual conduct. The excuse to constituents is: "I'm only one of 435 representatives in the Congress. I've done all I can do."[6]

Some are even more cynical. As one representative from the Southwest was reported to have said: "Being a congressman is 90 per cent form—you get attention, you view with alarm, you offer no solutions." Hopefully, this approach is the exception, not the rule.

(4)Lobbies

The second type of visit a congressman faces is not disposed of so easily: the visitor doesn't "go home." When a lobbyist (or "Washington representative" as they are euphemistically called) is involved the congressman generally has a more difficult time of it. A lobbyist is an individual who is retained to influence the passage or defeat of legislation. There's nothing new about lobbyists. Benjamin Franklin was a lobbyist who represented the colony of Massachsetts in the English Parliament.

There are several reasons why a lobbyist can't be set aside so easily. First, the special interest involved may have helped the legislator financially, and continued financial help may be expected. Second, the lobbyist knows the true score: he knows when the congressman is helping and when he really isn't. So merely introducing a bill will not be enough for most lobbyists. Third, the lobbyist may indeed represent real interests of a significant bloc of voters, and is ready and willing to communicate his or her opinion of the congressman's helpfulness to that bloc of voters and/or financial backers.

Lobbyists can give Congress valuable help with legislation. They can write the congressmen's bills for them; they can do necessary research, write testimony for a hearing, help with preparation for debate in the House or Senate, invite the congressman to a fund raiser or meeting with a client, pay the congressman an honorarium, and give endless other favors. They can also lobby others for him and therefore be the congressman's "friend." The Washington lobbyist thus is another possible source of that bill we will follow through Congress.

The comparative effectiveness of lobbyists representing corporate interests stems from their being specialists in areas which few congressmen or aides know well. The right information at the right time can be crucial to the wording and effect of legislation:

> "Every industry has its little quirks," says one Democrat. "Even if you are against them (the industry) you need their lobbyist to get your head on straight. The thing that runs through your head all the time is 'Can I defend this vote?' "[7]

In the words of another congressman:

> "I learn a lot from lobbyists because after they have given me all the arguments on their side I invariably ask this question: 'What are the three major arguments your opponents use and how do you respond to them?' This sometimes causes consternation. Then I will say, 'If you don't tell me, they will.' This usually provides me with additional information which would not otherwise come to my attention.' "[8]

More often than not, the congressman's legislative assistant (or "L.A.") plays the key role in meeting with lobbyists and developing the congressman's position on legislation.

Characteristically the L.A. is young, smart and fresh out of law school. He's cramped in a room filled with file cabinets and papers, and has to search all over the office suite to find a chair for the lobbyist to sit in. If the lobbyist has good sense, he or she will treat the young staffer with respect, and the staffer will usually be grateful to have an expert boil down the pros and cons of complicated legislation. The staffer knows the general rule that the more innocuous legislation appears, the more deadly it may be.[9]

Sometimes, lobbyists are connected with powerful law firms. Then they have increased clout. Not only do they speak for the specific client, but they may be influential with other power groups as well. And they can do legislative legal work for the congressman right on the spot, or can stand in the wings should litigation or other problems arise which might threaten to knock the bill off its course.

For the most part, attempts to prevent abuses by lobbyists have been abysmal failures. The only law regulating lobbying at the Federal level (except for foreign interests, which are regulated by a separate statute) is the Federal Regulation of Lobbying Act.[10] This legislation, which Senator Edward Kennedy has called "a scandal and a national disgrace" (and which Common Cause Chairman John W. Gardner has called "a sham and a hoax,"[11]) was enacted in 1946. It requires that all persons hired to influence legislation in the Congress register with the Clerk of the House of Representatives or the Secretary of the Senate. It also requires them to file quarterly statements disclosing the sources of their funding, the purposes of their expenses, and their lobbying objective. When the law was passed the Congress felt that it would violate the First Amendment of the Constitution (freedom of speech, the press, etc.) to attempt to bar a citizen, lawyer, business organization or trade union from lobbying. Hence the Act merely requires registration. And the Act is riddled with loopholes.

An organization doesn't have to register if lobbying is not its "principal purpose," even if it lobbies very extensively. It took the National Association of Manufacturers 29 years to register, which it finally did in 1975. And the Chamber of Commerce—with over 500 employees, Washington's largest lobby—reported less than $500 in expenditures under the lobbying act in 1975. (The two giant organizations have now announced their merger.) The Act is so unclear that "strict constructionists" (literal readers of the Act) feel free to report only cab fares and luncheon tabs with congressman, leaving out research or anything "informational."[12]

Another loophole in the Act is that the Supreme Court in the Harriss[13] case said the law applies only to those who 1) have direct contacts with members of Congress; 2) lobby through coordinated letterwriting campaigns; or 3) who personally have participated in the solicitation, acceptance or receipt of lobbying contributions. This leaves out the biggest part of lobbying: lobbying the congressional staff, rather than the members of Congress themselves.

Yet there is worse news: the law is virtually unenforceable. In the 30 years since it was passed, only four prosecutions have been brought by the Department of Justice. The Secretary of the Senate and the Clerk of the House have no power to investigate violations of the Act. They merely serve as repositories for the filing of the reports. A 1975 Government Accounting Office (GAO) study found that almost 50 percent of the reports were incomplete, and 61 percent were late.[14] If the Hill happened to stumble on any violations it could refer them to the Department of Justice. But there is no means to detect such violations. Because of these and other shortcomings in the lobbying law, the Department of Justice must stress "voluntary compliance" because of the lack of the necessary investigative and prosecutive tools to enforce it.

In addition, the lobbying laws don't cover anyone lobbying in the Executive Branch. Sometimes this can be the key to influencing legislation on the Hill. If an Executive Branch department or agency can be persuaded to support legislation, the Congress often will rely on that agency's position, and, barring substantial opposition, pass the legislation without further consideration.

Some of the best lobbyists are former government officials. Former Secretary of Defense Clark Clifford skillfully guides aerospace clients through the labyrinth of Pentagon officials until pay dirt is reached. And when the Ford Administration grappled with the question of whether to grant the Supersonic Transport (SST) landing rights in the United States, lobbyists Charles Goddell (former Senator from New York), William Ruckelshaus (former head of the Environmental Protection Agency), and Eugene Rossides (former Assistant Secretary of the Treasury) were deep in the battle. According to one tally in 1975, there were some 124 registered lobbyists who were former members of Congress.[15]

Some of the lobbying organizations are mighty indeed. Representative F. Edward Hebert of Louisiana was hot under the collar after having been deposed as Chairman of the House Armed Services Committee, one of the most powerful posts in the world. "Common Cause," (the "citizen's lobby") he thundered, "is running Congress."[16] Although this is hardly the case, Hebert was right in sensing one thing: the proverbial little guy may be better represented in Congress than ever before. This is due to the rise of the "public interest" lobbies in Washington.

Common Cause, for instance, spent $1.6 million in one recent year and has some 300,000 nationwide members, 80 Washington employees, close to 20 lobbyists, and just about as many causes. Ralph Nader's Public Citizen, Inc. has some 150,000 members and a lobbying arm called Congress Watch which focuses on consumer issues. The Consumer Federation of America, a Washington-based consortium of more than 200 consumer, labor and rural groups, has a handsome budget and a bevy of lobbyists plying the halls of Congress. And environmental groups such as the Sierra Club, Friends of the Earth, and Environmental Action spend thousands of dollars each year to influence legislation.

But the more traditional business-oriented lobbies still exercise great power in the Congress. The National Association of Manufacturers, with a staff of 200, the American Petroleum Institute, with a staff of some 400, can still spread out over the Congress like an oil slick.

One of the newest and most potent lobbying techniques is combining computers with grass roots lobbying. Grass roots lobbying produces an orchestrated groundswell from constituents which looks like a genuine popular movement. Organizations such as the Chamber of Commerce, with 2,000 local "congressional action committees," can produce a "voice of the people" at will. Some major lobbying organizations are taking their membership lists and putting them into computers programed to target letters to those constituents who have the most influence with particular congressmen and senators. If there's a banking bill on the floor of the House, these computers can help send off a barrage of mailgrams or letters to banking officials urging them to write to their congressmen to oppose (or support) such legislation. Because form letters are not used, these letter writing campaigns sometimes are difficult to distinguish from a real "grass roots" feeling. In the words of Senator Metcalf, "The most effective influence in legislation is the so-called secondary lobbying, that is, an indirect lobbying to people [asking them] to write their congressmen. . .I used to be able to keep track of the lobbyists of the Liquor Goods Association by the postcards I got from bartenders."[17] Under the Federal Lobbying Act this isn't lobbying because there is no direct contact with members of Congress.

> "Scene: It is 5 p.m. A U.S. senator, who has been wavering on the issue of gun control, has just announced he is changing his mind and may vote to support a control measure when it reaches the senate floor for a crucial vote the following morning.
>
> "Within minutes after the news spreads across Capitol Hill, an IBM 370 computer begins humming in the modern uptown office building. . . . It has been programed with the names of 5,000 'key people' in the senator's state and it is spitting out telegrams telling them of this latest move in the gun control fight.

"By 9 a.m. the next morning, the senator's phone is ringing off the hook. His desk top is covered with telegrams. Each one is different, eloquent and angry."[18]

There are other ways to put pressure on legislators. In 1975, when Congress was considering tougher emission control standards on cars, General Motors Corporation Chairman Thomas A. Murphy wrote all 1.3 million stockholders asking them to contact their representatives in Congress to oppose such emission controls.

D. Executive Branch Sources of Legislation

(1) Agencies

The Executive Branch consists of several departments (such as the Department of State, the Department of Agriculture, the Department of Health, Education and Welfare etc.) as well as various commissions and other agencies. All of these departments, commissions, bureaus, offices and agencies will be called "agencies" in this book, simply to avoid needless repetition.

Within these agencies there are literally thousands of programs and functions administered by hundreds of thousands of civil servants. With time, the laws that Congress has passed to run these programs simply don't work, become outdated, or trip all over each other. Or an agency may wish to start a new program or reorganize an old one that needs attention. When any of these things happens it may be necessary for the agency to draft corrective legislation and seek its passage. Agencies generate hundreds of such legislative proposals annually. In 1974, the Office of Management and Budget received 317 pieces of draft legislation from agencies with requests to send them on ("clear them") to Congress for its consideration. When the President or an agency sends draft legislation to the Congress it is called an "executive communication," which is the term generally used within the Government for legislative proposals suggested by the Executive Branch.

In some agencies, legislation is generated as a byproduct of its function. The Department of Justice, for example, routinely encounters situations in which legislation is declared unconstitutional, in whole or part, or is interpreted by the courts in a way the Department considers unfortunate. When this happens, the Justice Department may ask Congress to change the law. Such legal problems of course are not always the "fault" of the courts. Often legislation is drafted either so poorly (sometimes hurriedly) that serious ambiguities exist.

In other agencies, particularly small ones, proposed legislation is generated only rarely. Such agencies as the Foreign Claims Settlement Commission usually need legislation only when they are assigned new duties or wish to get rid of old ones.

What happens when an agency generates proposed legislation? Once personnel in any agency feel there's a need for legislation, the agency's lawyers might begin drafting proposals. Or they may first make sure the effort has a chance of becoming law. In some situations, agency legislation is drafted by a working group made up of persons from all parts of the agency although lawyers are still likely to predominate. The Administration's 1975 firearms legislation is one example of this sort. In 1974 the Attorney General appointed a Handgun Task Force of representatives of various offices of the Justice Department such as the Criminal Division, the Office of Legislative Affairs and others. Also included on the Task Force were representatives from the Treasury Department, which traditionally has had an enforcement role in firearms crimes. All along the line, the President's Domestic Council, the Legislative Reference Division of the Office of Management and Budget (LRD), congressional committee staff members and leading subcommittee members in both the House and Senate were consulted. Where there were differences in the positions of various parts of the Department of Justice, the Attorney General made the necessary decisions. The Attorney General then made a speech to a law enforcement group outlining some of the major legislative options being considered. The speech was well-covered by the national press, and reaction was gathered and considered in the drafting sessions. Then the Attorney General called in United States Attorneys from major cities and asked their opinions. Finally, after months of work, the legislation was ready to be sent formally to the Office of Management and Budget for legislative clearance.

In reality, however, the OMB's legislative clearance process had already been at work in the many conferences and discussions about the legislation with White House and OMB personnel prior to the formal submission to OMB.

Most pieces of legislation are not as important to the President's program as this one. Thus, they receive far less attention. Usually, only the routine procedures are followed: once any part of an agency has prepared a draft bill, it is sent to the general counsel's office for review. Some larger agencies have special offices of legislative affairs headed by an experienced lawyer to handle such matters. In both the Departments of Defense and State, for instance, there is an Assistant Secretary for Congressional Relations who supervises legislative matters.

The Form of Agency Draft Bills—OMB's Circular A-19

> "[Legislative clearance is] by far the oldest, best intrenched, most thoroughly institutionalized of the President's coordinative instruments—always excepting the budget itself..."[19]

To expedite the growing volume of legislation, OMB requires all Executive Branch agencies to follow detailed instructions in handling such proposals. These instructions have been put into OMB pamphlets and the latest one is called "Circular A-19 (Revised) Legislative Clearance and Coordination." This circular, which is routed to "The Heads of Executive Departments and Establishments," lays down the rules for legislative clearance. With Circular A-19, agencies theoretically know just what they need to do at each step of the way. Agencies produce draft legislation, plus comments on bills pending in the Congress, and enrolled (passed) bills; these are standardized in format, and contain the essentials. Circular A-19 applies to all the executive agencies, independent commissions, bureaus, offices, government-owned or controlled corporations, and the Government of the District of Columbia. It even applies to the "independent" regulatory commissions such as the Interstate Commerce Commission and the Federal Communications Commission, although these follow the rules far less consistently than the agencies and departments under direct Presidential control.

The functions of the Office of Management and Budget have already been mentioned;[20] these are the mechanics of fulfilling those functions:

Acting under instructions in Circular A-19, with all proposed legislation agencies send a transmittal letter called a "Speaker letter" (See Exhibit B for an example of such a letter). The Speaker letter is sent by a designated agency official. In large agencies, he is usually the head of the office of legislative affairs. In small agencies, he is the general counsel. This Speaker letter goes to the Speaker of the House of Representatives. A virtually identical letter is simultaneously sent to the President of the Senate (i.e.—the Vice President of the United States). The Speaker letter contains a general analysis of the legislation. This includes such things as changes the proposed legislation would make in existing law and how it relates to or differs from any previous agency proposals or bills currently pending in Congress. In addition, Circular A-19 requires agencies to include where appropriate other information in the letter, such as the results of consultation with other agencies, as well as the expected impact of the bill on state and local government, plus any other information required either by statute or administration policies.

EXHIBIT A --AN EXAMPLE OF A BILL AS INTRODUCED IN THE HOUSE OF REPRESENTATIVES.

.... CONGRESS
.... SESSION

H. R. ....

(NOTE. Fill in all blank lines except those provided for the date and number of bill.)

IN THE HOUSE OF REPRESENTATIVES

....

Mr. .... introduced the following bill; which was referred to the Committee on ....

A BILL

To clarify the terms of the Speedy Trial Act of 1974.
(Insert title of bill here)

Be it enacted by the Senate and House of Representatives of the United States of America in Congress assembled, That title 18, United States Code, Section 3164, is amended by adding at the end thereof a new subsection (d) as follows:

"(d) The periods of delay enumerated in section 3161(h) shall be excluded in computing the time specified in section 3164(b) for the commencement of trial."

EXHIBIT B -- A SAMPLE OF A ''SPEAKER LETTER'' REFERRING TO THE BILL SHOWN IN EXHIBIT A.

IDENTICAL SUBMIS
TO THE VICE PRES

Office of the Attorney General
Washington, D. C. 20530

June 21, 1976

The Speaker
House of Representatives
Washington, D. C. 20515

Dear Mr. Speaker:

Enclosed for your consideration and appropriate reference is a legislative proposal to amend Chapter 208 of Title 18, United States Code, Section 3164 of the Speedy Trial Act of 1974. The proposed legislation is needed to prevent the premature release of detained defendants which could well result in an increase in the number of fugitives, the rate of recidivism and the coercion of witnesses.

The simple amendment to Section 3164 would cure what the Department believes is merely an oversight in draftsmanship which, contrary to the intent behind the Speedy Trial Act itself, has occasioned diverse court interpretations. As in every traceable precursor and model of the Speedy Trial Act -- including the American Bar Association Standards and the Second Circuit Rules -- provision was made to eliminate from the time computation those delays attributable to the unavailability of an essential witness or to time consuming but necessary preliminary proceedings, such as examinations and hearings respecting the competency of the defendant or litigation questioning the propriety of search and seizure.

The Act provides, during the interim four year period, over which the limitations are gradually phased in for expedited trials for two classes of defendants -- those detained awaiting trial and those designated as "high-risks" by the Government, Section 3164(a). Trial must be had within 90 days of detention or designation, Section 3164(b). If that limit is not met the detention must be terminated, or, in the case of a high-risk designee, the conditions of release must be reviewed. The Act does not explicitly state that the 3161(h) exclusions apply to the 3164 limitations. On the other hand, it does not affirm the contrary.

It can hardly have been the intention of Congress to force the release of an alleged felon upon the expiration of 90 days from arrest, where much of the 90 days was consumed by commitment for a competency examination, removal hearings or pretrial motions or appeals. Even less likely is that Congress intended to impose more stringent limitations during the interim phase-in period than at its end. At the end of this interim, when the Section 3164 limits will no longer be applicable, the time to commencement of trial - 100 days - will be subject to the 3161(h) exclusions, and the Act will contain no provision requiring release from detention of dangerous offenders at the end of 90 calendar days, or otherwise.

Whether or not the restrictive construction is compelled by the present statutory wording, its adoption by the courts can lead to absurd results. In this connection it should be noted that the Ninth Circuit Court of Appeals recently directed the release of the alleged head of an international cocaine smuggling ring and one of his aides even though it recognized that "release of these two foreign nationals from custody is tantamount to an invitation to flee across the Mexican border, less than three hours away". The men were charged with participating in a conspiracy involving a half dozen transactions each involving as much as 20 kilograms valued at more than $500,000. The court conceded that "the wisdom of the result Congress decreed is questionable" but felt constrained by what is conceived to be the "straight forward" language of an "inartfully drawn" statute. United States v. Tirasso, ___ F.2d ___ (9th Cir.)(decided March 25, 1976).

The problem can be easily cured by an explicit statement of the excludability of delays enumerated in 3161(h) from the 3164(b) computations. The attached proposal represents this simple and explicit statement.

The Justice Department believes this proposed legislation represents a clarification of and not a departure from the Congressional intent of the Speedy Trial Act.

The Office of Management and Budget has advised this Department that there is no objection to the submission of this report from the standpoint of the Administration's program.

Sincerely,

Attorney General

Under Circular A-19, civil rights legislation, for instance, is required to receive "full consideration" whatever that means. And The National Environmental Policy Act (NEPA) requires that agencies prepare detailed environmental impact statements concerning major Federal actions including proposals for legislation. Finally, in certain cases agencies must give OMB five-year projections of additional funds to be required by new legislation. Such medium-range financial information, however, is usually not necessary for routine legislation.[21]

The Speaker's and the Vice President's transmittal letters that accompany the proposals to a committee for consideration complement the rules of the House and Senate which require that the assignment of bills to the appropriate House and Senate committee be handled through the Speaker's and Vice President's offices. Sometimes the assignment of a bill to one committee rather than another is crucial to its future. A committee chaired by a friendly legislator can schedule prompt hearings, order reports on it from the Executive Branch agencies involved, and build up a favorable case for enactment. On the other hand, an unfriendly committee chairman can purposefully do nothing as the bill dies a slow death.

In addition to the Speaker letter, the proposing agency often prepares something called a "section-by-section analysis." This is not a formal requirement of OMB, but is done to help OMB and the Congress. A section-by-section analysis is a brief explanation of the legislation on a line-by-line basis. (See Exhibit C for an example.) Sometimes a "Ramseyer" — named for former Congressman Ramseyer—is also included. This is a line-by-line comparison of changes which the proposed legislation makes in existing law (See Exhibit D.) A Ramseyer is used to highlight the proposed legislation in context. An otherwise innocuous bill, which looks as if it would simply change the number of a section in the law, or changes one number to another, may in fact change the entire tax structure or produce drastic results in other legislation. The Ramseyer serves a highly useful purpose in spotlighting possible effects.

EXHIBIT C — PORTIONS OF THE SECTION-BY-SECTION ANALYSIS OF A BILL BY A CONGRESSIONAL COMMITTEE

TECHNOLOGY ASSESSMENT ACT OF 1972

SEPTEMBER 13 (legislative day, SEPTEMBER 12), 1972.—Ordered to be printed

Mr. JORDAN of North Carolina, from the Committee on Rules and Administration, submitted the following

REPORT

[To accompany H.R. 10243]

SECTION-BY-SECTION ANALYSIS

Section 1.—Establishes the title as the "Technology Assessment Act of 1972."

Section 2.—Declares the purpose is for the Congress to equip itself with new and effective means for securing competent, unbiased information concerning the physical, biological, economic, social, and political effects of such applications; and to utilize this information, whenever appropriate, as one factor in the legislative assessment of matters pending before the Congress, particularly in those instances where the Federal Government may be called upon to consider support for, or management or regulation of, technological applications.

Section 3.—Creates the Office of Technology Assessment (the "Office") "within and responsible to the legislative branch." The Office shall consist of a Technology Assessment Board (the "Board") which shall formulate and promulgate the policies of the Office, and a Director who shall carry out such policies and administer the operations of the Office.

The basic function of the Office shall be to provide early indications of the probable beneficial and adverse impacts of the applications of technology and to develop other coordinate information which may assist the Congress. In carrying out such function, the Office shall:

(1) identify existing or probable impacts of technology or technological programs;

(2) where possible, ascertain cause-and-effect relationships;

(3) identify alternative technological methods of implementing specific programs;

(4) identify alternative programs for achieving requisite goals;

(5) make estimates and comparisons of the impacts of alternative methods and programs;

(6) present findings of completed analyses to the appropriate legislative authorities;

(7) identify areas where additional research or data collection is required to provide adequate support for the assessments and estimates described above; and

(8) undertake such additional associated activities as the appropriate authorities specified below may direct.

* * *

Section 4.—States that the Board shall consist of 13 members as follows: six Members of the Senate, appointed by the President pro tempore of the Senate, three from the majority party and three from the minority party; six Members of the House of Representatives appointed by the Speaker of the House of Representatives, three from the majority party and three from the minority party; and the Director, who shall not be a voting member. The Board shall select a chairman and a vice chairman from among its members at the beginning of each Congress. The chairmanship and the vice chairmanship shall alternate between the Senate and the House of Representatives with each Congress.

Section 5.—Defines the officials: The Director of the Office of Technology Assessment shall be appointed by the Board and shall serve for a term of six years unless sooner removed by the Board. He shall receive basic pay at the rate provided for level III of the Executive Schedule. The Director may appoint, with the approval of the Board, a Deputy Director who shall receive basic pay at the rate provided for level IV of the Executive Schedule.

* * *

Section 11.—Calls for the submission by March 15 of each year of an annual report to the Congress.

Section 12.—Authorizes appropriations not to exceed $5,000,000 in the aggregate for the two fiscal years ending June 30, 1973, and June 30, 1974, and a continuing authorization beyond 1974.

Section 13.—States that this Act shall become effective, and the members of the Board shall be appointed by the presiding officers of the Senate and House of Representatives as provided in section 4, sixty days following the date of enactment of this Act.

EXHIBIT D — EXAMPLE OF A "RAMSEYER," TO SHOW EXPECTED CHANGES IN PRESENT LAW.

Changes in Existing Law

In accordance with subsection 4 of rule XXIX of the Standing Rules of the Senate, changes in existing law made by the bill H.R. 10243, as reported, are shown as follows (existing law proposed to be omitted is enclosed in black brackets, new matter is printed in italic, existing law in which no change is proposed is shown in roman):

SECTION 3(b) OF THE NATIONAL SCIENCE FOUNDATION ACT OF 1950, AS AMENDED [42 U.S.C. 1862(b)]

(b) The Foundation is authorized to initiate and support specific scientific activities in connection with matters relating to international [cooperation or national security] *cooperation, national security, and the effects of scientific applications upon society* by making contracts or other arrangements (including grants, loans, and other forms of assistance) for the conduct of such [scientific activities when] *activities. When* initiated or supported pursuant to requests made by [the Secretary of State or the Secretary of Defense] *any other Federal department or agency, including the Office of Technology Assessment, such activities* shall be financed [solely] *whenever feasible* from funds transferred to the Foundation by the requesting [Secretary] *official* as provided in section 14(g), and any such activities shall be unclassified and shall be identified by the Foundation as being undertaken at the request of the appropriate [Secretary] *official.*

RELATED MATERIALS

Cost and Budget Data

The bill will authorize appropriations for fiscal years 1973 and 1974, not to exceed $5 million in the aggregate, and provides continuing authorization thereafter for such sums as may be necessary.

Committee Recommendations

A quorum being present, the bill was unanimously ordered reported favorably.

Once all of this information is compiled, the agency forwards its proposed legislation (with the related attachments) to OMB for "clearance" (i.e. a review by the administration before transmitting the legislation to Congress).

In the legislative clearance process, timing is everything. If agencies really get pressed for time such as when a hearing is suddenly scheduled, there is tremendous pressure on agencies to "cheat" by not sending proposed legislation to OMB for clearance. Thus, it is no surprise that OMB stresses the need for agencies to get their legislation to it as soon as possible. (OMB requires agencies to "make every effort to give OMB a minimum of three full working days for clearance of proposed report or testimony"[22] even in emergency situations.) Legislative clearance may take anywhere from ten seconds over the telephone with a staffer in the Legislative Reference Division (LRD) of OMB, to a few days or even six months or more if written proposals are submitted to OMB. The time required depends on such factors as the complexity of the issues involved, the number of agencies interested in the legislation, how long it takes the President's staff members to make up their minds on tricky policy questions, and whether OMB wishes to clear such a proposal to the Hill at that particular time in view of their tactical assessment of the chances of passage as well as partisan political considerations.

Agencies are sometimes tempted to avoid OMB in other ways too. In 1973, the Department of Housing and Urban Development (HUD) drafted and sent to OMB proposed legislation to give housing allowances to poor people. But when OMB didn't accept the idea, HUD made the proposals public in what some OMB officials thought was an effort to build up public support. OMB nevertheless held the line and refused to "clear" the HUD proposal.

In addition to agency proposals for legislation which may be submitted at any time, there is another major category of legislation coming from the agencies: the President's annual legislative program items. These make up a substantial part of Congress' agenda.

Annual Legislative Program Items

Usually, the President's legislative program is considered to consist of three basic Presidential "messages" (speeches) to Congress—the Budget Message, the State of the Union Address, and the Economic Message—as well as any special "messages."

OMB requires that each agency prepare simultaneously with its budget request a proposed legislative program for the coming congressional session. This legislative package is used by OMB to prepare the President's Budget Message which is transmitted (sent to the Congress) in January of each year. The President needs to know what programs agencies are interested in enacting so that if acceptable, estimated expenditures for them can be included in the Budget Message. These legislative submissions are also used in preparing the President's State of the Union Address. Traditionally, this address contains a shopping list of legislative items which make up the cornerstone of the President's legislative program. This annual exercise also helps the President prepare special messages to the Congress. These special messages are really just proposals for major legislation that were not transmitted with the State of the Union Address in order to focus greater attention on them. These messages at the beginning of a Congressional session give Congress the maximum amount of time to act upon the President's recommendations.

Presidents differ in their style of dealing with Congress. Some try to fill the congressional agenda with presidential legislation. Other let Congress lead—and take the heat. Theodore Roosevelt, for instance, called the Presidency a "bully [excellent] pulpit" and preached relentlessly, while Dwight D. Eisenhower tended toward a more deferential approach. But the Congress often wants it both ways. On some matters they wish to criticize the President for meddling when he tells them what and how to legislate. In other matters, they appreciate any technical or other help they can get. As one Republican committee chairman told an Eisenhower Administration witness in 1953:

"Don't expect us to start from scratch on what you people want. That's not the way we do things here—you draft the bills and we work them over."[23]

The annual legislative program submission works like this: each fall all federal agencies compile a list of recommended legislation, make 20 copies of that list, and forward it to OMB for review. This list includes the new items which the agency wishes to actively support even though they have already been introduced in the Congress. OMB also requires that agencies tell them what legislative proposals they might have under development even though high level policy decisions may not yet have been made on such legislation. In this way the agencies can send early warning signals to OMB to hold a place in the President's budget for such proposals even before it has been decided precisely what will be submitted.

As a final part of this annual exercise, OMB requires agencies to send a separate list of all laws affecting that agency which will expire within the next two years. Although most laws are passed with an indefinate duration, some programs are specifically created only for a limited period. This information helps OMB and the agencies to plan ahead so that they can propose an extension of an expiring law, if desired, at least one year ahead of its scheduled expiration. Financial requirements are also needed. OMB and the Legislative Reorganization Act of 1970 require agencies to send along a tabulation showing the dollar amounts required for the upcoming budget year and for each of the four fiscal years following the budget year.[24]

All of this legislative material is sent to the Legislative Reference Division (LRD) of OMB which in turn distributes it throughout OMB. One of the many places this proposed legislation goes is to the various OMB divisions in which budget analysts review the proposals as a part of the agency's annual program. The OMB budget analysts become reasonably knowledgeable in each phase of an agency's activities, and can therefore identify the approximate financial impact of proposed changes in ongoing programs. Major budget issues or problems stemming from the agency's proposals for legislation are identified so that they may be dealt with at the OMB's own (private) annual budget hearings on each agency's budget. If "cleared" by OMB, the proposed legislation goes to the Congress.

(2) OMB and Other Executive Office Agencies as Sources of Legislation

Sometimes OMB encounters problems of overlapping responsibility and jurisdiction among agencies, or notices on its own that certain programs should be changed. In that case OMB prepares its own legislative proposals. These are usually sent to the affected agencies for comment as a routine part of the legislative clearance process. OMB prepared 10 such proposals in 1974.

OMB is just one agency in the Executive Office of the President (EOP), and other EOP agencies also may submit proposed legislation which is routed through OMB.

(3) The White House as a Source of Legislation

Finally, there is the role of the White House staff in preparing the President's legislative program. Most of his personal legislative program is developed in agencies at the request of the White House or OMB staff. Presidents generally have a fairly firm idea of what they wish to accomplish, and these ideas may be transformed into messages to Congress seeking new legislation. The preparation of Presidential legislation is an interesting process and one which could consume a book of its own. This is discussed in detail later.[25]

E. Other Sources of Legislation

In addition to the Executive Branch agencies as a source of proposed legislation, there are other sources. The Judicial Branch for instance. Sometimes, the Judicial Branch sees a need to have various court rules changed, such as the Federal Rules of Evidence. Such legislation is usually submitted by the Administrative Office of United States Courts (AOC). This legislation travels a different route to Congress than legislation submitted by an Executive Branch agency. It goes straight to the Congress without clearance by OMB. This is because the Judicial Branch is a branch of the government co-equal with Congress and the Executive Branch, and is exempt from legislative clearance. The Judicial Branch as well as the Legislative Branch does, however, send its budget submission to OMB for inclusion in the President's annual budget. But these requests are not modified except for form. And this submission is merely for the sake of convenience so that the entire Federal budget may appear in consolidated form.

These then are the major sources of legislation. As the flow chart summarizing these sources shows (Chart 1), there may be other sources as well. But most legislative proposals flow from one of these primary rivers which in turn converge at OMB.

CROSS NOTE:

See Also CHART ONE

on page nine.

F. How the Office of Management and Budget Wields Its Powers

1) Regulating Agency Reports to Congress

Once legislation is introduced, what happens? Sometimes nothing; the legislation simply dies. In some cases, as mentioned earlier, the congressional sponsor may even hope that his own bill dies. But once legislation is drafted by the congressman or his staff in rough form it is referred to the House or Senate Legislative Counsel's office. Their job is to review the form of the legislation and make sure that it is properly worded to do what it is intended to do. Much of this work is very tedious, because changing one part of the law often requires corresponding changes in many other parts of it. Courts have been known to wrangle for years over the interpretation of one word. Accordingly, the work of the Legislative Counsel's Office is critical to producing the intended results in a way which will not further confuse the law. It is not uncommon for a law to be passed in one session, and then to be amended in the next because part of it was technically wrong or proved unworkable.

Sometimes, the Legislative Counsel's Office doesn't even get the benefit of a rough draft of the legislation. The congressman or an aide will call up and say, "write me a bill which does so and so." In that case, the LCO lawyer prepares the legislation. The congressman then drops the bill in the "hopper." The hopper is more than a metaphor; it is actually a little box located on the side of the rostrum in the House of Representatives. Printed blank forms are available for congressmen to use in typing the bill. Sometimes a member of Congress may insert the words "by request" after his name to indicate that the bill wasn't his idea.

Over on the Senate side, the process for introducing bills is more formal. At a time reserved for the purpose, a senator will call for introduction. Then he sends it by a Senate page [messenger] to the Senate Secretary's desk on the floor of the Senate. If there is an objection by any senator to the introduction of the legislation, it is postponed until the next day. If there is no objection, the bill is read by title for the first and second reading.

On the House side, bills are not read when they are introduced, but the title is entered in the House Journal and printed in the *Congressional Record*, which accomplishes the same purpose. The bill is then given a number by the Clerk and sent to the appropriate committee by the Speaker with the assistance of the Parliamentarian. It is then sent to the Government Printing Office where it is printed that same night and copies are available the next morning in the document rooms of both Houses. One copy is then sent via a page from the Clerk's office to the office of the chairman of the committee to which the bill has been referred for consideration.[26]

Each bill has a number printed on it so that it may be easily traced through the legislative process and the date of its introduction is also included. Bills are numbered consecutively according to their order of introduction. Sometimes, however, legislators ask to reserve certain catchy numbers such as S.1 or H.R. 1776. Members aren't shy about introducing bills. In 1975 alone 17,015 bills were introduced while only 682 passed the Senate and 754 passed the House.

At the same time the legislator drops the bill in the hopper he may prepare an address to be inserted in the *Congressional Record* outlining the reasons why he is introducing the legislation and spelling out what it purports to do. These remarks either may be made orally on the floor of the House or Senate or they may be written and given to one of the clerks in the chamber who will have them printed up in the *Congressional Record.* Some congressmen have objected to this procedure which makes it look as if the legislator were on the floor of the chamber when he introduced the legislation. In fact, he could have been out of the country and his printed remarks will never give a clue as to whether he was present.

Placing a statement about the legislation in the *Congressional Record* has several advantages. First, it tells other Members of Congress and congressional staffers just what legislation is being introduced and why; lobbyists are also alerted, if they hadn't already known of the bill. Second, these statements may be of assistance to courts and government agencies when trying to interpret the legislation. Finally, the statement's most practical value is to the congressman. He can obtain reprints of the *Congressional Record* free of charge and mail them free of charge under his franking privilege to his constituents or to the news media for personal publicity. Because of this free mail feature, the *Congressional Record* is filled not only with legislative business but also with trivia which is probably of interest, if to anyone at all, only to constituents in the particular district of the congressman ordering the material printed. The Record abounds with insertions about awards to young people, games the home teams won, and other items of dubious legislative importance.

Once legislation has been assigned to the appropriate committee, the committee is under no obligation to do anything with it. It is generally viewed as the sponsor's job to get the committee chairman or the staff interested enough to consider it at all. The first step in moving legislation is often for the staff to request the views of various Executive Branch agencies on it. These so called "views requests" are form letters or route slips from the committee to agencies which may have an interest in the legislation. Typically they say something like: "Attached please find a copy of H.R. 1111. Your views on this legislation are requested." Such a views letter may also ask the agency to comment in detail on particular parts of the legislation. In addition to requesting agency views, the committee may request the views of the Office of Management and Budget. In most cases, however, OMB's position is merely derived from the positions of the other agencies commenting on the legislation.

EXHIBIT E — AN EXAMPLE OF AN AGENCY REPORT ON PROPOSED LEGISLATION.

OFFICE OF THE SECRETARY OF TRANSPORTATION,
Washington, D.C., September 17, 1971.

Hon. WARREN G. MAGNUSON,
Chairman, Committee on Commerce,
U.S. Senate, Washington, D.C.

DEAR MR. CHAIRMAN: This is in reply to your request for the vie of this Department concerning S. 2020, a bill to amend section 220(of the Interstate Commerce Act to permit motor carriers to file ann reports on the basis of a thirteen-period accounting year.

The current language of section 220(b) of the Interstate Comme Act establishes the general rule that annual reports of motor carri shall cover the twelve-month period ending on the thirty-first day December in each year. If S. 2020 is enacted, such carriers could el between a twelve-month report ending on the thirty-first day of I cember and an accounting year report ending at the close of any the last seven days of the calendar year.

The enactment of S. 2020 would have no substantial impact on operations of this Department. Accordingly, although the Depa ment would have no objection to the basic concept of the bill, we ma no recommendation concerning its enactment.

The Office of Management and Budget advises that from the star point of the Administration's program there is no objection to the s mission of this report for the consideration of the Committee.

Sincerely,

JOHN W. BARNUM

(2) Preparation of Agency Reports

Committee requests for an agency's views on legislation are informal. But the way an agency reports to the committee is not. Both OMB, in Circular A-19, and the agencies in the own internal guidelines prescribe in great detail how agency reports on legislation are to be prepared, reviewed and finally "cleared" for transmittal to Congress.

In some of the larger agencies the process works like this:

The office of legal counsel or congressional liaison office of a department, bureau or agency receives a views request letter from a congressional committee and logs it in [records its arrival]. Any existing agency file on this proposed legislation will be found and attached to the views request. A form memorandum will be sent to the appropriate office or bureau in the agency asking for preparation of a draft agency report to the committee on the legislation. One office in the agency may be designated a "reporting unit" while another will be designated an "advisory unit." The reporting unit will write the report. Then, the advisory unit or units will receive the draft report and briefly comment on it in writing. The legal counsel or congressional liaison office will then take the proposed agency reply and the advisory unit's views on it, negotiate any differences of opinion, and then prepare a proposed agency report in final form. Sometimes, policy issues on an agency report or draft legislation will need to be thrashed out at a higher level. In the words of one high official in the Department of Health, Education and Welfare (HEW):

> "...settlement of disputes between assistant secretaries, career officials, or both is about the only way he [the Secretary of HEW] can gain any control in this circus."[27]

The form for such reports also is controlled by OMB's Circular A-19 and agency guidelines. Generally, such reports contain some or all of the following:

- A Recommendation—Usually this consists of a one or two-sentence summary of the position the agency takes on the legislation.

• A Summary—A brief statement of the contents of the legislation and its purpose.

• Effect on existing law—Any changes which the proposal may make in existing law.

• Discussion—Includes any references to similiar legislation and agency reports on such legislation in the recent past.

(3) OMB's Clearance of Reports and Testimony

As discussed above, all agencies are required to submit proposed reports for clearance to OMB before they are transmitted outside of the Executive Branch. A detailed discussion of the OMB's internal clearance procedures is given later in this volume.

Once the agency reports are cleared, the Congress has a pretty good idea of where the legislation stands in relation to the President's program. Unless the Hill has specifically asked for OMB's advice on legislation, the agency's report may be the only indication the Congress has of the Administration's position.

Members of Congress look at OMB's role in clearing reports and testimony in various ways. Congressman Jack Brooks of Texas has stated:

> "There is no question that OMB dicates the position taken by all government agencies on matters coming before congressional committees. The refusal of the Executive Branch to permit its witnesses to convey to congressional committees their forthright opinions on matters coming before us is detrimental to the entire governmental process."[28]

One veteran Hill staff director puts it like this. "We operate on the assumption that OMB and the White House are making all the decisions and the agency is making none.[29]

OMB's view is that OMB has no policies of its own. But it is virtually impossible to separate policy analysis done in OMB from the policy making which supposedly takes place only in the White House.

The agency's report is valuable in assessing whether the President will sign the legislation or veto it. Although the President is perfectly free to veto legislation he has supported or to sign legislation which he has objected to vehemently, usually such turnarounds don't happen unless the legislation is substantially changed during its journey through the Congress. Accordingly, the Congress often can use the legislative clearance process to tell which legislation is worthwhile pushing and which may bog down for lack of Administration support.

And a President will certainly get criticized if he reverses his field and vetoes a bill he said he would support. Indeed, if President Ford's experience with the 1975 Common Site Picketing Bill is any indication, a President can get himself virtually crucified by such a reversal. In that case President Ford apparently let Labor Secretary John Dunlop pass the word that Ford would sign the Common Site Picketing Bill, which was supported by organized labor. With Ford's backing, Dunlop spent months negotiating the contents of the bill with labor, management and the Hill. When the bill passed Ford vetoed it, apparently for political reasons stemming from strong business opposition. Labor felt betrayed. Dunlop felt betrayed and resigned his Cabinet post. Clearly, when a President reverses his field on legislation he does so at considerable political risk.

If no agency's report is opposed to the legislation there is an excellent chance that it will pass. In many cases, routine legislation with favorable agency reports is whisked through the Congress without debate. Accordingly, lobbyists often pressure agencies to generate favorable agency reports. If all agency reports are favorable it is difficult for an opponent of the legislation to have anything to hang his hat on in objecting to the legislation when it comes to the floor of the Congress.

Under OMB guidelines, oral testimony also is covered by the legislative clearance process. Thus, all testimony must be cleared through OMB just like reports.

Clearance Delays.

There is one important difference between legislative clearance for agency reports on pending legislation and legislative clearance for agency draft bills. OMB will usually clear an agency report on pending legislation even if it is opposed to the agency's viewpoint. The agency's report will merely indicate that OMB doesn't agree with the agency. But draft bills are not treated in the same way. When OMB objects to a bill which the agency has drafted, it simply doesn't get cleared; that is, it doesn't reach Congress; it dies at OMB.

Sometimes, however, the agency tries an end run around OMB and finds a friendly legislator who will introduce the legislation without OMB clearance. Then reports can be ordered on it. At that point, OMB will clear the agency's views on the legislation. But the report is likely to state that OMB is opposed to the agency's position. Worse, OMB may detect such an agency attempt and refuse to submit the report on that legislation unless OMB is pressured to do so by the Hill. And OMB has many reasons it can give for prolonging its consideration—or dragging its feet, as some legislators might call it. Clearance requires time. A controversial report on legislation may require many months for clearance. Reports need to be sent to other agencies. Once responses are received they may be in conflict, which will require an exchange of conflicting reports, conferences among the agencies, and ultimately with OMB. One example of such agency coordination was HEW's 1973 proposed legislation to regulate the distribution of medical devices. OMB sent the HEW draft to the Department of Commerce. The Department asked that the number of products subject to pre-market review be reduced, and OMB changed the bill accordingly. "If you're going to pounce on an industry," said a source in the Food and Drug Administration, "OMB wants the Department of Commerce's point of view. That's a fair check and balance."[30] If the agencies cannot agree on their positions then the White House might be asked to step in directly to meet with the agencies and make a policy decision. Any of these steps can be used not only to reach accomodation, but also as an excuse to the Hill. Sometimes after waiting without results, the legislator feels that the chances of such legislation clearing OMB, not to mention the authorization and appropriations committees of the Congress, are so slim that he simply writes the bill off as a lost cause.

Occasionally, OMB does indeed decide to kill legislation by foot dragging. In the late 1960's the White House was preparing for a new tariff reduction round with its allies under the GATT (General Agreement on Tariffs and Trade). It is a principle of tariff negotiations that you have to generate some real pressure on the other countries at a tariff session to get what you want. To do this, the Administration made a conscious decision to prevent the clearance of agency reports on routine tariff legislation. This built up pressure among our trading partners to get concessions from us. In return we could ask for some favors from them. Month after month OMB was told by the White House to let reports on tariff bills remain uncleared. These reports gathered dust on the floor under a table in the Old Executive Office Building. Although some pressure from individual legislators was felt, the Administration got what it wanted in the process.

OMB's clearance powers can be used by a President to create something legislators want. This in turn can be exchanged for favors. How does this work? One classic case, which was rumored but never proved involved President Lyndon Johnson. According to this story, LBJ needed some votes to push the nomination of Abe Fortas to the Supreme Court through the Senate. Opposition to the Fortas nomination was rising. But the President didn't have anything to trade for those votes. So he decided to create something. He orally passed the word to key Administration officials that all reports on legislation and other administrative actions on projects of interest to certain senators should be stopped dead in their tracks. The usual agency reports and clearances on bread and butter projects that are so dear to members of Congress just never left the Executive Branch. After a month or two, LBJ had a host of presents he could offer key Senators if they would vote his way on the nomination. LBJ had proved that the President's legislative powers are limited only by the imagination.[31]

Reclearance

OMB's "advice" to agencies on their reports and pending legislation generally "applies to all sessions of each Congress but does not carry over from one Congress to the next."[32] A Congress lasts two years, with at least two sessions. Thus, once an agency has cleared a bill, this clearance applies to substantially similiar bills in the same Congress. There are some exceptions to this rule. If, for example, significant changes have occurred in the President's program or his relations with Congress, agencies are advised to check with OMB to make sure that the clearance still stands. To be on the safe side and to complete its files, OMB requires agencies to send them a copy of all reports sent to the Congress even when clearance has already been obtained on a similiar report. Generally, any legislative items which have not been cleared by OMB by the time the Congress adjourns are filed without action. In some cases, however, Congress may request OMB to comment on pending legislation because it will be re-introduced in the next Congress. OMB usually complies with such requests.

G. OMB's Processing of Enrolled Bills

One of the most important parts of the Office of Management and Budget's legislative clearance process concerns enrolled bills—those passed by both houses of Congress and sent to the President for approval or veto. If OMB weren't a part of this process, it couldn't make its muscle felt with the agencies in the report-clearing stage. Let's suppose that an agency wishes to submit a favorable report on a Medicare bill. OMB however, doesn't like the price tag on it, so they make the agency insert language in its report saying that although the agency favors enactment of the legislation, it is not in accord with the program of the President. If the legislation nevertheless was passed and went straight to the President without the views of OMB, the President would be more likely to sign it. But if the enrolled bill has on top of it OMB's views reminding him that he had opposed it earlier, and that he had informed Congress he did not approve of it, OMB's advice in clearing reports on the legislation carries a lot more weight. And that's just what happens.

Under the Constitution, the President has 10 days (including holidays but excluding Sundays) to act on enrolled bills presented to him. Because the time limit for presidential action on enrolled bills is so short, OMB has developed special procedures for dealing with them. In fact OMB has bought more time by getting into the picture before the 10-day clock begins to run.

Under current procedures, the 10 days the Constitution provides the President on enrolled bills is generally agreed to begin when the enrolled bill is "presented" to an authorized White House employee. Thus, the President does not have to personally receive the bill. But even before the bill is delivered, OMB receives a facsimile of it. The Government Printing Office runs off numerous copies of the bill at the same time it is printed for the Congress. Thus while the clerks in the House and Senate are getting the President of the Senate and the Speaker of the House to sign the official copy of the enrolled bill, OMB has already begun processing it.

The first step in OMB's processing is for the enrolled bill fascimilies to be logged in and sent to the Legislative Reference Division. LRD then sends copies of the bill to interested agencies for their comments. Generally, these agencies are the same ones which were originally asked to report on the legislation when it was moving through the Congress. Under OMB guidelines each agency prepares an "enrolled bill views letter" on the bill. This letter must be sent to OMB within 48 hours of receipt by special messenger. These views letters are designed to help the President reach a reasoned decision on whether to approve an enrolled bill. They are privileged communications—not revealed by the White House—and accordingly agencies are urged to be as candid as possible in their remarks to him. To make sure that top agency personnel with policy responsibility review these enrolled bill letters, they must be signed by a Presidential appointee (i.e.—a high-level official). If agencies are recommending a veto, they must include a draft veto message with their enrolled bill letter. On those occasions when Congress has already adjourned and the President cannot return the bill with a veto message in the usual fashion, a "memorandum of disapproval" for a "pocket veto" (veto by inaction) must accompany the agency's request for disapproval. In some situations, either OMB or any agency requesting approval of an enrolled bill includes a proposed signing statement for use by the President.

Enrolled bill views letters typically run from one to three pages and contain an analysis of the significant features of the bill. Usually the key agency involved in the legislation is designated by the OMB staff to write a more detailed analysis of the bill, while other agencies with less interest contribute a shorter views letter. Agencies are also expected to compare the bill with Administration proposals; analyze any changes that will occur in existing law; identify factors which may make it particularly desirable for the President to act on it before a certain date; estimate the first-year and the recurring cost or savings; cite the

EXHIBIT F -- FORMAT FOR OMB ENROLLED BILL MEMORANDUMS

EXECUTIVE OFFICE OF THE PRESIDENT
OFFICE OF MANAGEMENT AND BUDGET
Washington, D.C. 20503

MEMORANDUM FOR THE PRESIDENT

Subject: Enrolled Bill H.R. 8000 - Tort claims suits
Sponsor - Rep. Celler (D) New York

Last Day for Action

June 5, 1961 - Monday

Purpose

A very concise statement in 1-2-3-4- style of the principal features of the enrolled bill. Usually not more than one or two sentences. Comments, views, issues, agency differences, urgency, etc., should go into the two following sections.

Agency Recommendations

Office of Management and Budget	Approval
Department of Justice	Approval (Signing statement attached)
Postal Service	Approval
Department of State	No objection
Department of the Treasury	No objection
Department of Commerce	Disapproval (Veto message attached)
Department of the Interior	Defers to Justice

Discussion

The discussion should be as brief as possible and yet contain the essential background information and basic data which the President should have in deciding action on the bill. If pertinent and significant, such matters as the following should be covered here: (1) origin of the bill, (2) differences, if any, from the Administration's proposal, (3) changes in policy or deviations from established policy, (4) important agency comments or differences, (5) significant provisions of the bill, (6) estimates of costs or savings, and relationship to the budget, (7) references to any attached draft veto message, memorandum of disapproval, or signing statement.

Assistant Director for
Legislative Reference

Enclosures

relationship of the first-years' estimate to the President's proposed budget; and make a clear-cut decision at the end of the letter as to whether the bill should be approved or disapproved. These views letters are then attached to an OMB "enrolled bill memorandum" to the President. This memo summaries agency views and recommends approval or veto of the legislation. Exhibit F.

To do all this within 48 hours may sound difficult. And sometimes it is. But unless the bill has changed substantially since the agency last reported on it or the bill is unusually complicated, the agency can usually write its views letters quite quickly using prior reports on the legislation as a guide. Sometimes, the agencies cannot meet the 48-hour deadline. If their letters still have not arrived within five days of the arrival of the bill at the White House, the OMB enrolled bill memorandum to the President goes forward without the agency's formal views. These views however, usually will be known by that time, and will be included in the memorandum. According to one former LRD Director, OMB gets its enrolled bill views memorandum to the White House within the five-day period some "97 percent of the time."[33]

In the case of private bills which benefit one individual or a small group rather than the public in general, agencies are encouraged by OMB to dig around for precedents to show that allowing an exception in this case will not cause the "floodgates to open" and produce a rash of similiar private bills. As the old legal maxim goes, "Hard cases make bad law." That is, when you stretch the law just to accomodate a particularly worthy case, you may create a precedent for similiar cases with less merit.

Once OMB receives an agency's views on the enrolled bill, a staff member of LRD takes these views, analyzes them, and writes a memorandum ostensibly from the Assistant Director of OMB for Legislative Reference to the President. This "enrolled bill memorandum" summarizes the agency views and presents OMB's best judgment on the merits as to whether the legislation should be approved.

According to the usual format, these OMB memoranda usually run at least two to three pages, except for very simple legislation such as private relief bills which may only take one page. At the top of this memo is a list of all the affected agencies and how they stand on the bill. This gives the President a thumbnail lineup on the legislation. In deciding whether to recommend approval, OMB is very careful. This is one of the most sensitive and difficult functions performed in the government, and OMB takes it seriously. If all of the agencies favor approval of the legislation and it is "in accord with the President's program" or has been cleared on a "no objection" basis i.e., the President does not oppose it—there is no problem; approval will be unanimously recommended. Most bills presented to the President fall into this category. Sometimes, however, one or more agencies urge a veto. If the agencies which favor a veto will not be affected substantially by the legislation, then OMB will usually side with the majority of the agencies which favor enactment. If key agencies are split on whether to approve, OMB's job is far more difficult. OMB then weighs such factors as the relationship of the legislation to the President's program, the reasons for requesting veto or approval—including whether agency responses are more in the nature of a "knee jerk" institutional response—or whether the agency is really spotlighting a serious problem.

Enrolled bill memoranda are also privileged communications between OMB and the White House staff. OMB staff are encouraged not to discuss their contents with anyone but White House staff. Often, the President's decision on enrolled bills generates great controversy, and the agencies' positions are kept from the public to keep such controversies from escalating before the President has made up his mind on the legislation.

Once the enrolled bill memorandum goes to the White House it is assigned to White House staff members for further comments. Then it moves to the President for action. In that five days which the White House usually has, the White House staff checks with political contacts, party leaders, Congressional leaders, private interest groups and anyone else to determine whether the President should sign the bill. Generally, OMB focuses on the merits of the legislation in their enrolled bill memorandum, while the White House staff looks to the political side of the equation.

Deciding whether to veto legislation is often tricky business. In 1976, Representative Wayne L. Hays (Dem. from Ohio) told the President's chief White House lobbyist that if the President vetoed an extensive revision of the campaign finance laws he would kill emergency funds for the U.S. Information Agency. Said Hays, "Two people can play this veto game, and if I don't bring up the USIA authorization bill, that is a kind of veto because if they don't get $4 million. . .soon, they'll be out of business."[34]

While some Presidents, such as Thomas Jefferson and Millard Fillmore never vetoed anything, Franklin D. Roosevelt vetoed 635 bills in twelve years, making him the all-time champion. But even FDR's veto rate was topped by Grover Cleveland, who shot down bills at the rate of 73 a year.

H. The Legislative Liaison System

> "I had heard a lot about lobbyists before I came to Washington and expected to be beseiged when I arrived. I was. To my amazement the first ten lobbyists who came to see me were from the ten Executive Departments, offering assistance, literature and advice on their legislative programs."
>
> —A freshman congressman.[35]

If OMB is the military command center for legislation in the Executive Branch, then the agencies' legislative liaison officers are the foot soldiers. Each of the Departments and most other federal bureaus, agencies and what-nots have such officers and legislative liaison offices. These offices are staffed with close to 600 lobbyists who draw salaries of some $15 million each year.

The Pentagon, for instance, has separate offices near Congress for each of the armed services. For the Army alone there is a million-dollar lobbying operation employing almost 300 people.[36] In 1973, the Office of the Secretary of Defense handled some 168,300 written informational queries and 510,000 telephone requests.[37]

The White House has a 12-man branch office on the Hill. And even the CIA has lobbyists prowling congressional corridors. Not all of a liaison's duties are strictly legislative. The State Department's 25-man, $600,000 liaison staff, for instance, serves as a travel bureau for congressmen traveling abroad:

> "Urgent cables go out from the liaison office notifying U.S. embassies that Senator______ needs hotel reservations in Ceylon, that Senator______ is a vegetarian . . . or that Congressman______ wants tickets for the opera *Aida* in Austra."[38]

Generally, however, the liaison's functions include more mundane duties:

- Coordinating Legislative Programs—handling the agencies' legislative programs through OMB, the White House and the Congress;
- Service Function—serving the Congress by answering requests from members of Congress and constituents;
- Intelligence Function—keeping their own agency and OMB posted on key legislative developments;
- Technical Support—providing expert technical services in drafting legislation; and
- Protective Function—staying close to Congress for self-interest and patronage reasons.

As long as there have been agencies there have been legislative liaisons. But the institutionalization of the liaison function is a relatively new development. Until the twentieth century agencies dealt directly with the Congress with little if any White House coordination. Even after the Bureau of the Budget [the direct ancestor of the present Office of Management and Budget] was established in 1921 and made a part of the Executive Office of the President in 1939, cabinet officers, bureau chiefs and other officials dealt directly with members of Congress with little if any guidance from the Budget Bureau or the White House.

After World War II, the Department of Defense created an Office of the Secretary of Defense for Congressional Liaison. This centralized congressional relations which previously had been handled separately by each of the armed services. In 1949, the Department of State followed suit by creating the Office of Assistant Secretary for Congressional Relations. This followed a recommendation by the Hoover Commission for better cooperation between the State Department and the Congress. By 1955, congressional liaison offices were operating for the Post Office Department. Finally, the last of the then-existing Executive departments—the Department of the Interior—came on board with a liaison office in 1963.[39]

Congressional liaison offices lobby, and lobby hard.In the words of the Army's Chief lobbyist, "I believe the key to successful legislation is knowledge, and that means educating the congressmen. So I make a special effort to keep the Hill offices informed about Army programs."[40]

The Army has found that one of the most effective ways to educate congressmen is to get them away from Washington and out in the field. Army legislative liaisons offer lawmakers quick helicopter rides to Aberdeen, Maryland, where the Army tests new weapons. "They can leave at seven in the morning and we'll have'em back to vote by noon," says one liaison officer.[41]

And military lobbyists aren't above using a little old fashioned flattery to keep up good relations with the Hill. One senator and his wife received two letters from the Air Force liaison office congratulating them on their thirteenth wedding anniversary. "Wonderful couples like you make our association on Capitol Hill both pleasant and inspirational," wrote the Air Force Director of legislative liaison. But not all the liaison's job is puffery. The Army House liaison office handles about 3,000 telephone calls a month; the Army's Senate office gets about 1,200, and another 4,000 written inquiries concerning the Army go to the Pentagon.[42]

Some congressmen and students of government argue that such Executive Branch lobbying violates the spirit if not the letter of the federal lobbying laws. These laws define a lobbyist as:

> "any person. . .who. . .in any manner whatsoever, directly or indirectly, solicits, collects, or receives money or any other thing of value to be used principally to aid. . .in the accomplishment of any of the following purposes:
>
> > "(a) The passage or defeat of any legislation by the Congress of the United States.
> >
> > "(b) To influence, directly or indirectly, the passage or defeat of any legislation by the Congress of the United States."[43]

Section 227 of the Federal Regulation of Lobbying Act requires registration of lobbyists with the Secretary of the Senate and the Clerk of the House. But this section also states that it does not apply "to any public official acting in his official capacity." Accordingly, there seems to be no question that agency lobbyists are exempt from the registration provisions of the Federal lobbying statute. And the registration provision is the only provision that counts.

Nevertheless, as the role of the congressional liaison continues to grow, there will be more and more discussion of the propriety of Administration lobbying efforts. On the one hand agencies should be able to make their positions known on legislation when requested to do so by the Congress. And most information services are desirable and helpful to members of Congress. On the other hand, political arm-twisting by agency or Administration officials is more difficult to justify.

Congressional liaison offices are located in various places in each agency. But all are close to the top. Most liaison officers are Assistant Secretaries in their own right. Others, such as liaisons for the Agriculture and Commerce Departments are in Deputy-Under-Secretary or Special-Assistant slots.

Congressional liaisons serve as a focal point for Hill inquiries. It's no secret that if a constituent wants a quick answer from an agency, the Hill can get it faster. In most agencies there are formal or informal guidelines requiring that congressional requests be handled on an expedited basis, usually within ten days. And when an emergency strikes, a congressional liaison can do wonders.

One morning, at the Rayburn House Office Building, the colonel who heads the Army's liaison office in the House of Representatives was on the phone with Rep. Dan Daniels of Virginia. One of the Congressman's constituents had suffered a heart attack during the night and his anxious widow wanted to get word to her son, an Army Captain stationed in Germany. Within a few minutes, the Colonel was giving instructions to Army headquarters in Europe via transatlantic phone. Within an hour he was able to report to the Congressman that everything was set. The Captain would be notified shortly and a seat would be held for him on a military transport plane leaving the following day for the states.

That's the kind of service the Hill has been accustomed

to getting, and that's the kind of assistance the liaison system can give.

The Army's liaison office does other things as well. They may be found guiding Army lobbyists around to key congressmen's offices just before the big votes on Army authorization or appropriation bills. Or they may be arranging for military briefings for House members on 30-minutes' notice; or setting up field trips for congressmen and their aides.[44]

Congressional liaisons spend much of their time on the Hill pushing or following their favorite bills through the torturous legislative process. Sometimes liaisons act as troubleshooters for an agency, ironing out misunderstandings or setting policies. Sometimes they gather intelligence vital to their agency's mission and the survival of their programs. And sometimes they have to act as "step-and-fetch-its" for congressional committees and key committee members.

While the liaison officer may be busy on the Hill, his staff can be aiding congressmen in other ways:

> "[Some] agencies help Congressmen get local publicity by advising them in advance of federal expenditures in their districts. This advance warning system permits the Congressmen to 'announce' the federal grant or contract award to the press, thus gaining credit for securing federal money that they likely had nothing to do with.
>
> "HEW, for example, has a special 'grants notification unit,' which keeps four full-time workers busy tipping off Congressmen." [45]

Generally, liaison officers keep out of the way of budget and appropriation matters. These are left to the budget shops in each agency. And usually liaisons avoid the technical side of drafting legislation—the dotting of the "i's" and crossing of the "t's." These matters are left generally to the legal counsel's office.

It is difficult to estimate the volume and cost of congressional liaison operations. One survey in 1963—over ten years ago—estimated that some 737 agency and executive office personnel were directly involved in processing congressional information. This effort cost nearly $8,000,000.[46] Those figures could well be at least double that today. But such surveys are inherently misleading. Virtually any employee in any agency may be asked from time to time to assist in answering a congressional "referral" or inquiry.

One thing is clear. As the Hill relies more on congressional liaisons to provide information quickly, additional personnel will be needed to serve the Congress. It is no wonder that the congressional liaison offices are used so frequently. Anyone who has ever tried to call a federal agency for information or read a federal government organizational chart to find out whom to call knows what frustration is. And congressmen's offices are no exception. Even they don't know where to start sometimes. So they call a liaison office.

By far the largest liaison office is in the Department of Defense (DOD). This office has hundreds of employees who monitor the course of legislation and lobby it when necessary. And the Department spends millions of dollars each year to keep this operation functioning—a drop in the bucket compared with the hundred-billion dollar annual budget of DOD. DOD also has an extra advantage in the lobbying game. Congressman may be commissioned in the reserves and taken on acting-duty tours to such pleasure spots as Hawaii, Paris, or Hong Kong.

Regardless of an agency's size, all congressional liaison officers have a hand in making departmental policy. Liaison officers routinely review reports and correspondence on their way to the Hill. These officials are sensitive to congressional temperment and by a discrete word change here or there they can avoid trouble for the agency.

Congressional liaison officers often are recruited from

the Hill where they gained first-hand experience with the workings of the Legislative Branch. Sometimes there is more flexibility in the liaison officers on issues than among line bureaucrats who have worked closely with policies of a department and are wedded to them. Bureaucrats occasionally see liaisons as public relations persons who would sell the agency's position down the drain for a couple of votes here and there. But generally agency bureaucrats rely heavily on their liaison officers to steer their programs through the difficulties of Capitol Hill.

The liaison contacts with the Hill vary with the agency. Some agencies, such as the Departments of State and Defense, must deal with all members of Congress. All of them have to vote time and again on matters of foreign policy or military spending. Other agencies spend most of their time dealing with the few committee members who care about their programs and can mean life or death to the agency's future. The Department of Interior, for instance, is primarily concerned with members on the House and Senate Interior Committees, as well as the House Committee on Merchant Marine and Fisheries.

Some congressional liaison officers deal almost exclusively with members of the President's own party. Others deal with members on both sides of the aisle. Usually, some accomodation must occur with members of both parties on any major issue before it comes to the House or Senate floor. This is particularly true in the case of Republican administrations, which for many years have had to deal with Democratic control not only in the House and Senate but also as a consequence in the important committee and subcommittee chairmanships. And if the chairman of a committee is against a program, the agency will have a hard time even getting hearings scheduled on it, much less getting the desired results.

Generally, liaison officers try to do their work as early in the legislative process as possible. This gives the agency the most leverage and the least visibility. It also helps to produce legislation favorable to the agency before members of Congress take public positions on it and get locked in on the issues involved. Thus, much of the liaison's work is done with the sponsors of legislation and in committee sessions as the bill is first being shaped. Once the legislation gets to the floor of the House or Senate changes may be more difficult to make.

Sometimes the liaisons' interests are dictated by geography. The Department of Agriculture, for instance, is usually more concerned with the 150 or more rural congressmen than with urban ones. Lately, however, with this department administering other programs such as Food Stamp distribution, this emphasis is changing. In most cases, liaison officers must keep in touch with a substantial portion of the 535 members of the House and Senate.[47]

Over the years, legislative liaisons have had an increasing impact on relationships between the Hill and the White House. Among their effects:

- They can help weaker bills survive by "hiding them" in other bills, or otherwise wrapping them in the cloak of an Administration-supported program;
- They may reduce bickering both inside and among agencies by their conciliatory efforts;
- Liaison operations may help to identify legislative priorities. More important bills can be given White House support when necessary, while lesser ones can be pushed as a part of an agency's legislative program.
- Legislative efforts can be pooled by liaisons supporting each other's legislation.
- Their service and intelligence functions can help to smooth out differences and misunderstandings between the Hill and the agencies.[48]

The increasing use of liaisons probably has aided the Executive Branch more than the Legislative Branch. For many years there has been concern over the need for Congress to maintain its Constitutional powers vis-a-vis the Executive Branch. Although legislative liaisons may get the Congress information faster, they also help the Executive Branch to keep up with if not ahead of the Congress. Some have suggested that the liaison function needs closer attention and reform. One possibility would be to staff the liaison office with both Hill and agency personnel. This would give the legislative oversight committees on the Hill or other congressional staff a chance for on-the-spot inspection of the administration of agency programs.[49] But there is a thin line between inspection and interference. And while the formulation of laws is within Congress' purview, the administration of laws is reserved by the Constitution for the Executive Branch. Thus, if this were done the Legislative Branch might be infringing on the separation of powers between it and the Executive.

In any event, there is no denying that liaison officers provide the Congress a full spectrum of services:

> "Presidential lobbyists arrange special White House tours, at the request of Congressmen, for favored constituents. The National Gallery provides reproductions of its famous masterpieces to decorate Congressional offices. The National Park Service offers scenic photographs through its liaison office. And the CIA's lobbying team delivers copies of foreign news broadcasts to members of Congress who are mentioned in them."[50]

Agency liaison officers report not only to their agencies but also to OMB and the White House. During the Nixon Administration some felt that Hill affairs were neglected. When William E. Timmons, Nixon's legislative aide, made appointments for legislators for instance, they were sometimes kept waiting. "Nixon didn't like politicians, and that included congressmen," according to Barber Conable of New York. "The result was that these [congressional relations] people became second-class citizens as far as the rest of the White House staff was concerned. Because they handled dirty goods and had dirty hands, they were so treated." [51]

President Ford's legislative team on the other hand, seemed to take a different approach. John O. Marsh, Jr., who worked with Ford on legislation, served in the House for many years and understood how Congress operated. And with former House Minority Leader Ford having served as a mediator in many Hill battles there was a friendlier White House reception for legislators. That is not to say that there weren't troubles from time to time such as in 1976 when the White House and the Hill were trading charges over leaks of classified information by the House and Senate Intelligence Committees. But generally liaison operations helped President Ford maintain low-key, businesslike relations with the Congress.

I. OMB and The White House

The Office of Management and Budget doesn't always play a major role in the Administration's legislative programs. OMB's power is weakest where those in the White House are strongest. People like Secretary of State Henry A. Kissinger and former Treasury Secretary George P. Schultz were also simultaneously Assistants to the President, and more frequently gave orders to OMB than they took them. When the Nixon Administration's trade bill was on the House floor, Schultz—not OMB—chartered the Administration's position. And in matters of foreign affairs, OMB deferred to Kissinger.

Sometimes OMB officials liaison with the Congress at a substantial risk. Former OMB Assistant Director Dwight A. Ink is one case in point. Ink enjoyed a reputation on Capitol Hill as an Administration spokesman who knew how to make compromises. But one day Ink was transferred to GSA. "Ink got bounced to GSA because he was too close to Congress," said one Democratic staffer. "He was viewed as not partisan enough and therefore not loyal enough."[52]

"It's amazing that our basic process for reviewing legislation has changed as little as it has over the years," says former Director for Legislative Reference Wilfred H. Rommel.[53] Nevertheless, during the Nixon Administration, there was one significant change in the legislative clearance process. Before Nixon, OMB's key decisions on legislation were often made within the Legislative Reference Division (LRD) or—as it was then called—the Office of Legislative Reference. Now, these decisions are made in OMB's program divisions by political appointees rather than the non-political, professional civil service staff of the LRD.

Roger Jones, former Director of what is now the Legislative Reference Division, has noted that when he was active in legislation, he felt required to notify the White House on legislative issues only when they touched on matters of express Presidential interest. These issues, however, have grown enormously. "Now there are too many people in the White House who are trying to bite you with the President's teeth," says Jones.[54]

There is no question that some of the formal neatness in the relationships between the Bureau and the White House is gone. In the days when Jones handled legislation, he would act pretty much on his own with an occasional check with the counsel to the President. Now, Associate Directors have to check here, there, and everywhere—they check with the Domestic Counsel, the Counsel to the President, various economic and other officials, and any other White House policy advisors that might be interested. In Jones' view, "Communications between the White House and OMB are downright messy." Yet, "Where the President of the United States is concerned," says Jones, "I don't feel you can afford to be messy."[55]

Throughout the Truman and Eisenhower Administrations, the Budget Bureau kept a tight reign on the flow of information from the Executive Branch to the Congress. Under such leaders as Jones and Phillip S. (Sam) Hughes (his successor) politics was pretty much kept out of OMB's handling of legislation.

In the 1960's Presidents Kennedy and Johnson let their personal advisors "intervene" on key legislative issues. But most of the legislative decisions still came from the nonpartisan staff of the Office of Legislative Reference. "We were pretty deep into substance in our office," said Hughes, who served in the Office of Legislative Reference from 1957 until 1966. "It was a hell of a lot more than a post office that just moved papers around."[56]

Just what role OMB and its predecessor, the Bureau of the Budget should properly play has been a favorite subject of political scientists for years. Some 20 years ago Arthur Maass argued that there were three types of staff a President needed. First, "a small personal staff of top politi-

CHART TWO: STEPS IN O.M.B. CLEARANCE OF AGENCY REPORTS ON PENDING LEGISLATION

CONGRESSIONAL COMMITTEE

1. The committee sends out a request for the views of relevant federal departments and other agencies on each pending bill.

9. Federal agency reports and testimony are made a part of the committee's record and final report.

DEPARTMENT OR OTHER AGENCY

2. The agency prepares its draft report on the bill with the assistance of its legislative liaison office.

3. A proposed agency report on the bill is sent to OMB for ''clearance.''

8. Each agency sends a ''cleared'' report on the bill to the Congressional committee.

7. OMB transmits its clearance advice to the agencies.

OFFICE OF MANAGEMENT AND BUDGET (O.M.B.)

4. OMB's Legislative Reference Division reviews the proposed agency report, and coordinates it with the reports of other departments and agencies.

6. The White House gives OMB the necessary advice.

THE WHITE HOUSE

5. If the President's position on the pending legislation is not known, OMB sends for White House ''advice'' as to the Presidential stance.

CHART THREE: PROCESSING AN ENROLLED BILL

1. CONGRESS enrolls a bill when both houses have passed the bill. To become official, a copy (printed) must still be signed by an officer of each house, but meanwhile. . . ↓

2. THE GOVERNMENT PRINTING OFFICE immediately prints copies and rushes some of them to OMB.

3. THE OFFICE OF MANAGEMENT AND BUDGET of the Executive Branch sends copies of the enrolled bill to every department and agency of the federal government that is presumed to have an interest in the subject matter of the bill. ↓

4. EACH DEPARTMENT OR OTHER AGENCY, upon receiving a copy of the enrolled bill from OMB, has just 48 hours to prepare a ''views'' letter recommending Presidential approval or disapproval and get the letter to OMB. ↓

5. THE OFFICE OF MANAGEMENT AND BUDGET has five days to summarize agency views on the enrolled bill, prepare its own recommendation, and send all of this to the White House. ↓

6. THE WHITE HOUSE STAFF obtains other views on the enrolled bill, particularly those of a partisan political nature, and sends its recommendations along with the OMB packet to the President for his action. ↓

7. THE PRESIDENT has three reasonable courses. He may sign the bill into law. He may veto the bill by returning it to the Congress with a veto message. Or, if Congress is not in session any longer, he may ''pocket veto'' the bill by not signing it, and usually by issuing a statement as to his reasons.

cal advisors." Second, a permanent civil service "general staff" such as the Budget Bureau to implement policy decisions. And third, a staff to generate ideas for the President's programs.[57] The Bureau, he argued, wasn't suited to play the third role: it had a tendency to postpone, mediate or muddle through controversial decisions by cracking bureaucrats' heads rather than making firm policy decisions. This was because it didn't want issues going to the President or to any other group, lest the Budget Bureau lose power.

Let's illustrate this point. Suppose there's an important difference of policy between two Cabinet secretaries on an issue. OMB discovers this when the departments send up conflicting agency reports on pending legislation. Under the old system the Budget Bureau would have decided that there was no applicable policy directive. But rather than bother the President, it would try to settle the matter. The Budget Bureau Director then asks the Secretaries of the two Departments to attend a conference in his office. At the conference, in addition to the Secretaries and the Director, there are Budget Bureau officials—an Assistant Director, and several other officers. The Director talks about the desirability of settling the issue without bothering the President and presents a staff memo spelling out the differences in the two agencies' positions; suggested compromise positions are also listed. After discussion that reveals clear-cut, unreconcilable differences in the basic approach of each agency, the discussion turns to areas of possible compromise. Each Secretary gives on some minor points and takes on others. But the most important points disagreed upon are postponed for later determination. Nevertheless, the Director declares the matter settled, directs action to "clear appropriate letters to Congress on the legislation," and later reports to the President that "he has settled certain differences" between the two departments on legislation.[58] Yet such conferences didn't settle policy issues: they avoided them. And any compromises centered around the "bureaucratic or institutional aspects of the

EXHIBIT G —

EXAMPLES OF ADVICE USED IN OMB REPORTS ON PENDING LEGISLATION

Standard

Enactment of S. 909 would be (would not be) in accord with the program of the President.

Enactment of this legislation would be (would not be) consistent with the Administration's objectives.

There is no objection from the standpoint of the Administration's program to the enactment of H.R. 909.

Accordingly (in view of the above), the Office of Management and Budget recommends (against) enactment of H.R. 909.

The Office of Management and Budget has no objection to enactment of this legislation.

Qualified or conditional

Enactment of legislation along the lines of these bills would be in accord with the program of the President.

Subject to your consideration of the above suggestion (subject to consideration of the above recommended changes by your Committee), you are advised that, etc.

The Office of Management and Budget concurs in the views of the Department of Commerce in its report on H.R. 101, and accordingly recommends, etc.

The Office of Management and Budget would favor (oppose) enactment of S. 101 if (unless) amended as recommended above (in the report of the Department of Justice).

While the Office of Management and Budget favors the objectives of the bill, your Committee may wish to take into consideration the comments and suggested amendments of the Department of the Interior in its report on the bill (the Office of Management and Budget believes the Committee should consider the comments and suggested amendments of the Department of the Interior in its letter to the Office of Management and Budget commenting on the bill, a copy of which is enclosed).

On the understanding that this bill would not authorize regulation of intra-state commerce in Alaska, the Office of Management and Budget would not object to its enactment.

EXHIBIT H -- OMB REPORT TO CONGRESS LETTER

EXECUTIVE OFFICE OF THE PRESIDENT
OFFICE OF MANAGEMENT AND BUDGET
Washington, D.C. 20503

August 19, 1975

Honorable Harley O. Staggers
Chairman, Committee on Interstate
and Foreign Commerce
House of Representatives
Washington, D. C. 20515

Dear Mr. Chairman:

This is in response to your request of July 17, 1975, for the views of this Office on H.R. 7988, a bill "To amend the Public Health Service Act to revise and extend the program under the National Heart and Lung Institute, to revise and extend the program of National Reserach Service Awards, and to establish a national program with respect to genetic diseases; and to require a study and report on the release of research information."

We concur with the views expressed by the Department of Health, Education, and Welfare in its report on H.R. 7988 indicating that it would have no objections to enactment, provided the bill is amended in a number of significant respects. The report strongly recommends that the Department proposal for National Research Service Awards, introduced as H.R. 7049, be incorporated in Title II of H.R. 7988. In addition, the Department identifies serious objections to the provisions of Title III for the study by the President's Biomedical Research Panel on the release of research information. The Department further notes that Title IV of H.R. 7988 would duplicate existing authority for genetic disease programs and would not improve program administration.

Accordingly, we do not object to enactment of H.R. 7988, provided it is amended as proposed by the Department of Health, Education, and Welfare.

Sincerely,

(Signed) James M. Frey

James M. Frey
Assistant Director for
Legislative Reference

problem—those aspects that would assume importance for a budget examiner. . .", not a policy man.[59]

According to Maass, the "permanent and career nature" of the Bureau made it overly cautious and not well-suited for important policy decisions. Finally, it was too well insulated and isolated from political pressures in the Congress and other groups.

Maass argued that the Bureau's own institutional interests came to the front too often and that another mechanism or group was needed to develop Presidential policy. Apparently, years later, someone took his advice.

When President Nixon moved into the White House in 1969, John D. Erlichman became his key advisor on legislative matters. With the establishment of the Domestic Council in 1970, Erlichman's role became institutionalized. The Domestic Council soon came to coordinate much of the Administration's domestic policies and legislation. The result was a major challenge to OMB's authority for control over legislative clearance. Says one OMB examiner, "I'd come to work and learn that 'There was a meeting at the White House last night, and it's all settled.' The bill I've been negotiating for weeks has been pulled up from the Office by the White House staff."[60]

Traditionally, decisions by the Budget Bureau on behalf of the President were deemed to be final. Of course the affected agency could always appeal to the President. But the Bureau had a long memory, and winning against the Bureau was rare. Indeed the prejudice developed in the Bureau for turning an agency down would be such that the negative reaction might be assumed even before the merits of the case were heard. As one former Director puts it:

> "If the President reverses his Budget Director fairly frequently, the latter's usefulness to the President will be gravely impaired if not destroyed, for it will have become evident that he has failed in his effort to tune in on the President's wave length, and his desk will become only a temporary resting place for problems on the way to the President."[61]

In the second Nixon Administration, the Domestic Council was reduced from thirty-five professionals to twelve. And when Domestic Council head John Erlichman resigned in 1973[62] in the wake of the Watergate scandals, OMB began to regain some of its former powers.[63] But this time the power shifted to the directors of the program divisions within OMB. These new directors were a result of the 1970 reorganization which transformed the Bureau of the Budget into the Office of Management and Budget. In this reorganization, associate directors—who were political appointees—were placed in key OMB roles. The change in the way legislation was handled was immediate. According to former OMB legislative head Rommel, "if there is a policy issue. . .it goes to a policy officer, not a career person."[64]

OMB has four program divisions: National Security and International Affairs; Natural Resources; Energy and Science; Economics and Government, and Human and Community Affairs. Both OMB associate directors and Domestic Council associate directors perform their functions in similiar, if not overlapping areas.

In general, the Domestic Council keeps its attention focused on the Congress, interest groups and state and local governments, while the budget remains a major concern of OMB. But there is no doubt that there is considerable overlap between the Domestic Council's activities and those of key OMB personnel.

A case can be made for putting political decisions at OMB into the hands of politicians, responsive to the President. This still leaves a basic question unanswered, however. Are the associate directors just politicians, and no more, or are they professionals as well? The full results are not yet in, but some early returns are encouraging.

One case in point is Paul H. O'Neill, OMB's Associate Director for Human and Community Affairs under Nixon and Ford. O'Neill is typical of OMB officials who have made their weight felt by professionalism, working long hours and avoiding publicity. In 1973, when President Nixon was to deliver his housing message, O'Neill was in his office early that morning making sure it came out the way the President wanted it. When Nixon vetoed a veteran's health bill in 1973, O'Neill negotiated a compromise bill with the House Veteran's Affairs Committee. When the Department of Defense helped write a bill to use helicopters to evacuate civilian accident victims, O'Neill shot it down. And when the Senate and House Government Operations Committees wrestled over the creation of a consumer protection agency, O'Neill was in the thick of the negotiations.[65]

Like other key OMB staffers in the Nixon Administration, O'Neill maintained close ties with the White House policy staff, especially the Domestic Council. At 7:30 a.m. three days a week, he would go to White House meetings on current legislation chaired by the Domestic Council head. "Paul O'Neill speaks virtually with the voice of the White House," said one commentator. And few apparently would contradict that estimate.[66]

The close ties of the OMB associate directors with White House staff sometimes lead to friction with their own professional staff members. In one budget examiner's view, "Budget examiners have been demoted to the lowest level of staff work."[67] But others disagree.

If OMB decisions are second-guessed and agencies appeal to the President, someone has to settle these disputes. And so the White House staff will continue to play a key role in legislative clearance. OMB's legislative clearance role has survived attacks from above and below. From above, the White House sometimes cramps its style. And friendly agencies can always strike their own bargains with each other, leaving no dispute for OMB to mediate. This doesn't bother OMB because in reality there are always plenty of disputes. And OMB is pleased to have agencies solve their own problems.

Legislative clearance has been going on in one form or another for more than 50 years. And everything that has happened suggests that it will be here 50 years from now.

Part Two: How The President Moves His Legislation

A. The Art of Presidential Persuasion

When the President takes office he gets a magic box. With this box he can send signals to U.S. Armed Forces throughout the world. These signals are instantly transmitted and instantly obeyed. Nuclear war requires such devices.

But when the President wants the Congress to pass a bill he has no magic box. What then is his power? President Truman once claimed that presidential power was merely the power to persuade. The theory behind this notion is that the American government is not a system of separate branches with *separate powers.* Rather, it is a system of *separate branches* with *shared* powers. Even President Dwight D. Eisenhower, who often deferred to Congress, once said: "I am part of the legislative process." Presidential persuasion this is the catalyst of the legislative process. But as we shall see, it is more. The Congress won't budge for the President, much less move in the direction he wishes, unless the President can persuade Congress that his program is good for *them.* It doesn't hurt if the proposals are *also* good for the country.

But the power of "persuasion" is more than country charm and reasoned argument. It is status, authority, and bargaining power. When the President calls a member of Congress into the Oval Office or to his White House living quarters and asks him for help "because the country needs it," saying "no" is not the first thing that comes to one's mind.[68]

The President's position of being powerful in many spheres—from a prime time television figure, to political party leader, to head budget drafter, to the person who appoints the Cabinet and can veto legislation—gives him powerful advantages when bargaining. Too many people wish for what only the President can give them, and fear what the President can do to them or take from them.

Persuasion, however, is not a one-sided coin. The President must give up some things to get others. There has never been a President who hasn't had some major frustrations in the face of a defiant Congress. When the Congress is run by the opposition party, he might as well retire for his four years unless he is prepared to bargain—and bargain hard—for whatever he wishes from Congress. On the other hand, what the Congress wishes, the President can resist—if necessary, by his veto power. The rules of *this* game are known to all participants and to the rest of us as well. Each side plays some cards, holds back others, and wins or loses one hand at a time for different stakes. "You can't win them all," the expression goes, yet not only can the President be frustrated legislatively by the Congress, he can also be driven to distraction by acts of his own Administration. "The members of the Cabinet," said former Budget Director Dawes, "are the President's natural enemies."[69] Once Cabinet members and their subordinates have built up a web of ties to constituent groups and Congressional committees, they can frustrate the President at every turn. Franklin Delano Roosevelt knew what he was talking about when he made this classic statement:

> "The Treasury is so large and far-flung and ingrained in its practices that I find it almost impossible to get the action and results I want—even with Henry [Morgenthau] there. But the Treasury is not to be compared with the State Department. You should go through the experience of trying to get any change in the thinking, policy, and action of the career diplomats and then you'd know what a real problem was. But the Treasury and the State Department put together are nothing compared with the Navy. The admirals are really something to cope with—and I should know. To change anything in the Na-a-vy is like punching a feather bed. You punch it with your right and you punch it with your left until you are finally exhausted, and then you find the damn bed just as it was before you started punching."[70]

And every President since F.D.R. has had the same problems. Harry Truman had his Douglas MacArthur, and nearly every modern President had J. Edgar Hoover to contend with.

The President can move his legislative program through the Congress in various ways. First, he can work directly with (or on) the Congress. He can ask his legislative liaisons and agency officials to nudge the Congress gently in the right direction. He can get his White House aides to assist in this process. And he can place some phone calls, spread some patronage, and make some horse trades himself when necessary. Or he can do other things.

A ride on the Presidential yacht Sequoia can be a persuasive experience, especially after a couple of drinks and promises. But few can boast of the treatment that Senator Byrd of Virginia got from John Kennedy—Kennedy paid a personal helicopter visit to Byrd's Virginia estate to help celebrate Byrd's birthday.

Second, the President can work indirectly on the Congress. He can solicit help from powerful individuals, groups and lobbies. They in turn, can contact key members. And when the going gets rough, and the Congress is being stubborn, he can appeal over the heads of the Congress to the people and urge them to get Congress moving by writing letters, making phone calls or casting their votes in the next election to get him more responsive legislators.

When legislation moves through the Congress it usually has a "tilt" either toward the Executive Branch or the Legislative Branch—whichever originally sponsored it, and cares enough about the bill to push it. This tilt means that the legislation needs continued support from either the Executive or Legislative Branch to survive and move toward enactment.

When there is combined pressure for enactment from both the Executive and the Congress simultaneously, the bill stands even a better chance. It moves toward that middle "jet stream" shown in Chart 4 and the tailwind behind it keeps it moving despite the many obstacles on the legisla-

CHART FOUR: PRESSURES ON LEGISLATION

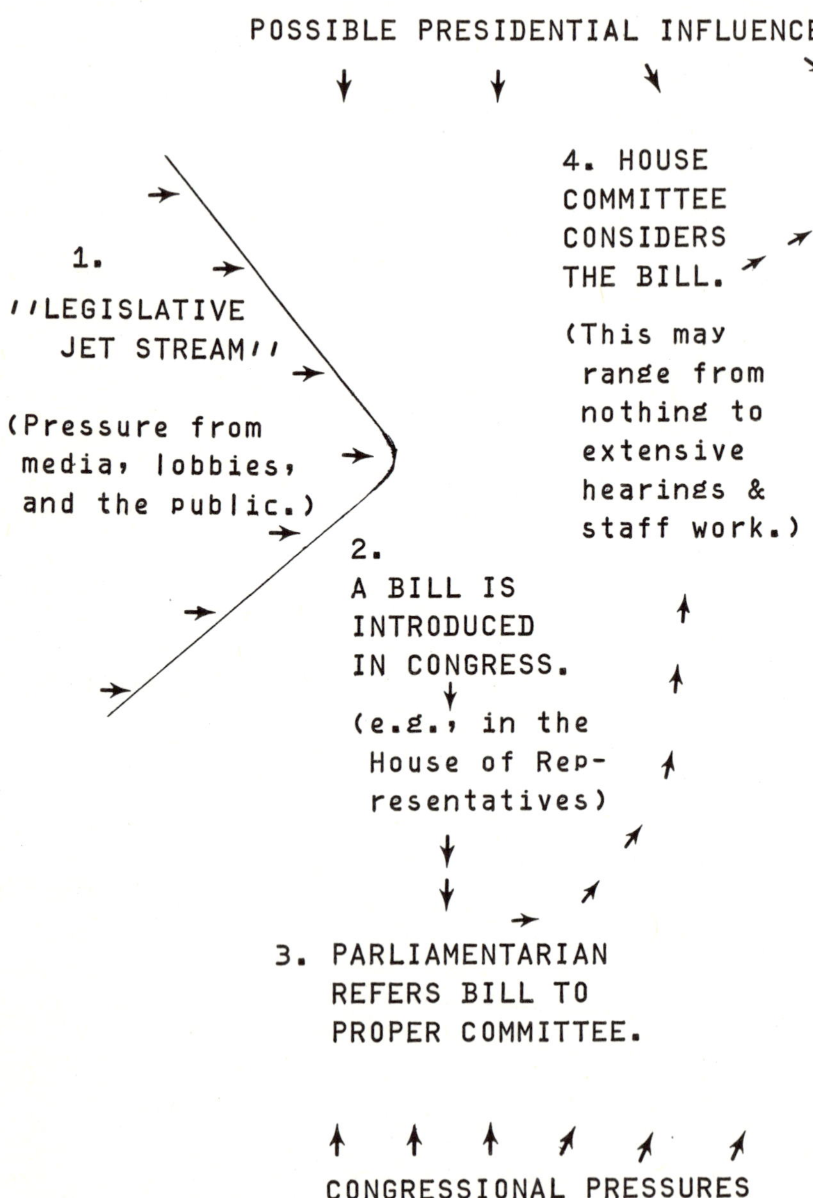

5. RULES COMMITTEE SCHEDULES FLOOR CONSIDER-ATION.

6. HOUSE OF REPRESENTATIVES VOTES; IF BILL PASSES, IT GOES TO THE SENATE.

7. THE SENATE RECEIVES BILL, AND FOLLOWS A PROCEDURE LIKE THAT OF HOUSE.

8. THE SENATE VOTES ON THE BILL. IF IT PASSES IN IDENTICAL FORM TO THE VERSION WHICH PASSED THE HOUSE, IT GOES TO THE PRESIDENT; IF IT DIFFERS, IT GOES TO A JOINT CONFERENCE COMMITTEE.

9. A JOINT HOUSE-SENATE CONFERENCE COMMITTEE IS APPOINTED TO NEGOTIATE DIFFERENCES BETWEEN BILLS OF THE TWO HOUSES.

10. FINAL PASSAGE BY BOTH HOUSES.

11. ENROLLED BILL GOES TO THE PRESIDENT FOR APPROVAL OR VETO (See Chart 3, p.64)

tive course. If, in addition, there is public pressure from the grass roots, pressure groups, the media, or other sources outside of the government, the bill can move even faster through the Congress.

B. Harnessing Public Opinion

The Presidency is most effective when it can rally public support behind its policies. Theodore Roosevelt moving against the railroads and Franklin Roosevelt combating the Great Depression and reforming the economy are samples of the results that can be achieved when the public is actively behind the President.[71] There is another side to this as well. Most Presidents have repeatedly had to decide whether to follow popular public opinion down an ill-considered road, or to stand fast and wait it out. When George Washington as President in the final decade of the eighteenth century, issued his proclamation of neutrality in the face of an overwhelming demand for a declaration of war on England and George III, it wasn't easy. Even his safety was in jeopardy:

> "Ten thousand people in the streets of Philadelphia," John Adams reported, "day after day threatened to drag Washington out of his house, and effect a revolution in the Government, or compel it to declare war in favor of the French revolution and against England."[72]

One of the first things the President wishes to do is to keep track of public opinion so that he can use it effectively to push his legislative program.President Lyndon B. Johnson used to carry public opinion polls around in his pocket so that he could use them to show congressmen and the press how popular his programs were. Most recent Presidents have relied heavily on trusted aides and scouts sent to the hinterlands. Presidents also glean information from their meetings with congressmen and politicians, and with ambassadors, businessmen and others on the international scene. William McKinley got his information from traveling Cabinet members; Franklin Roosevelt got much of his from his wife's jaunts, and Harry Truman once dispatched his old friend Leslie Biffle, the Secretary of the Senate, disguised as a farmer, to the corn belt to sample public opinion. The Presidential press summary, which is prepared daily in the White House, isn't new. Louis Howie compiled a daily press summary for Franklin Roosevelt which included editorial comments from as many as 750 newspapers representing every city with more than 25,000 population. Roosevelt figured he had an infallible way to tell if he was doing the right thing on any issue. If the publishers opposed him, he knew he was on the right track. President McKinley used to put in two hours after breakfast reading about his administration. From his hometown newspaper, the Canton, Ohio *Repositor*, to the New York, Washington, and Chicago papers and half a dozen more, McKinley kept on top of what the press was saying about him. Letters to Presidents and visitors also keep the President posted on public opinion. Truman sometimes set aside four hours a day for seeing people. If he made 95 appointments per week, he might see some 250 people with opinions on every conceivable issue.[73]

With in-house tools such as speech writers and television crews and with ready access to prime television time, the President can dominate the news and push his views. When the President can succeed in giving the people a message of hope in a time of dispair, of firmness when the times are uncertain or of courage when reasonable men are afraid, he can create great public enthusiasm which can be rapidly translated into legislative victories. Simplifying complex issues and driving them home in skillful phrases is not only a demagogue's major resource, it is the President's too. Theodore Roosevelt's phrase "malefactors of great wealth," Wilson's castigation of "a little group or willful men," and Franklin Roosevelt's "We have nothing to fear but fear itself," live in the public's memory.[74]

The President can reign while in his castle—the White House—but he can really feel the glory of his job when he travels on a grand tour. George Washington started the tradition by traveling through the South for two months in 1791. And all Presidents since that time have gotten a taste of the hustings. Modern Presidents, with their entourage of press aides, political aides, local congressmen, and fancy cars and airplanes (followed by other cars and airplanes filled with the press) resemble a comet: there is more tail than head.

Presidents are easily led to believe that if they can only talk face-to-face with "the people," the logic of their position will crumble congressional opposition. Sometimes they are right. But sometimes they aren't. Franklin Roosevelt, in his first hundred days, took advantage of the people's demand for action by fireside chats and twice a week press conferences. But Roosevelt knew that such appeals had their limits:

> "The public psychology and, for that matter, individual psychology cannot, because of human weakness, be attuned for long periods of time to a constant repetition of the highest note in the scale . . . people tire of seeing the same name, day after day, in the important headlines of the papers and the same voice, night after night, over the radio."[75]

Perhaps Roosevelt had learned this from other Presidents, such as Wilson who toured around the country to promote the League of Nations and killed himself in the process. His 40 speeches and unscheduled appearances on the platform of the Presidential train did him in, and three days before the end of his planned 25-day tour, Wilson collapsed in Colorado with a stroke. And not all who come to hear, see, and cheer a President agree with his policies, much less take the time to tell their representatives in Congress how they feel. Many show up out of curiosity. And some will always say, "Why doesn't he stay home in Washington and get some work done." But if the President can put it all together and build up public enthusiasm, he can keep his legislative program in the jet stream of public support.

C. Basic Approaches to Congressional Leadership

Much of the nation's legislative agenda comes from the President simply because the Executive Branch agencies have working access to Federal problems that need to be solved and those problems can be easily identified and organized into legislation for the President's annual budget and other messages.

There are various ways of viewing the President's role in legislation.[76] To some, his immense involvement in legislation is not only inevitable but desirable. Butressing this approach is the view that Congress consists of 535 diverse people running around in little circles protecting their constituents. The idea is that they simply don't have the time to see the whole picture. Only the President, the theory goes, can see that. Generally speaking, members can't get themselves together to perform a major role in national leadership. Under this concept, the President initiates and the Congress reviews his proposals. Certainly there is widespread support for such an approach in foreign affairs legislation, where it is presumed to be difficult for the Congress to keep secrets, conduct negotiations, and act quickly.

On the other hand, the abuses of the Nixon Administration have encouraged a rethinking of the President's relations with Congress. Perhaps Congress should try to lead more. And the Budget and Impoundment Control Act of 1974 at least gives Congress the means to look at the whole budget and spending picture at once. Indeed, that legislation gave the Hill its own budget bureau: the Congressional Budget Office. And if the Congress wants to reassert itself, it can simply do so.

Yet many factors contribute to legislative conflicts between the President and the Congress. First, institutional rivalry is a long historical tradition: the President views the Congress as obstructionist and the Congress looks at the President as a would-be dictator. Secondly, they have different electorates. The President is a nationally elected figure, while the Congress is made up of locally elected politicians. In many cases, the House of Representatives emphasizes rural areas rather than urban ones because the powerful committee jobs go to those re-elected most often, and these legislators have usually had rural constituencies. Thus Presidents generally have been more responsive to urban problems and power blocks than has Congress.

Third, Congress is made up of two Houses. Each has a different view of the world. The House of Representatives, elected each two years, can come in on the President's coattails and vote for his proposals. The Senate is less sensitive to volatile issues that engage the public's attention for awhile and pass on. And the Congress is well organized to defeat legislation. Not only must a bill that is introduced in the House of Representatives survive agency reports, hearings and votes on the subcommittee and committee levels, it also may have to clear the Rules Committee before being scheduled on the Floor of the House. And then it must go through the whole process again in the Senate. Along the way, one disgruntled member of Congress, one stubborn committee chairman, or one wary member of the leadership can work a backroom trade and cause most bills to disappear without a trace. And if legislation is purposefully sent to a hostile committee, the bill may never emerge from the "dim dungeons of silence." [77]

Another way to look at Presidential-congressional relations is by using the exchange theory. According to the exchange theory, political interactions depend on political expectations of mutual gain. Only when such gain seems likely, do the President and the Congress transact business. "The basic assumption of the exchange theory is that people calculate their own interests rationally, and act on these calculations." [78] This approach is different from others we have been looking at. Constitutional experts tend to view relations between the President and the Congress in the context of their legal powers granted by the Constitution and statutes. To others, such as Richard Neustadt in *Presidential Power,* Presidential leadership to a very important extent is a matter of manipulation and persuasion. But exchange theory supplements such approaches: the norm is that the President is constantly playing the role of a trader, looking for a quick swap to get his legislative program through Congress. He's perpetually a used-car salesman or, in older parlance, a "horse trader." The President must deal. His reputation in domestic affairs often depends on getting results from the Congress. On the other hand, while the Congress will listen to deals, it usually says no. This is because helping the President's prestige by moving his programs doesn't do much for individual Congressmen. Their lifeblood is pushing projects of more limited interest through the Hill for their constituents. Thus, the usual pattern is the President requesting and the Congress denying legislation. Indeed, Congress can kill bills in so many interesting and delightful ways that it is amazing they pass any at all.

Of course, some Presidents have been content to let the Congress alone. These have typically been classified as weak executives. President Taft's philosophy tended toward such a limited view of the President's role:

> "The true view of the executive function is, as I conceive it, that the president can exercise no power which cannot be fairly and reasonably traced to some specific grant of power or justly implied and included within such express grant as proper and necessary to its exercise. Such specific grant must be either in the federal constitution or in an act of Congress passed in pursuance thereof. There is no undefined residuum of power which he can exercise because it seems to him to be in the public interest . . .. [79]

Theodore Roosevelt's view, however, is the one followed by most recent Presidents. This is the view of the strong executive:

"I declined to adopt the view that what was imperatively necessary for the nation could not be done by the president unless he could find some specific authorization to do it. My belief was that it was not only his right but his duty to do anything that the needs of the nation demanded unless such action was forbidden by the Constitution or by the laws ... I did not usurp power, but I did greatly broaden the use of executive power."[80]

Some Presidents see their track record of fights with the Congress as a sign of masculinity. As John Kennedy put it:

The time—and the people—demand ... a vigorous proponent of the national interest—not a passive broker for conflicting private interests ... They demand that he be the head of a responsible party, not rise so far above politics as to be invisible—a man who will formulate and fight for legislative politics, not be a casual bystander to the legislative process."[81]

And there is perhaps a third type of President, the paternalistic one, who like Eisenhower and Washington seeks to rise above party politics to benefit all the people by building national consensus and harmony.

When the President applies pressure on the Congress, it sometimes works and sometimes backfires. When Richard Nixon started running into trouble with his nomination of Judge Clement Haynesworth to the Supreme Court, he disregarded all warning signs and plowed straight ahead. Massive White House mail campaigns were initiated to flood the Senate with "grassroots" support for the nomination. Key constituents were asked to call their senators. Presidential aides threatened to encourage opposition candidates to run against obstinate senators. Aides also threatened to withdraw the President's support in the election and to stall selected public works projects. Those who couldn't make up their minds to vote were invited to meet with the President, and hints were made that White House access might be cut off if they voted wrong. In the words of one senator, "I expect pressure. I know that we're not playing beanbag down here. But some of this was rough." One Republican told the public that there was a veiled threat that a detailed review would be made of the income tax return of senators who voted against the President.[82] But all of these threats failed. Indeed, they produced a reaction on the Hill that sealed the doom of the nomination.

Sometimes in dealing with Congress, Presidents can be insulting. Richard Nixon, for instance, openly snubbed the Democratic-controlled 93rd Congress. In January, 1973, Nixon announced his proposed fiscal year 1974 budget. This pruned or dismantled some 100 social programs of the Truman, Eisenhower, Kennedy and Johnson Administrations. He sent his State of the Union Address to the Congress to be read by clerks. This action, defying the tradition that such addresses be given in person to the Congress, was apparently meant to signify that the legislative seat of power had shifted from the Congress to the White House. Finally, he announced wholesale reorganization of the Executive Branch in defiance of the Congress which had earlier refused to grant him legislative authority to carry out such a reorganization.

While the President can expect to get turned down by the Congress on his domestic proposals, he usually can expect to receive more serious consideration on his international ones. From 1948 to 1964, for instance, the White House prevailed some 70 per cent of the time in proposals dealing with defense policy and foreign affairs. Over the same period, less than 50 per cent of the more than 2,000 domestic proposals of the Presidents met with success. Unless sending boys to fight is an issue, Congress usually views the impact on constituents as less direct in foreign policy legislation than in domestic legislation. Thus, they tend to support the President's initiatives. But with the growing restiveness of Congress over playing second fiddle in any legislation, the trend toward passivity may be reversed not only in domestic legislation but in matters dealing with foreign policy as well.

In wartime or other national emergencies, all bets are off. The usual rules change, and the President generally wins. Indeed, he becomes downright belligerent if he finds opposition to programs he sees as essential. In 1942, President Roosevelt demanded price controls from the Congress:

> "I ask the Congress to take this action by the first of October. Inaction on your part by that date will leave me with an inescapable responsibility to the people of this country to see to it that the war effort is no longer imperiled by threat of economic chaos.
>
> "In the event that Congress should fail to act, and act adequately, I shall accept the responsibility, and I will act . . . .
>
> "When the war is won, the powers under which I act automatically revert to the people—to whom they belong."[83]

Dictatorships have been announced in less arrogant terms.

D. The President as Party Chief

Being party leader is somewhat like organizing a bag of fleas; the difficulties are never-ending, and not many Presidents have mastered the art. But those who do, such as Jefferson, Wilson and Roosevelt, have almost certainly earned themselves a solid place on the list of great Presidents. The role of party chief is both a source and a tool of the President's legislative power.

The nature of national parties makes the President's task difficult. Compared to parties in other countries, the American political party is a weak force. It consists not of one relatively cohesive national party, but of 50 state parties loosely tied together basically only once every four years for the massive struggle of a Presidential campaign. Parts of the party apparatus are controlled by a host of congressional campaign committees, caucuses, steering committees and policy committees. Other parts are controlled by county chairmen or lesser satraps. At best, the President is a chief among chiefs.[84] So uncontrollable is this apparatus that some Presidents, such as Richard Nixon, gave up altogether and formed their own re-election committees virtually independent from the party structure. The fact that the Democratic Party includes both Senators James Eastland and Edward Kennedy, while the Republican Party has both Ronald Reagan and Jacob Javits, shows how politically diverse and potentially unpredictable a base of support the President's party can be.

Nevertheless, a shrewd President can take this amorphous mass and turn it into a real force to achieve his legislative programs. To do so he must be able to manipulate party resources, including funds and organization, and exploit to the fullest any policy moves his Administration makes. Because this task is so difficult and depends so much on the personal skill of each President and his interest in doing so, no really successful Presidential party leader has been able to pass this gift intact to another to provide a continuity of party power.

The party role was tacked onto the Presidency after the office was built. The Founding Fathers made no provision for it, and Washington even removed himself from party functions on the grounds that they were incompatible with the nature of the office. Because political parties were only developing during Washington's Administration, he could ignore the natural tension which being the chief of state and chief of party continually generates.

As chief of state the President must transcend any limits his party may put on him. But he must always remain conscious of the role the party played in getting him into office, particularly if he wants to be re-elected.

The congressional arm of the President's party often causes him particular frustration. Senate Republicans made Eisenhower work with their leader Senator William Knowland, who opposed much of Eisenhower's foreign and domestic policy. President Lyndon B. Johnson had no choice but to work with Senate Majority Leader Mike Mansfield, who opposed his Vietnam war policy.

Because of the nature of American political parties, many Presidents have adopted a practical approach to circumvent their power. After all, once your party elects you, they can't do much for you except oppose your programs and embarrass you. Accordingly, most Presidential programs are designed to have bipartisan support. For survival's sake, the President must make accommodations. This is particularly true of the Republican Presidents in recent times. Not only do they come from a minority party, but they are vigorously opposed by the majority party in both houses of Congress. Presidents become elected by appealing to voters both in and out of their party. Likewise they can best govern by proposing legislative and other programs which appeal to the broadest segment of voters. No one can miss the lesson of Senator Robert Taft ("Mr. Republican") being denied the Republican nomination because he could not attract a large segment of Democratic and independent voters into his column.[85]

Some have categorized Presidential approaches to the Congress according to party politics. Randall Ripley has suggested, for instance, that there are four basic approaches:[86]

1. *A Presidential partisan majority* in which the President and a majority of both houses of Congress belong to the same political party. In this situation, the President and the party leaders can spend their time getting the support of other party members to enact the President's legislative program. Franklin D. Roosevelt's coattail Congress of 1933 was such a creature. In the House there were 313 Democrats to 117 Republicans, and in the Senate, there were 60 Democrats and only 35 Republicans. If the party members are anywhere close to the President's political beliefs, he can almost ignore the minority party and simply use his majority.

2. The *Presidential-bipartisan majority* situation is one in which the President and congressional leaders must seek support for their programs from the minority party. In 1963-1965, for example, John F. Kennedy and Vice President Lyndon Johnson had to work to hold the Democrats in line and get sufficient Republican votes to enact their programs.

3. In the *congressional majority* situation, the President and the majority are of the same political party. But the President yields some of the legislative leadership to the Congress. He suggests legislation and they act on it, in their own fashion. Congressional leaders play more of a role in fashioning legislative programs, and the President lets his agencies have a freer reign in setting Administration priorities. From 1953-1955 Eisenhower's Republican majorities in Congress provided a good example of this situation. Eisenhower submitted a few legislative proposals in 1953 and a great many in 1954, but he didn't dictate to the Congress what to do with them. Publically, he rarely asked for support for his programs except in foreign affairs legislation. Congressional output, however, was quite low, for the legislative process produces most when a friendly

and energetic President meets a friendly and energetic Congress in a time of national need.

4. The *truncated majority* occurs when the majority party of one or both houses of Congress is not the President's party. About half of the Presidents in the twentieth century faced this unpleasant situation, which begs for the President to adopt a bipartisan approach. Any other approach is likely to court disaster, or at least inaction. From 1959 to 1961 Eisenhower faced such a Congress. The Democratic political leaders were partisan. Their approach was to make a record for the 1960 Presidential campaign. They passed many bills they knew Eisenhower would not sign. If he vetoed them, they had an issue, and attempted to override the veto. If they failed, they still had an issue. But there was a difference between foreign and domestic legislation. In foreign affairs they usually worked with Eisenhower in a bipartisan spirit.

There is another way to look at the President's party role. That is to see the President's party in Congress as a separate group—one which may or may not agree with the President, depending on the issues. Lyndon Johnson, as President, certainly had more trouble with liberal members of his own party over the Vietnam war than with many Republicans. And so there tends to be a congressional wing in both parties and a Presidential wing in one. And majorities must be made wherever possible—they do not automatically exist under a party label. Indeed, some have suggested that the Congress only follows Presidential leadership in three types of situations: First, where there is a crisis in the nation, such as the existence of two World Wars or the Great Depression; secondly, in the area of national security and international affairs where the Constitution gives the President a more dominant role than in other areas of legislation. (This situation has changed somewhat, however, since the Vietnam war. Since that time Congress has, with such actions as the War Powers Resolution, begun to play a more active role in international affairs. Whether this trend continues remains to be seen. But some have already pointed out that the War Powers Resolution may be read to give the President a freer hand than he otherwise would have had in committing troops abroad.)

Finally, when the President is lucky enough to have working majorities (not just majorities in party name only) in the Congress, he can really be their leader. Certainly the Roosevelt Congress of 1933-1935 and the Johnson Congress of 1965-1967 fit into this category. But such situations are short-lived. Presidents must act while they can. As a result of the Republican gains in 1967 and the Vietnam war, Johnson's impressive legislative leadership bogged down and he ended up resigning.

Johnson saw this coming. As he told a group of Administration lobbyists in 1965:

> "I have watched the Congress from either the inside or the outside, man and boy for more than forty years and I have never seen a Congress that didn't eventually take the measure of the President it was dealing with ... I was just elected by the biggest popular margin in the history of the country, fifteen million votes. Just by the natural way people think and because Barry Goldwater scared the hell out of them, I have already lost two of these fifteen and am probably getting down to thirteen. If I get in any fight with Congress, I have lost another couple of million, and if I have to send any more of our boys into Viet Nam, I may be down to eight million by the end of the summer."[87]

(1) The Election Treadmill

Even when the party is doing what it should do best—campaigning to elect a Presidential candidate–the relationship between the party and the Presidential candidate is an uneasy one. The party, for instance, generally reserves the right to approve its own platform. There are exceptions, such as where a powerful incumbent has already proven the success of his platform in the polls. Franklin D. Roosevelt had no problem getting the 1936 Democratic convention to support his platform. "I would like to have as short a platform as possible this year," he said, and "I would like to have it based on the sentence of the Declaration of Independence, 'We hold these truths to be self-evident.' "[88] The convention cheered his platform into acceptance with waves of ovations. On the other hand, if Lyndon Johnson had come to the Democratic convention of 1970 as a candidate, it is unlikely that the same group which nominated George McGovern would have rolled over for all of President Johnson's policies.

It is not surprising that many Presidential nominees have viewed the party with some distrust and formed their own personal organizations to conduct much of the preconvention campaign. John Kennedy, for instance, relied heavily on the support of Robert Kennedy, a Harvard brain trust headed by Archibald Cox, volunteers from his earlier campaigns, pollster Lou Harris, and his family. Some have quipped that his campaign included everything but the Democratic party.

A similar uneasiness exists between the President and his party's House and Senate Campaign Committees. Mid-term elections are often the time when the party leaders and the President are both eager to emphasize differences between their policies. Nevertheless, the President usually has led the congressional mid-term elections with support for his party's candidates. The results of such leadership, like legislative leadership, are mixed. In 1918 Woodrow Wilson began the practice by appealing for a Democratic Congress. His party lost control of both houses—not an auspicious start. Franklin Roosevelt conducted a hard-hitting campaign devoted to purging the Congress of wayward dissenters. The purge not only failed, but backfired. The Democrats lost 70 seats in the House and 7 seats in the Senate. Roosevelt tried again in 1942 and had similar results. Truman ended up about the same. Eisenhower gave it all he had in 1954. He traveled some 10,000 miles, gave 40 or so speeches, and lost 18 Republican seats in the House, 1 senator, and control of both houses. Kennedy had better luck in the off-year 1962 election. Apparently when the country rallied behind him during the Cuban missile crisis, it helped the Democrats in the election. In 1966, LBJ figured that with his popularity, the best thing he could do for his party was to stay home and act "Presidential." He probably was right.[89] Presidents Nixon and Ford had similar luck in their off-year elections.

Clearly the President can help his party just about as much as his party can help him—and that's generally not very much.

By its nature an election leaves behind a loser. In varying degrees, this loser is a wasted national resource. Some suggestions have been made for recycling losers. Clinton Rossiter once suggested a plan under which each losing candidate for the Presidency who received at least 25 per cent of the popular vote would end up with a seat as a senator-at-large for four years. Thus, the titular party leader of the opposition party would have a better opportunity to continue a vigorous policy dialogue with the winning candidate.[90] But perhaps the loser is best forgotten.

In good times, when the President is running with the wind of a strong popular mandate, political defiance by a mere congressman can be fatal to the congressman. But in bad times, being party chief may hurt the President's legislative program. If a President is unpopular, House members who are up for re-election will go to great ends to disassociate themselves from his program,[91] and this may bring even more legislative opposition than would be expected from members of *opposing* parties: the dissident from the President's party has to *prove* his distance from the unpopular President.

(2) *Presidential Patronage*

The President has few levers he can pull to move a recalcitrant Congress. One of the oldest and most basic of these levers is patronage. When all else fails, offering a man a job can work wonders. Abraham Lincoln used to find the White House stairs, rooms, hallways and even closets filled with job seekers. In 1885, an estimated 110,000 out of the 126,000 federal jobs were under patronage. The Civil Service Act of 1883 gradually reduced the number of patronage jobs until today the President only controls a few thousand positions by patronage. But the loaves and fishes of patronage are still valuable.

Patronage is tricky business. William Howard Taft once lamented that every time he made a job appointment, he created "nine enemies and one ingrate." Even after all the patronage that Franklin Roosevelt disbursed, complaints poured in from state party organizations that not enough Federal jobs were going to Democrats.

Sometimes when the President uses his patronage powers to reward the party faithful, he alienates the rest of the voters. In 1975, President Ford nominated former Republican Party Chairman George Bush to head the CIA. Both Ford and Bush found themselves skewered by the Congress and the press and the nomination survived only after Bush promised to take himself out of Presidential politics in the 1976 election.

Nevertheless, patronage is a wonderful oil for releasing stuck legislative gears. When nothing else will work, it can be dispensed equally to friend and foe alike to bring the desired results. President Kennedy knew he needed some favors to dispense to wayward Democrats. House Public Works Committee Chairman Charles A. Buckley controlled the pork barrel. Buckley wasn't exactly the image of the "typical" Kennedy man; as an old-line Democratic leader from the Bronx, he could be downright arbitrary and unprogressive. But Kennedy needed the pork. And so Buckley joined Kennedy in his Presidential Box at the Inaugural Ball. Necessity makes strange bedfellows.

(3) The Development of the President's Party Role

When George Washington left the Presidency, he left a few choice words behind. In his farewell address he said of party spirit:

> "It serves always to distract the public councils and enfeeble the public administration. It agitates the community with ill-founded jealousies and false alarms; kindles the animosity of one part against another; foments occasionally riot and corruption. . . ." [92]

In short, George Washington didn't like political parties. There is a natural, inescapable tension between the President as national leader and party leader. As President Taft once said:

> "I am afraid I am a constant disappointment to my party. The fact of the matter is, the longer I am President the less of a party man I become . . . . It seems to me to be impossible to be a strict party man and serve the whole country impartially."[93]

Any President's success in party politics is a mixture of many ingredients: his skill at quick maneuvering, his intuative sense, his public popularity and his personality. The party game can't be played by rules because there are none. At least no fixed rules. It can be played successfully only with a sense of the shifting sources of power.

Some Presidents reveled in their role as party leader. Jefferson, Franklin Roosevelt and Kennedy, for instance, seemed to enjoy the game and usually played it with consummate skill and finesse. John Quincy Adams and John Tyler were uncomfortable as party leaders and as such were failures. In the middle were Presidents such as Eisenhower, Lyndon Johnson and Gerald Ford, who often adopted a stance of the Presidency over the party.[94]

Politics is no stranger to America. But political parties are something else. National parties first cropped up during the Revolutionary War. Those Americans who were against Britain were called Whigs. Those who were loyal were called Tories. When independence came, the Tories disappeared, but politics didn't.

Conservative groups that advocated a strong Federal government generated the Philadelphia Convention of 1787, which produced the Constitution. Supporters of the Constitution were called Federalists. Those opposed came to be known as Anti-Federalists. Generally speaking, the wealthier parts of the Eastern seaboard were Federalist, while the farm communities tended to be Anti-Federalists. With the successful ratification of the Constitution, and the relative success of its operation, the Anti-Federalists fell into the background in the early Presidential elections.

The unique American system of electing the President indirectly through an "Electoral College" never envisioned political parties. The whole theory behind this electoral system was to screen out the dangerous parts of democracy without giving the appearance of doing so. Congress and the state legislatures ended up with most of the power. As originally set up (until the Twelfth Amendment was enacted in 1804) the system worked like this: Each state could choose electors equal to the number of the state's senators and representatives in Congress. The state could pick them in any way, either by popular vote, by an election in the legislature, or by a mixed arrangement. The electors in turn voted for two people for President. One had to be from another state. The two houses of Congress would then meet in joint session and tabulate the votes. If one person captured the majority he was the President, and the person with the next highest tally became the Vice President. The House would settle any tie by a vote of its own. But for such a vote each state would have one vote. If that failed to produce a majority, the House would then decide from the five highest.[95]

The first election was no problem. There were no primaries, no nominating conventions, no campaigning, no national balloting, and no opinion polls. Washington won 66 to 0. Not much of a fight, but a great victory. Adams won the Vice Presidency by a closer vote but didn't appreciate it. He called his new position, "the most insignificant ... that ever invention of man contrived, or his imagination conceived."[96]

National political parties got started at the top of government, not at the grassroots. They grew in part out of opposition to the policies of Alexander Hamilton, the first Secretary of the Treasury, who offered a financial program for the urban establishment that aroused suspicion in the rural areas. When Hamilton recommended that the depreciated Revolutionary War national securities (paper currency) called "Continentals" be redeemed at full value in hard currency after the war, that state debts be assumed by the Federal government, that a United States Bank be established, and that an excise tax on liquor and a protective tariff be enacted, he stirred up opposition in the hinterlands. Although these measures were designed to instill confidence and put the new Federal government on reputable financial footing, they upset rural interests who saw increased taxes as the end result.[97]

Hamilton made no apologies about his views. The business and financial classes were to be a bulwark against the masses of rural citizens who "seldom judge or determine right."

Thomas Jefferson, on the other hand, favored agrarian policies. He saw America as a nation of farmers and wanted to keep it that way. He opposed the monied interests and saw the extension of Federal power as a threat to states' rights. Later, he was to use that power to its fullest limits, in part because it benefited a nation of farmers.

When John Adams won the closely contested election of 1796, he jelled the opposition into Jefferson's corner by his strong-minded approach to governing. Adams as President (1787-91), however, continued the philosophy about political parties laid down by Washington. In his trite inaugural speech he pointed to dangers if "anything partial or extraneous should infect the purity of our free, fair, virtuous and independent elections."[98] He particularly railed against any election that might be determined by a single vote. Adams knew a lot about that. He was elected by only one vote in the electoral college.

Jefferson (President, 1801-09) has been called the greatest party manipulator of all U.S. Presidents. For Jefferson, state and local party organizations which were loyal to him were the key to political power. While the President and his Cabinet formulated the President's legislative program, his party members in the Congress transformed that program into law. He once called those who wouldn't help, "wayward freaks, which now and then disturb the operations."[99]

Jefferson also knew how to adopt an above-the-battle stance. Who could have explained it more diplomatically than Jefferson when he said:

> "But every difference is not a difference of principle. We have called by different names bretheren of the same principle. We are all Republicans, we are all Federalists."[100]

Jefferson was a take-charge man in congressional affairs. And he was wiley. While formally catering to congressional egos by abolishing the "monarchial" policy of delivering annual messages in person, he went for the congressional jugular vein—the party machinery. He presided over caucuses of congressional party leaders. And he invented the concept of the "floor leader" and used such leaders to shepherd legislation through the Congress. So successful was he that in eight years in office he didn't have to veto a single bill.

John Randolph, the House Ways and Means Chairman and Jefferson's floor leader, knew how to deliver the goods. Jefferson would dine with Randolph at night and watch Randolph move his legislation through the Congress by day. Randolph managed such key bills as the appropriations legislation to purchase Florida, the repeal of the Judiciary Act, and the charges of impeachment brought against Supreme Court Justice Samuel Chase. But when Randolph botched the prosecution of Chase, Jefferson moved to strip him of his leadership post. Randolph knew he was in trouble. " . . . every engine has been set to work to undo me in the estimation of my constituents, and not without effect," he moaned.[101] Jefferson's son-in-law eventually moved into Randolph's congressional district, ran against him, and beat him. Jefferson was definitely a political winner. But there were losers too. A whole string of them.

Richard Nixon, who was riding high with his party in 1972, was virtually railroaded out of office by the same party leaders in 1974. He was not alone.

John Quincy Adams (President, 1825-29) was one of the most abysmal political failures imaginable as a President. In 1824 he squeaked into the Presidency by the narrowest margin in the House of Representatives. His enemies claimed that he won only because of a corrupt bargain with Henry Clay in which Clay swung the necessary votes in return for becoming Secretary of State. From this auspicious beginning Adams went straight downhill. Jackson promptly said: "The Judas of the West has closed his contract and will receive the thirty pieces of silver."[102] As if that weren't enough, Adams ended up with a Cabinet with no one in it who had openly supported him for President. When one senator started berating Adams on the Senate floor, Adams' own Vice President, John C. Calhoun, simply sat there and took it all in. Adams got so mad at Calhoun for this that he adopted as his pen name "Patrick Henry" and wrote a slashing letter to the press. Not to be outdone, Calhoun took the pen name "Onslow" and wrote back.[103]

Andrew Jackson (President, 1829-37), on the other hand, was as strong a party leader as Adams was weak. Under Adams, the Federalist party had faded into oblivion. Under Jackson, the two-party system again emerged. The National Republican Party, called the Whigs, adopted a conservative stand. The rest of the Jeffersonian Republicans assumed the name Democrats, and under their leader Jackson forged "Democracy" into a powerful force for Presidential legislation and party politics.

Jackson took party leadership one step beyond Jefferson. When the Congress challenged him during his first term, he used the veto power more times than any previous President to preserve his legislative program. This set up his important re-election campaign in 1832. To boost his power both in Congress and the Presidency, he used patronage to its fullest to place "Jackson men" in positions of power.

When the Congress refused to confirm Martin Van Buren, Jackson's nominee as minister to Great Britain, Jackson worked with Van Buren to wrest the Presidential nominating convention from the control of Congress. The nominating convention wound up ratifying Van Buren as its choice for the Vice Presidency, and thus Van Buren assumed that job and the Presidency of the Senate that goes with that position. The Senate learned a lesson.

The party convention, used so successfully by Jackson, emerged out of a slow democratizing of politics begun many years before. In local elections, nominating conventions by a candidate's friends had been used in the North. In the South, the convention system had begun to replace the more or less haphazard self-nominating process. Jackson took the convention and forged it into his tool.

In 1837, Jackson had the personal pleasure of watching his hand-picked candidate for President, Martin Van Buren, sworn into the Presidency. Again, Jackson had used the party convention to accomplish this over his congressional opposition. To top off the pleasure of it all, Van Buren was sworn in by Chief Justice Roger B. Taney, whom the Senate earlier had twice refused to confirm to public office.[104]

Because of Jackson's adroit use of party power to achieve Presidential programs,he has been called the "first modern President." Through his brilliant leadership, popular support for Presidential programs was channeled through party leaders who broke down all opposition.

At the other extreme was John Tyler (President, 1841-45). So feeble was his party support that Clay dubbed him "a President without a party." Tyler's Whig party had so few representatives in the Congress that it was laughingly called "the Corporal's Guard." When things got rough, only one or two supporters came to Tyler's aid, and all but two of his Cabinet members were aligned with his arch rival, Clay.

Because Tyler had no party, his legislative program was at the mercy of Clay. A stand-off resulted. Time and again the President vetoed legislation while the Congress responded by ignoring Tyler's proposals. But there was more.

While Clay was busy pushing through Congress his "American System" to stimulate the economy, Tyler openly opposed it as an affront to states' rights. Clay so attacked the President that one wag said, "The vocabulary of the language seems to have been ransacked for words to express their angry denunciation ."[105] When Tyler and Clay tangled over legislation to create a new national bank, political bedlam resulted. Tyler vetoed the bill. Congress passed it again. Tyler vetoed it again. Finally Clay ordered all of his supporters on Tyler's Cabinet to resign, which they did.

Tyler, who was called "a vast nightmare over the Republic," by the *Richmond Whig*, was finally memorialized when a flu epidemic spread across the country. The Whig press called it the "Tyler Grippe."[106]

Today it is commonplace for Presidents to try to lead not only the people and their party but the Congress as well. It wasn't always that way, especially after Lincoln's death. The open conflict that developed between his successor Andrew Johnson (President, 1865-69) and the radical element of his own Republican Party in the Congress ended any hopes that Johnson may have had for leading Congress. Johnson ended up avoiding impeachment by the skin of his teeth.

For the next twenty years or so Congress was in its glory. The seniority rule, the growing importance of the Speakership in the House of Representatives, and the committee system in both houses forged Congress' power into an unwieldly but unchallengeable tool. Party programs came from the Congress. Little came from the Presidency. Woodrow Wilson, as a youthful student of this situation, wrote in his book *Congressional Government* that the Congress should be reformed toward a British parliamentary system. The President would be a public official—an administrator—and little more. According to Wilson's ideas, congressional committees would make the policies and the President would carry them out. In fact, if it weren't for the necessity for the President to be around to veto bills once in awhile, "he might not... be a permanent officer."[107] He would be a "part of the official rather than the political machinery of government," concluded Wilson.[108]

Wilson, of course, was just interpreting Presidential history up to that time. With Andrew Johnson's impeachment problems, and the track records of Presidents Ulysses S. Grant (1869-77), Rutherford B. Hayes (1877-81), and Chester A. Arthur (1881-85), Wilson had every reason to conclude that Presidents should let Congress run the country.

Later, when Wilson had the chance to observe Presidents Grover Cleveland (1885-89 and 1893-97), William McKinley (1897-1901), and Theodore Roosevelt (1901-09) in office, his views changed radically. All of these man had been effective party leaders when they were state governors. And all of them later demonstrated their political skills in the White House. Wilson concluded that the President must be the party leader, because:

> "... he is at once the choice of the party and the nation ... He is the party nominee, and the only party nominee for whom the whole nation votes.

Thereafter the Presidency continued to unfold in this direction , leaving behind in the dust the weaker age of Andrew Johnson, Grant, Hayes, and Arthur.

The epitome of the powerful party leader was Franklin D. Roosevelt (President, 1933-45). He was living proof that an active party leader could be an active and powerful President. Roosevelt knew where all the levers of party power were and how to pull them. He knew that his unprecedented popularity, which put him into the White House four times, was strong enough to change the very sturcture of the Republic. He lost some votes and he won some, but he knew that his support with the people and the party was strong enough to withstand gigantic battles.

Roosevelt had no fear of running his own party. He handpicked his party chairman, James A. Farley, and ran much of the party's patronage operation himself. Farley once moaned, "While I transmitted a great many recommendations for appointment to the White House and to other Cabinet officials, only a small part of them actually were approved."[110] When Roosevelt became dissatisfied with Farley's preparations for his second campaign, he promptly infiltrated some of his own men into Farley's staff and began sending them instructions over Farley's head.

Roosevelt knew how to reach the public. He once told his party friends on the National Emergency Council:

> "Don't tell them in Georgia what is being done in Alabama . . . take the nearest project to where you are speaking in Georgia and tell them about that."[111]

But Roosevelt could also make political mistakes. It is conventional wisdom that Presidents should stay out of local primaries. Most folks don't appreciate the President charging in to meddle in local issues. But Roosevelt couldn't resist trying to purge the Congress of a handful of Democratic and Republican opponents in the election of

1938. For several years, many of Roosevelt's greatest schemes had been declared unconstitutional by the Supreme Court. In 1937, Roosevelt tried to pack the Court by requesting that Congress add one new member for every justice who had served ten years, was over seventy, and would not retire. The Congress turned him down and Roosevelt turned his wrath on the Congress. Taking to the stumps in the 1938 election, Roosevelt told the voters which legislators had supported him in Congress and who had not. He went to Texas to praise young Congressman Lyndon B. Johnson and elaborately ignored other Democrats who had refused to support him. But Roosevelt failed miserably. Nearly all of the candidates he asked the voters to defeat were elected. As Jim Farley put it, "It's a bust."[112]

Nevertheless, Roosevelt transformed the Democratic Party from the minority to the majority party. And he used his own brand of political glue. This consisted of patronage and programs to bind together Northern labor leaders and Southern states-rightists and a host of other minorities into a party with a purpose. The Democratic Party claimed to be the party of the people and for their welfare. The Social Security Act, the National Labor Relations Act, and other legislation gave the intellectuals, the workers and many other groups something with which to identify. Roosevelt used his party popularity to create programs and his programs to create constituencies. When the 1936 elections rolled around Roosevelt pulled out his familiar formula:

> "Henry," he said to Henry Wallace, "through July, August, September, October, and up to the fifth of November, I want cotton to sell at 12 cents. I do not care how you do it. That is your problem." [113]

When a Works Projects Administration (WPA) cutback in funds threatened to cut many persons off the payroll in October of that same year, Roosevelt put it to Treasury Secretary Morganthau like this:

> "You tell Corrington Gill that I don't give a God damn

where he gets the money from but not one person is to be laid off on the first of October."[114]

The President merged presidential legislation and politics, and the constituencies responded. The president of the NAACP (National Association for the Advancement of Colored People) responded: "... he had done more for the Negro than any Republican President since Lincoln."[115]

Most Presidents first win over their party, then use their political power to push their programs through the Congress. But sometimes, particularly for "hero Presidents," party activity is distasteful and awkward. Dwight D. Eisenhower (President 1953-60) was a good example of this. He could have come to the Presidency through *either* party because his popularity was broader than either one. Like Washington, Eisenhower preferred to place himself above the battle in presidential politics. Eisenhower's views about politics came from at least two sources. First there was his political philosophy. This favored returning Federal activity to the states whereever possible, encouraging private enterprise, and balancing the budget. Because he avoided pushing serious social changes until the consensus for them overwhelmed the Congress, the need for partisan politics was minimized.[116]

The other source for Eisenhower's views was strictly practical. He probably could not have controlled the Congress even if he had wanted to do so. Eisenhower faced a Congress that had been controlled by the opposition party for a longer time and by a greater majority than any President had faced since Zachary Taylor (1849-50). Even during Eisenhower's first two years, when the Congress was in Republican hands, the Republicans only boasted a majority of 11 in the House and 1 in the Senate. For Eisenhower, bipartisanship was merely a requirement of sanity. As Sherman Adams, his powerful assistant once said, "Whenever he [Eisenhower] thought any one of us became too harsh, he would remind us that we were not going to get anywhere in Congress without Democratic votes."[117] And when Eisenhower looked at his party head in the Senate, William Knowland of California, he could only hear the words of

Sherman Adams: "It would have been difficult to find anybody more disposed to do battle with much of the President's program in Congress."[118] Not that Eisenhower's precarious position was anything new for a Republican. The last time that the Republicans had controlled the Congress and the Presidency had been in 1931, a quarter of a century earlier.

Eisenhower delighted in his non-political status. And he talked about it—not only to the American people but even to his own party faithful. To one group of Republican workers he bravely admitted, "Everybody knew I wasn't a politician—and I'm not yet."[119]

For Eisenhower, there was a clear distinction between his party and his legislative program. He allowed himself to be photographed with at least 100 Republican candidates during the 1954 Congressional elections. But he rarely retaliated against them if they failed to vote for his programs. For some strong Presidents, such as Kennedy and Johnson, voting against the President's program was voting against the party. But Eisenhower was bi-partisan in dealing with the Congress and partisan while stumping for candidates.

President John F. Kennedy (1961-63) took a different view of politics. His political machine, comprised of his brothers Robert and Edward, plus Kenneth O'Donnell, his brother-in-law Stephen Smith and others, believed that the way to get programs through a Democratic Congress was to elect Democrats who would support his programs. Kennedy lavished attention on candidates who could help him in Congress. In the big northern urban areas where the Kennedy machine was well-tuned, Kennedy picked his candidates and tossed them patronage. In New York, the goodies went to those who opposed two top Democratic chiefs, Carmine DeSapio, the New York City leader, and Michael Prendergast, the state chairman. Jonathan B. Bingham was named U.S. Representative to the United Nations Trusteeship Council. Thomas Finletter, who also opposed the DeSapio leadership, became Ambassador to the North Atlantic Treaty Organization (NATO). At Kennedy's inaugural, he made it quite clear whom he favored and whom he didn't in New York. While Congressman Charles A. Buckley, Democratic leader of the Bronx, sat in the Presidential Box, Prendergast and DeSapio danced with the other 15,000 packed on the ballroom floor.[120]

When Kennedy campaigned for his candidates, he got something in return: his programs were brought to the people. With a spectacular entourage of airplanes, press secretaries, instant press releases, and busloads of aides in all shapes and sizes, the Kennedy presence generated a wave of interest and enthusiasm.

And Kennedy was not above a frontal attack on sacred Republican traditions. In 1963 Democrat Kennedy tried to take Abraham Lincoln away from the Republican Party. The White House invited a thousand persons, including prominent blacks in every field, to a gala celebration of the 100th anniversary of the Emancipation Proclamation. The Republicans were stunned.

When Kennedy died in Dallas in 1963, he died while doing the party's work. His mission was to calm rival Democratic factions in Texas. We'll never know if the Kennedy formula of urban politics over Congressional politics would have worked. But for a while, it shook up the party and focused attention on the "New Frontier" programs.

Lyndon Johnson's Presidency (1963-68) was something else. Johnson's political experience as a congressman and Senator from Texas had surprisingly little partisanship in it. He came from a basically one-party state (in those days) where consensus was the road to results. He assumed leadership in the Senate during the bipartisan Eisenhower years. And he topped off his bipartisan experience with a bipartisan philosolphy: "Come let us reason together" was one of Johnson's favorite phrases.

With this background, it's not surprising that Johnson had little experience as a partisan party leader. And the 1966 elections revealed his problem. In the off-year elections of 1966, the Republicans gained 47 seats to the House and eight governorships. To analyze what had gone wrong and to prevent such a political disaster from recurring,

Johnson called Democratic governors together at his Texas ranch. The governors told him that the "Great Society" might be designed to get votes from minorities, but that it was tripping over itself in carrying out the programs: getting Federal benefits was one thing, but taking them away if the State misbehaved (according to racial and other Federal guidelines) was quite another. The governors made it clear that they were on the receiving end of both the carrot and the stick of the Great Society, but they had no voice in setting these policies. This position was taken more by Southern governors than Northern ones, because minimum Federal standards bit the Southern hand more frequently. Johnson soon began to learn about party frustrations.

The Democratic National Committee slid into a decline under Johnson; national political committees are only as powerful as the President wishes them to be. And Johnson, pressed by campaign deficits from 1964, cut the budget of the Committee sharply. In 1966, this cutback resulted in the failure of the Committee to sponsor a national registration drive, and the White House added insult to injury in bypassing the Committee on patronage appointments. As former Texas Governor John Connally tells it, even the State party leaders were sometimes bypassed on LBJ's patronage appointments.[121]

Party money problems were also great under Johnson's reign. The President's Club, run by the National Committee, drained funds from state and local party coffers. Johnson's 1966 President's Club, for instance, siphoned off $700,000 from New York State. This was twice the amount that the Democratic candidate for governor spent in his whole campaign against his opponent, Nelson Rockefeller, who had millions to spend. And Johnson's centralization of party funds in Washington may have prevented some of the local party organizations from obtaining the money they needed to encourage new candidates to run in local races.[122] In addition, LBJ's aloof position during the 1966 elections earned him few plaudits from party leaders. While the campaign was going on, LBJ was out—first to the Far East, and then to the hospital. Such Democratic hopefuls as Governor Pat Brown in California, and Sen. Paul Douglas in Illinois ended up with no firm presidential endorsements.

Johnson's efforts to centralize campaign functions under his wing is partially explained by the Kennedy phenomenon. When Robert F. Kennedy began gearing up for the presidential nomination, Kennedy's strength naturally came from the grassroots party organizations. To the extent that LBJ could use the lawn mower on those grassroots, he was only acting in his best interests.

It is ironic that the President has become so powerful in legislative affairs, for his legislative powers are ultimately dependent on Congress. Indeed, all of his Executive powers are dependent on the Congress. Does this sound extreme? Consider a little game that constitutional law expert Charles L. Black, Jr. likes to play. It's a game that gives some interesting insight into the true nature of American government and the Constitution. He asks his audience to "identify the irreducible minimum of the American Constitution" in order to see its "deep structure." They would consider how much of our Constitution is indispensible to the formation and continuance of the government, and how much is just detail work.[123] Black then goes through the Constitution article-by-article using this test. When he comes to Article II—the one dealing with the Presidency—he would point out that the President has very little power of his own:

- His treaty making power is in the hands of the Senate;
- He has the power of appointment but only in offices the Congress creates and only for those nominees which the Senate approves and that Congress is willing to pay for;
- He is the Commander in Chief of the Armed forces, but only the Congress can raise an army, create the draft, provide for its maintenance, and promote its officers.[124]

And when the President starts taking the Congress for granted they can politically paralyze him—cut off his salary and stop passing the appropriations he needs to run his

Branch of government. And this principle applies to all of the President's legislative powers. How can the President recommend measures to Congress and give a State of the Union address, if they won't let him into the chamber? How can he approve legislation if they don't pass anything he can afford to support, and how can he veto legislation if they have the majorities to override such vetoes?

- The House as well as the Senate now regularly participates in foreign affairs legislation. This trend has accelerated since 1972, when legislation was enacted requiring the President to submit Executive Agreements to both Houses of Congress. Previously, the Congress got involved only through the Senate's treaty power.
- House and Senate members increasingly participate in international affairs legislation.[125] There is a growing appreciation that external issues affect internal interests.
- More staff experts have been hired by the Congress. Many have expertise in the Executive Branch and can compete with the President's experts.
- Members of Congress are more willing to make Executive Branch secrets public. This counteracts the President's claim that "I know more about this than you do."
- Many laws now provide for a Congressional veto of Presidential policies.

Despite recent events, the Congress generally has been giving its powers away—delegating them since the turn of the Century. This trend can be reversed if the Congress simply has the will to act. Legislation is a function shared by two branches of government. Whichever branch has the will to muster the necessary popular support can govern. It's up to the Congress to inventory and analyze the President's growing legislative powers, freeze that growth wherever necessary to prevent a further decline in Congress' role, streamline its own legislative tools, and play a more active role in initiating and shaping legislation. Near the end of this book we will return to this subject of Congress' efforts to reassert the powers it has let slip to the Presidency.

PART THREE: The Constitutional Basis for the President's Role in Legislation

A. Presidential Power at the Constitutional Convention

"All legislative powers granted herein shall be vested in a Congress of the United States . . ."—Article I, Constitution

"[the]. . . one great object of the Executive is to control the Legislature."—G. Morris of the Constitutional Convention

There is no question that the founding fathers were worried about the great power the Constitution granted to the President. And his legislative powers caused particular concern. But when they finally voted on the President's role in legislation, virtually every one of their key decisions favored a vigorous chief legislator.

This approach is understandable when we consider the men who played the greatest part in writing the Constitution's Article II, the portion dealing with the Presidency. First, there was James Wilson, who campaigned for a chief executive who could operate with "energy, dispatch, and responsibility."[126] And Gouverneur Morris, who directed the battle for a strong chief executive on the Convention floor, and then insured its victory by writing the final draft of the Constitution. Finally, there was James Madison, who was doubtful at first, but "swung around slowly but decisively to Wilson's advanced, but sensible views."[127]

Experience had taught these Revolutionary leaders that, as Jefferson had written in his *Notes on Virginia,* "173 despots would surely be as oppressive as one."[128] They had worked with the colonial governorship. They knew the problems that had developed under the state constitutions and the Articles of Confederation. And so it was natural that the U.S. Constitution was cast under the persuasive influence of such exponents of balanced government as Locke and Montesquieu. These were the elements for the Presidency provided by the Constitution:

1. *An Independent Executive.* First, the President would have his own electorate, separate from that of the Congress. This would prevent the legislature from overwhelming the President. Most delegates considered this an essential move to correct a major defect in the Articles of Confederation. As Lyndon Johnson was later to boast, "I am the President of all the people."

2. *A Fixed Term of Office*. Second, the President was to have a fixed term of office which would prevent his being ousted easily by the Congress. Unless impeached by the House and convicted by the Senate, the President was to remain in charge of the Executive Branch for a full, fixed term. Thus, his power was to be both separate and equal to that of the Legislative Branch. Alexander Hamilton felt so strongly about the merits of this decision that he devoted one whole issue of *The Federalist* to arguing for its acceptance, which, he insisted, would guarantee the "personal firmness" of the President and the "stability" of his administration.[129] Although a fixed term was important it was enhanced by the possibility of relection to an infinite number of terms. Without such a policy, the legislative power of the President would be greatly diminished as be became a lame duck toward the end of his term. This of course has since been limited by Constitutional amendment.

3. *No Executive Council.* Third, the President escaped without a legislative or executive council to share his powers. This was surprising because at the time of the convention every state constitution had such a council. One disgruntled delegate, convinced that the executive should be restrained by such a council, grumbled that even "The Grand Signor himself had his Divan."[130]

4. *An Independent Cabinet.* Fourth, the Convention delegates inserted a clause in Article I which prohibited a "person holding any office under the United States" from being

a "member of either house during his continuance in office." This hotly debated clause was finally accepted after a motion to strike it failed on a tie vote. This unique clause prohibits the development of alliances through interlocking between the Cabinet or other segments of the Executive Branch and the Congress and gives the President total authority over actions of his cabinet.

No doubt other provisions could have been added to increase the President's power. Even today Presidents long for an item veto, with which to veto only *parts* of bills, but this was not provided. Nevertheless, some Presidents have claimed the power to selectively enforce or not enforce certain parts of laws they sign. (This is discussed in detail later in this book.) A longer term of office could also have been given the President. But overall, the President was given powers which were very considerable. Based on these, the Presidency today has firmly established a role that is not only chief executive, but also chief legislator. This is despite the unequivocal language of the first Article of the Constitution which states that "All legislative powers herein granted shall be vested in a Congress of the United States."

The Constitution lists the President's major powers. He has the power both to approve and veto legislation, the power to make treaties, to nominate ambassadors, justices of the Supreme Court and all other officers of the United States. And regardless of whether they heed, he has the duty to "give to the Congress information of the state of the Union and recommend to their consideration such measures as the shall judge necessary and expedient . . ." Finally, he has the power to convene, and adjourn Congress under limited circumstances.

Each of these powers has undergone development since the Constitutional Convention. Some have been eroded, but most have been augmented. One power which has steadily grown in strength is the veto power.

B. Presidential Power Since the Constitutional Conventi

"Every order, resolution, or vote to which the concurrence of the Senate and House of Representatives may be necessary . . . shall be presented to the President of the United States; and before the same shall take effect, shall be approved by him . . ."—Article I, Section VII, The Constitution.

1. The Veto Power

In many ways the veto power is the President's strangest legislative power. The Congress could threaten to take it away if they wished: What if the Congress passed only one giant bill each year, containing all necessary measures? Under the Constitution, the President has no item veto. He must approve the whole bill or return it. What would he do in that case—let hundreds of vital measures die simultaneously by a veto or sign a bill which would contain many mini bills he opposed? Or take another case. Concurrent resolutions are not even presented to the President. What if the Congress conducted all of its legislative business by concurrent resolutions rather than bills?

(a) *History of the Veto Power.*

The veto power has a venerable history. In one form or another it has existed since before Christ. When the word "veto," meaning "I forbid," was uttered by the Roman tribune, the plebians were often protected from harsh patrician legislation.[131]

In sixteenth-century England while the Parliament's powers engulfed the King's, the King still maintained his veto power. During the reign of Henry V, for instance, the King's approval was withheld with the expression "Le roi s'avisera",—which meant "The King will think it over."[132] The English veto power was different from the President's, however. The King's veto was absolute. It could not be overridden. The King of England in theory still has a veto power over parliamentary acts. The last time an English monarch exercised this power over laws for England, however, was in 1707. One commentator has said that this power is now so withered that if Parliament were to send the King a bill providing for his own execution he would have to approve it.[133]

In colonial America, the veto power was a familiar and hated tool. The Declaration of Independence made this clear. After the phrases dealing with the right of a free people to establish a new form of government, the Declaration began spelling out the abuses which made the break with England appear necessary. The very first abuse was the King's use of the veto power:

> "The history of the present king of Great Britian is a history of repeated injuries and usurpations, all having, in direct object, the establishments of an absolute Tyranny over these States. To prove this, let Facts be submitted to a candid world:
> "He has refused his Assent to Laws, the most wholesome and necessary for the public good."

Although the King of England denied himself the power to veto domestic legislation after 1707 he continued to veto colonial acts. The King of England and as well as the governors of all but two of England's American colonies had the veto power. And the King could veto colonial acts even when they had been approved by the governors. Thus, when the Constitution was drawn up, the founding fathers knew the potential tyranny of the veto.

The veto power as written into the Constitution is perhaps the President's most important domestic power. Woodrow Wilson considered it to be such when he said the President is no greater than his prerogative of veto makes him. While the power of the Legislative Branch is to enact laws, the power of the President is to veto them. The veto is the President's great equalizer with the Congress. It is his power to go over their heads and appeal to the people. One of the strengths of the veto is that it takes two thirds of each house of Congress to override it. Until 1845, in President Tyler's term, not one bill was passed over a President's veto. In the first 78 Congresses almost 1,000 bills were

EXHIBIT I: EXAMPLE OF A PRESIDENTIAL VETO MESSAGE

TO THE HOUSE OF REPRESENTATIVES:

I am returning without my approval H.R. 4035, the Petroleum Price Review Act, because it would increase petroleum consumption, cut domestic production, increase reliance on insecure petroleum imports and avoid the issue of phasing out unwieldy price controls.

H.R. 4035 would go counter to the Nation's need to conserve energy and reduce dependence on imported oil. It would increase petroleum imports by about 350,000 barrels per day in 1977, compared to import levels under my phased decontrol plan. It would even increase imports by about 70,000 barrels per day over continuation of the current system of mandatory controls through 1977.

The provisions in this bill to roll back the price of domestic oil not now controlled, to repeal the "stripper well" exemption from price controls and to establish a three-tier price system which would require even more complex regulations would be counterproductive to the achievement of energy independence.

The bill does contain an Administration requested provision which would continue the coal conversion program through December 31st. Since coal conversion authorities authorized last year in the Energy Supply and Environmental Coordination Act expired June 30th, I urge rapid enactment of a simple one year extension of these authorities.

Last Wednesday, July 16, I submitted to Congress a compromise plan to phase out price controls on crude oil over a thirty-month period. Coupled with administratively imposed import fees, this plan will reduce the Nation's imports by 900,000 barrels per day by 1977. It will reduce our vulnerability to another embargo by adding slightly over one cent per gallon to the price of all petroleum products by the end of 1975 and seven cents by 1978.

If Congress acts on this compromise and on other Administration proposed energy taxes, including the "windfall profits" tax and energy tax rebates to consumers, the burden of decontrol will be shared fairly, and our economic recovery will continue.

I veto H.R. 4035, because it increases our vulnerability to unreliable sources of crude oil and does not deal with the need to phase-out rigid price and allocation controls enacted during the embargo. I urge Congress not to disapprove my administrative plan of gradual decontrol. If it is accepted, I will accept a simple extension of price and allocation authorities. If decontrol is not accepted, I will have no choice but to veto the simple six-month extension of these authorities now being considered by Congress.

THE WHITE HOUSE July 1975

EXHIBIT J: EXAMPLE OF A PRESIDENTIAL SIGNING STATEMENT

STATEMENT BY THE PRESIDENT

I have signed S.J. Res. 98, which provides that the flag of the United States of America may be flown for twenty-four hours of each day in Valley Forge State Park, Valley Forge, Pennsylvania.

Enactment of this measure is a fitting tribute to the determination and valor of the men who served in the Continental Army at Valley Forge. These men endured the rigors of cold, disease, and starvation during the winter of 1777-1778, to later fight and win the Battle of Monmouth, an important victory in the struggle for independence. As we approach the year of our Nation's Bicentennial anniversary, this Joint Resolution by Congress reminds us again of the unselfish sacrifices made by many American men and women who have served in our Country's Armed Forces. They have fought to establish and preserve, for Americans and free people everywhere, the right to liberty, justice, and the pursuit of happiness.

vetoed and only about 6 per cent were passed over the veto.[134] Clearly, the President's veto power is a potent one.

There are some exceptions. When vetoed bills are overridden they often are important bills. Some of those passed over a veto include the Volstead Act (which imposed Prohibition) and the Taft-Hartley Labor Relations Act.

President Andrew Johnson's term provides a case study for major veto overrides. Johnson, who himself was almost "overridden" by the Congress, lost many key veto fights: a series of acts dealing with Civil War Reconstruction, the admission of Nebraska as a state, and acts relating to the President's power to remove office holders, and the jurisdiction of the Supreme Court.[135]

The two-thirds-vote provision of the veto is potent. As few as 18 Senators (one third plus one of a quorum, which is 51 Senators) may be needed to uphold a veto while the maximum needed is 34. Then the legislation is dead. This is true even if all 435 Members of the House of Representatives support it. Thus it is no suprise that vetos are rarely overridden.

The veto power provoked substantial debate at the Constitutional Convention. George Read proposed vesting an absolute veto power in the Executive, while Hugh Williamson would have required a two-thirds vote by Congress to pass *any* legislation. Edmund Randolph's plan for the veto included a Council of Revision which could veto any bill passed by the legislature. Elbridge Gerry offered an amendment to Randolph's plan to give the President a veto unless overridden by two thirds of each house of Congress. Two months later this was changed to three-fourths, but was later changed back on the grounds that requiring more than two-thirds to override a veto would put too much authority in the hands of the President.[136] Early in the Nineteenth Century futile attempts were made to change the two-thirds provision to a simply majority, which obviously would make the veto power extremely weak, but not *entirely* meaningless, since most legislation is passed by merely a majority of those *present*, not a majority of all members. This part of the Constitution has always had its supporters and opponents.

(b) *The Veto Process*

The word "veto" does not appear in the Constitution, but the concept is there. Article I, section VII of the Constitution [see Appendix] describes the veto power in the second longest paragraph in the Constitution. This paragraph says that once the Congress enacts legislation, the President has three options within ten days:

First, he may sign the measure (traditionally by writing the word "approved" on it and signing his name). This makes it law.

Second, he may withhold his signature from the bill and return it to the house of Congress in which it originated along with a message stating his reasons for disapproval. This is a "regular" veto. If both houses pass it again by at least two-thirds majorities of their membership, the measure becomes law without the President's signature.

Third, the President may do nothing. In this case it becomes law automatically within ten days if the Congress remains in session.[137] If the Congress has adjourned, however, the bill dies. This is a pocket veto.

While this procedure may sound simple, it is actually anything but simple. Numerous problems have arisen over what each of the three steps involves. Under the "necessary and proper" clause of the Constitution,[138] the Congress has the power to enact legislation to clarify ambiguities in the Constitution. But in regard to the veto power it has not done so.

Let's review the basic types of legislation which the Congress may present to the President, and then look at a few of the unresolved issues involving the President's veto power. At the beginning Congress jealously guarded its legislative powers. When the first Congress decided what to put in the "enacting clause" [the opening words] of each bill introduced, they decided upon:

> "Be it enacted by the Senate and House of Representatives of the United States of America in Congress Assembled . . . "

—They left out the President, intentionally. Next, they tackled how constitutional amendments were to be proposed by the Congress. Here too they left out the President. By custom constitutional amendments are proposed by the Congress and sent to the states without prior approval by the President.

Congress traditionally uses four types of measures for conducting its business:

- First, there are House and Senate bills for ordinary acts. These may either be *public bills* relating to broad subjects, or *private bills,* sometimes called "private relief" bills, which relate to individuals or groups for whom Congress is providing relief or special benefits. One example is a private bill providing a government pension to a widow who cannot qualify for one under the usual legal requirements. Virtually all legislation is in bill form. See Exhibit A for an example of a bill. Bills originating in the House are designated by the letters "H.R." followed by a number. Senate bills are designated by the letter "S." followed by a number. The form for all bills is identical. They begin as follows:

  "Be it enacted by the Senate and House of Representatives of the United States of America in Congress assembled, that," etc.

- Second, there are *joint resolutions,* which are often used for ceremonial or other functions, but are also used interchangeably with bills, and if signed by the President will have the force of law. Accordingly, they are presented to the President for his approval except when they deal with constitutional amendments. The form of joint resolutions, like the form of bills, reflects the Congress' primary role in legislation. They begin:

  "Resolved by the Senate and House of Representatives of the United States of America in Congress assembled, that . . . ." [Exhibit K] Joint resolutions originating in the House are designated "H.J. Res." followed by their number. Those originating in the Senate are designated "S.J. Res." In form, joint resolutions are usually distinguished by the use of "whereas" clauses indicating the necessity for the resolution, and "therefore" clauses stating the resolves. Joint resolutions follow the same legislative procedures as bills except for the joint resolutions proposing constitutional amendment; these must be approved by two-thirds of both houses and are sent to the General Services Administration for submission to the States for approval. They are not presented to the President for approval.

• Third, there are *concurrent resolutions.* These usually are not legislative in character, but express findings of facts, opinions, and purposes of the Congress. The term "concurrent" does not mean they are simultaneously introduced in both houses; it simply means that both houses have considered them, unlike simple resolutions of a single house.

• Fourth and finally, there are *simple resolutions.* Those of the House are designated "H.Res.", those of the Senate, "S. Res." These resolutions are used for internal administrative matters ("housekeeping") or other matters concerning the operation of only one house. They are not presented to the President, but are attested to by the Clerk of the House or the Secretary of the Senate and are published in the *Congressional Record.*

(c) *Presenting Legislation to the President*

The Constitution requires that every bill in order to become law must "be presented to the President." What does this mean? As previously mentioned, this is currently interpreted as meaning that the President's ten-day clock begins to run when the enrolled bill is presented to an employee at the White House who date-stamps it and issues a receipt for its delivery.

In simpler times there were few problems in delivering a bill to the President in plenty of time for him to consider it. Then came the Twentieth Century. President Wilson was the first President to leave the hemisphere during his term of office. Although both Presidents Franklin D. Roosevelt

EXHIBIT K: EXAMPLE OF A JOINT RESOLUTION

94TH CONGRESS
2D SESSION

S. J. RES. 191

IN THE SENATE OF THE UNITED STATES

APRIL 28, 1976

Mr. TUNNEY introduced the following joint resolution; which was read twice and referred to the Committee on Foreign Relations

JOINT RESOLUTION

Relating to Presidential authority to prohibit the importation into the United States of goods and materials from Rhodesia.

Resolved by the Senate and House of Representatives of the United States of America in Congress assembled, That the United Nations Participation Act of 1945 (59 Stat. 619; 22 U.S.C. 287–287e) is amended by adding at the end thereof the following new section:

"SEC. 10. Provisions of section 10 of the Strategic and Critical Materials Stock Piling Act (53 Stat. 811; 50 U.S.C. 98–98h–1) notwithstanding, the President may prohibit or regulate the importation into the United States, its territories or possessions the importation of goods or raw materials from Rhodesia for such time as the United Nations' sanctions directed at that country remain in effect.".

EXHIBIT L: PORTIONS OF A CONCURRENT RESOLUTION

94TH CONGRESS
2D SESSION

H. CON. RES. 619

IN THE HOUSE OF REPRESENTATIVES

APRIL 27, 1976

Mr. ROUSSELOT submitted the following concurrent resolution; which was referred to the Committee on the Budget

---

CONCURRENT RESOLUTION

Resolved by the House of Representatives (the Senate concurring), That the Congress hereby determines and declares, pursuant to section 301 (a) of the Congressional Budget Act of 1974, that for the fiscal year beginning on October 1, 1976—

(1) the recommended level of Federal revenues is $363,000,000,000, and the amount by which the aggregate level of Federal revenues should be decreased is $14,800,000,000;

(2) the appropriate level of total new budget authority is $394,200,000,000;

(ADDITIONAL SECTION 1 MATERIALS OMITTED)

(page 2)

SEC. 2. Based on allocations of the appropriate level of total new budget authority and of total budget outlays as set forth in paragraphs (2) and (3) of the first section of this resolution, the Congress hereby determines and declares pursuant to section 301 (a) (2) of the Congressional Budget Act of 1974 that, for the fiscal year beginning on October 1, 1976, the appropriate level of new budget authority and the estimated budget outlays for each major functional category are as follows:

(1) National defense (050):

(A) New budget authority, $112,000,000,000.

(B) Outlays, $100,600,000,000.

(Remaining items omitted here.)

SEC. 3. The Congress hereby determines and declares, in the manner provided in section 310 (a) of the Congressional Budget Act of 1974, that for the transition quarter beginning on July 1, 1976—

(First items in section omitted)

(4) the amount of deficit in the budget which is appropriate in the light of economic conditions and all other relevant factors is $15,200,000,000; and

(5) the appropriate level of the public debt is $646,200,000,000, and the amount by which the temporary statutory limit on such debt should accordingly be increased is $19,200,000,000.

and Harry S. Truman went abroad while the Congress was in session, they had few problems with signing legislation because Congress was controlled by the President's political party. If the President were out of town, the party leaders could arrange for the legislation to be held up for a few days and presented to the President when he returned. Professor Corwin relates one instance some years ago when a bill was approved by the President some 23 days after final adjournment of the Congress.[139] This didn't work all the time, however. When President Wilson suffered a stroke in 1919-1920, some 28 bills automatically became law through the operation of the ten-day rule.[140] But President Franklin D. Roosevelt on one occasion vetoed a joint resolution claiming that this "was presented to me on November 25, 1943." In fact, the item was presented to the While House while he was abroad on November 18, 1943.[141] Clearly he was seeking a more liberal interpretation of the "presentation" language. Obviously, such conflicts breed litigation. If the Congress wanted to insist that the President's time had run out and the bill had become law without his signature, it could prove troublesome. By the same token, near the end of a session, the President might attempt to pocket veto a bill by telling his staff not to present it to him until the Congress had adjourned. In that case he could conceivably—even if not very convincingly—claim the bill had died.

Who may sign the legislation presented to the President when the Presidency is changing hands? Let's suppose that a bill arrives at the White House and the clock starts running on its ten-day countdown. If the President's term runs out first, can the incoming President sign the legislation or veto it? The Supreme Court seems to have hinted that an incoming President cannot act on the legislation. We have a partial answer in some of President Truman's actions. After Roosevelt's death in 1945, Truman approved bills which were presented to Roosevelt. But Truman was never challenged for doing so, and so the issue remains somewhat in doubt.

(d) *Adjournment*

(i) *Before Approval*

For nearly 150 years it was generally believed that the President had no power to approve legislation after the Congress had adjourned or while it was in recess. Indeed, "it was the practice of Presidents to go to the Capitol on the last day of each session to sign the final bills which he intended to approve." An act was presented to President Andrew Johnson in 1864 while the Congress was in recess. Johnson promptly refused to sign it on the grounds that he had no authority to do so.[142] This inconvenience so irked President Grant that he suggested a constitutional amendment preventing the Congress from voting for the passage of any laws in the last 24 hours of the session unless it was reviewing those already vetoed.

In 1869, President Lincoln received a bill for his signature just after the Congress had adjourned. He signed it within the ten-day period, but this wasn't considered good enough by the Congress. When the new Congress formed, the House adopted a resolution requesting the Judiciary Committee to inquire whether the act was in force. They concluded that it was not, reasoning that constitutionally if the President could hold the bill for ten days after adjournment before approving it, he could just as well hold it for ten months.[143]

President Cleveland's Attorney General came out with some interesting reasoning as to why the President couldn't sign legislation after adjournment. In his view, the President was a "part of the Congress" in its legislative role, and when they adjourned, so did he—at least for legislative purposes.[144] This view continued well into the Twentieth Century, and as late as 1916 former President Taft maintained that it was clear the President could not sign a bill after adjournment. However, President Wilson started what finally proved to be stampede in the other direction by signing several bills after adjournment. His actions were butressed with a convenient opinion by his Attorney General that such a practice was legal. Finally, the Supreme Court helped to straighten this situation out when in 1932 they ruled (in *Edwards v. United States*) that the President did have the right to sign bills after adjournment.[145]

(ii) *Adjournment Before Disapproval—The Pocket Veto*

In recent times, the most controversial facet of the veto power has been the pocket veto. The pocket veto arises when the Congress passes legislation and then adjourns before the President has acted upon that legislation within the ten-day period. In such cases the act does not become law but dies. And the Congress gets no chance to override the veto. They must legislate from scratch with a new bill.

The pocket veto was rarely used by early Presidents. Contributing to this was the fact that until the Second World War adjournment within a session of Congress was unusual. There were only eighteen pocket vetoes before the Civil War, and Jackson produced seven of these. All took place after the final adjournment of the Congress or after the adjournment of a session of Congress.[146] Thus none occurred while the Congress was merely in recess.

The Supreme Court has spoken only twice on the subject of pocket vetoes. In the *Pocket Veto Case* of 1929[147] the Court held that a pocket veto was just as valid at the end of a session of Congress as at the end of a Congress. This finding was partially based on the argument that if the Congress was in adjournment, no officer or agent was authorized to receive the rejected bill. Thus, it was dead.

A few years later, Franklin Roosevelt vetoed a bill and sent it back to the Secretary of the Senate while the Senate was in a three-day recess. The beneficiary of the bill then ran into court claiming that the bill must have become law because the Senate was incapable of receiving it when it was not in session. In 1938, the Court, modifying their earlier decision, held in *Wright v. United United States*,[148] that the Secretary of the Senate did have the power to receive the President's message during the recess, and thus the bill was validly vetoed.

Lyndon Johnson, however, may be the only President to "take back" a veto. In 1964 he purported to pocket veto a bill relating to the Court of Claims by returning it to Congress with a "memorandum of pocket veto." Two days later he recalled his veto and signed the bill! By then the Congress was in adjournment for the Democratic National Convention. Thus, the President's action didn't arouse much reaction. But what might have happened if he had done this on an important measure? Hopefully, this isolated act will not be used as a precedent for further presidential acts of doubtful validity.

One of the most interesting collisions on the pocket veto took place between Senator Edward Kennedy and President Nixon. In 1970, the Congress overwhelmingly passed the Family Practice of Medicine Act which authorized grants to hospitals and medical schools. The Senate had passed this legislation by 64 to 1, and the House by 345 to 2. This bill was presented to the President on December 14. On December 22, both houses of Congress adjourned for the Christmas recess. Before adjourning, the Senate specifically authorized the Secretary of the Senate to receive messages from the President. On Christmas Eve President Nixon announced he was disapproving the Act, ostensibly by pocket veto. This was intended to avoid the virtual certainty that the veto would have been overturned when the U.S. Congress returned from its recess. Senator Kennedy maintained that the act became law following the expiration of the ten-day period. The President, on the other hand, argued that this was a pocket veto and the act had died. By treating the Christmas break as if it were *sine die* (final) adjournment at the end of a session, Nixon could employ an absolute, irreversible veto. This was the first time any President had tried such a feat.

Senator Kennedy sued the President. In Kennedy's words: "If the pocket veto clause applies to a five-day adjournment, why should it not also apply to an adjournment of three days, or a weekend, or one day, or even overnight?"[149] In *Kennedy v. Sampson,*[150] the Court of Appeals agreed with the Senator that the pocket veto could not be used during a five-day Christmas recess because the recess did not prevent the return of the bill to the Congress. The Court made it clear that the length of the recess wasn't the issue. Indeed, said the Court:

> "The length of an intrasession adjournment per se does not prevent the return of a disapproved bill for reconsideration. The Constitution sets no time limit on the right of Congress to override a presidential veto."[151]

When President Nixon pocket vetoed another bill during the January 1974 intersession adjournment of Congress and President Ford pocket vetoed a bill during a 31 day intrasession adjournment for the November 1974 Congressional elections, Kennedy brought a second law suit. This time President Ford announced a change in policy: he had "determined that he will use the return veto rather than the pocket veto during intra-session and inter-session recesses of the Congress."[152] Kennedy had finally won: the President had announced he would obey the law.[153]

(e) *Measures Subject to the Veto Power*

The Constitution requires "Every Bill which shall have passed the House of Representatives and the Senate"[154] to be presented to the President. The Constitution doesn't define the term "bill." During the Constitutional Convention, Madison pointed out that this language might permit Congress to bypass the President merely by enacting resolutions instead of bills. He suggested that the words "or resolve" be added after the word "bill." Although his motion was rejected, Randolph's proposal that a second sentence be added was adopted.[155] That sentence, which is now part of the Constitution, says:

"Every Order, Resolution, or Vote to which the Concurrence of the Senate and House of Representatives may be necessary (except on a question of adjournment) shall be presented to the President."—Article I, Section 7.

Unfortunately this didn't do enough. Confusion immediately sprang up regarding whether proposed constitutional amendments, in the form of joint resolutions, needed to be presented to the President. In 1794, the Congress passed a joint resolution proposing an amendment to the Constitution, and didn't send it to the President. Indeed, neither were any of the ten original constitutional amendments that became the Bill of Rights presented to President Washington before they were sent to the States for ratification. Washington didn't object to this, but when the Eleventh Amendment went through this way the Supreme Court was asked to decide—in the case of *Hollingsworth v. Virginia*[156]—Whether such a presidential bypass was constitutional. They held that it was, on the grounds that the Congress was acting not as a legislative body but as a constituent body, whatever that means.

Like joint resolutions, concurrent resolutions also are not sent to the President. Often they are used to terminate rather than to enact statutes. One example is the Lend-Lease Act of 1941.[157] Frequently, legislation contains its own termination date. In the case of the Lend-Lease Act, however, Congress provided that the Act would terminate "... after the passage of a concurrent resolution by the two Houses ..."[158] And the Civil Defense Act of 1950 provided that "The provisions of this title shall terminate on June 30, 1954, or on such earlier date as may be prescribed by concurrent resolution of the Congress."[159]

There's something strange about this. If the President's signature is required to enact legislation, why isn't it equally necessary in order to repeal legislation?

Another variation of this practice is found in the Reorganization Acts. These Acts, which have been used to authorize reorganizations in the Executive Branch, sometimes provide that the plans submitted by the President in response to the authorization given by the Act become effective after a given date unless they are rejected by a concurrent resolution. This, to some extent at least, is legislation in reverse. The President legislates and the Congress vetoes. In political and practical terms, such a practice makes sense. In constitutional terms, it raises serious questions. In 1904, when the concurrent resolution issue arose, the President pro tempore of the Senate verbally threw up his hands and said:

> "Within the experience of the Chair of the Senate no concurrent resolution has ever been sent to the President of the United States, nor has he ever signed one. The Chair has endeavored faithfully to find out how concurrent resolutions escape the provisions of the Constitution. He has not been able to succeed." [160]

There appears to be no question that this practice is sanctioned in history but not specifically in the Constitution.

One theory for treating concurrent resolutions differently from bills and joint resolutions is that they are not "legislative in nature and have no effect beyond the confines of the Capitol." But this is hardly an answer. Concurrent resolutions have been used to influence policy by terminating administrative actions. And one concurrent resolution, the War Powers Act of 1973, enables Congress to terminate by concurrent resolution a presidential commitment of troops abroad if the commitment is not authorized by the Congress.[161] Whether this is an *increase* in Congress' power vis-a-vis the Chief Executive and Commander in Chief, or a *decrease* in its constitutional power to declare war (through recognition of an implied right of the President to comit troops unless "vetoed" by Congress) is unclear.

At one time, some members of Congress believed that the President's veto couldn't reach private bills. But President Grant, who vetoed 29 private bills, and President Cleveland who vetoed many more, put an end to such wishful thinking.

On the theory that levying taxes and providing appropriations are basic powers of the purse entrusted particularly to the Congress, some early legislators felt that revenue and appropriations measures were also immune to the veto. This theory, however, was cut to ribbons by Presidents James Madison (1809-17), James Monroe (1817-25) and Andrew Jackson (1829-37), all of whom vetoed expenditure bills, and by President Rutherford B. Hayes (1877-81) who became the first President to veto a general appropriation measure on policy grounds.

(f) *Grounds for Veto*

These days, when Presidents occasionally veto legislation for little more than political advantage, it comes as a shock to learn that many Presidents thought they could only veto legislation if it was unconstitutional. George Washington, for instance, felt that he could veto legislation only on the "clear and obvious ground of propriety," and declared that he gave his signature to "... many bills with which my judgment is at variance."[162] Jefferson, who didn't veto even one bill during his two terms, apparently felt much the same. President William H. Taft (1909-13) took off in the other direction by maintaining that the could *not* veto legislation on constitutional grounds at all because it was the role of the Supreme Court to determine its constitutionality. President Jackson argued that it is just as much the role of the President and the Congress to decide what is constitutional as it is the Court's. And Jackson proceeded to practice what he preached. He vetoed twelve bills in eight years—more than all of his predecessors' vetoes put together. His Bank Veto Message of 1832 advanced not only constitutional but social and economic reasons for his action, and became a campaign document for the coming election.[163] In recent years Presidents have used the veto power more than their predecessors. In contrast to Jefferson's record of no vetoes, we have Franklin Roosevelt's record of 633, and Truman's of 250.

President Eisenhower is often deemed a conservative in his views of the role of the President vis-a-vis the Congress. But on the veto, which he used 181 times, he showed no hesitation, and once said:

> "By the Constitution, I am part of the legislative process. I think that the American public expects its President always to exercise his best judgment in giving his approval or disapproval or qualified approval or disapproval in such cases. That's exactly what I do . . . I think it is a disservice to veto anything merely because it has failed in some detail to go along with the the expressed views of the President. On the other hand, as quickly as it gets out of line I think the President is not doing his duty unless he does express disapproval."[164]

(g) *The Item Veto*

The Constitution provides in the simplest language, "Every bill . . . shall . . . be presented to the President . . . If he approves he shall sign it, but if not he shall return it . . . "[165]

There appears to be little doubt that the President cannot approve one part of a bill and reject the rest. The Constitution does not provide an item veto, but many Presidents have wished for such power and a few have acted as if they had it. Until the Civil War, the country apparently was without widespread discussion of this issue. But with the adoption of the Confederate Constitution and state constitutions providing for item vetoes, the possibility of a Presidential item veto became obvious. Some states today go farther and allow the governor not only to veto appropriations bills, but also to reduce the items in such legislation.[166]

During the Civil War the Congress began adding legislative riders to appropriations bills. This cornered the President into vetoing the whole bill, which would cause delays in necessary appropriations, or approving a bill with undesired parts. President Grant took issue with this policy by proposing a constitutional amendment allowing the item veto. And Grant in effect exercised an item veto through selective enforcement of at least one public works bill.

When Grant got into a fight with Senator Stephen Douglas of Illinois over Douglas' criticism of the fact that a public works bill hadn't helped his state at all, the President replied when signing another bill that he would refuse to spend funds on projects which were "of purely private or local interest . . ."[167] Presidents Hayes and Arthur also supported an item veto amendment but would have restricted their proposal to appropriations bills.

(h) *The Veto Power as An Offensive Weapon*

The veto power is often thought of as a negative power. It shoots down legislation. But the use of the veto is just the tip of the iceberg. The times when its use is merely threatened can mold legislation within certain bounds acceptable both to the Congress and the President. This makes the veto power a creative force. When President Ford told Congress in 1975 that he would veto a tax cut unless it was accompanied by a corresponding reduction in expenditures, he was both shaping legislation and trying to build a campaign platform for his reelection.

The veto power may also be used to punish particular congressmen. One example of this was President Roosevelt's three-time veto of routine livestock legislation introduced by Senator McCarran of Nevada, who had taken an active role in opposing the President's court reorganization bill and other measures.

The item veto threatens the basic structure of the Constitution. If the will of Congress can be reversed by a President declaring various parts of laws null and void, the Constitution might be little more than a cover for a dictatorship. In 1969, the Attorney General and the Secretary of Health, Education and Welfare issued a statement that the Administration had decided not to enforce Title VI of the Civil Rights Act of 1964. This title required the government to cut off federal funds to school districts which continued racial discrimination. When the government was taken to court, it argued that Title VI was permissive—it didn't require the government to enforce it. But a unanimous court of appeals disagreed. In *Adams v. Richardson*[168] the court held that the language was mandatory, and the Secretary of HEW was ordered to enforce the law.

In 1973, the Nixon Administration acted again to ignore the law. This time it struck against the Office of Economic Opportunity. The OEO, which was established to wage Lyndon Johnson's "war on poverty," continued in a diminished status in the Nixon Administration. In sending his 1974 budget to Congress however, Nixon simply omitted funds for OEO programs and ordered the newly appointed Acting Director of OEO to begin dismantling the agency. The courts found that Nixon's efforts "would in effect give the President a veto power through the use of his budget message"—a veto power not contemplated in the Constitution. The Administration, continued the court "really argues that the Constitution confers the discretionary power upon the President to refuse to execute laws passed by Congress with which he disagrees." If this were the case, "no barrier would remain to the executive ignoring any and all congressional authorizations, if he deemed them . . . contrary to the needs of the nation."[169]

But the item veto issue has two sides. It is wrong for a President to exercise an illegal item veto. But it may also be wrong for the Congress to so load up bills with non-germane amendments that the President is forced to retaliate. The Congress should not try to steal the President's veto power. When the Congress starts combining small, unrelated bills into big ones, they are trying to change the rules of the legislative game. It is not clear that combining bills is unconstitutional. But it does tend to upset the balance of powers in a way not envisioned in the Constitution.

Of course, a President's veto or veto threat may backfire. President Ford's veto of the common situs labor bill in 1975 cost him the resignation of his Secretary of Labor, John Dunlop. Rumor had it that Ford's energy chief Frank Zarb, who worked 16-hour days to put together the Administration's energy bill in 1975, would have resigned if Ford had vetoed that measure.

The veto power has had a way of getting tangled up in election-year politics. When the Congress convened in January, 1976 one of its first items of business was taking up the $45 billion omnibus appropriation for health, welfare and labor programs which the President had vetoed before Christmas. Ford wanted that veto to be sustained. It would stake out a conservative position for him on welfare policies right before his first primary fight with fellow Republican challenger Ronald Reagen.

But the Democrats were waiting for Ford. They wanted to portray him as the great nay-sayer, while the Democrats fought for jobs and social programs. And the veto was overridden by a wide margin. Ford's Budget Director James Lynn went away licking his wounds—"They've only been in session for six days, and they've already added $1 billion to the budget. With this kind of performance, it's going to be a long year."[170]

(i) *The "Legislative Veto"*

Under the Constitution, only the President has a veto power. In recent years, however, there has been a trend toward giving the Congress a veto over actions of Executive Branch agencies. This has been called the legislative veto.[171] A legislative veto occurs when an administrative decision, usually exercised by the President or an agency, is submitted to the Congress for review and approval. Congressional approval may come from the whole Congress, one house, or even by a committee, subcommittee, or handful of members. Sometimes approval is expressed when the Congress does nothing: the decision stands unless the Congress overrides it within a set time period such as 30 or 60 days. Other times, the Congress must take some affirmative action to indicate approval. Generally, however, Congressional approval or disapproval can't modify or amend an administrative decision, it can just take it or leave it *in toto.*[172]

Constitutionally, the "legislative veto" presents problems. According to some, it violates the legislative process set forth in the Constitution and breaks down the separation of powers. And it may illegally delegate powers to individual members of Congress and committees that only the Congress as a whole can legally exercise. Opponents of the legislative veto argue that our Constitution spells out a government of limited powers. Only those powers specifically granted to the Congress may be exercised by it, because the rest are specifically reserved to the states or to the people by the Tenth Amendment.

But there are strong arguments in support of the legislative veto. First, although the legislative veto is not specifically sanctioned in the Constitution, it may be implied in the "necessary and proper clause" of the Constitution. Second, there are several powers that Congress exercises in legislating which are not specified in the Constitution, such as the power to hold legislative investigations, and the power to pass concurrent resolutions and not present them to the President.[173] Thus the legislative veto might just be another implied power.

But another argument against a legislative veto is that it infringes on the President's veto power. It is a form of legislation. Therefore it must be presented to the President for his approval or rejection. Finally, there is the question of whether Congress may legally delegate such veto power to one house, a committee, subcommittee, or the doorkeeper if necessary. But the Congress has done it and has not been stopped. Perhaps this is the simple answer to a complicated problem. Will the courts stop a practice which has been tolerated by the President and used by the Congress? Probably not. Were the Supreme Court to declare the "legislative veto" illegal, it would be directly challenging the two other branches of our government. Regardless of the theoretical merits, the Supreme Court is not such a glutton for punishment.

A bill to give Congress veto power over present, past, and future rules and regulations written by federal agencies and departments was narrowly defeated in the House of Representatives on September 21, 1976. The bill would have allowed one house of Congress to veto any proposed rule or regulation of almost any federal department or agency within 60 days of promulgation, provided the other house did not object within 30 legislative days of the veto. It would also have allowed one house to veto existing rules by passing a resolution forcing the agency to reconsider the rule, after which the agency would have 60 days either to withdrew the rule or regulation, or to issue a new rule. The legislative veto bill was considered under a procedure that required a two-thirds vote to pass it , and the vote was 265 to 135, showing majority support for such an extension of Congressional powers.

Many members at the Constitution Convention were concerned about the veto power. In general, their worries were of two sorts. The first, a concern of Madison, Wilson and others, was that the veto might regularly be overturned by the Congress and prove to be virtually worthless. The opposing view, held by Benjamin Franklin and others was that the veto might be so potent that it could revive the English and Colonial experience and lead to despotism.[174] In fact, neither of these worries has materialized. The veto has been a consistently useful, though limited, tool.

2. Treaty Power and Executive Agreements.

> *"He [the President] shall have power, by and with the advice and consent of the Senate, to make treaties, provided two-thirds of the Senators present concur . . . "*—
> Article V, section II, the Constitution

The treaty power was seen by the Founding Fathers as one area in which the Executive and the Senate could cooperate. The delegates to the Constitution Convention were not pleased with the Articles of Confederation which allowed only Congress to control foreign affairs.

And so they took the middle ground: The President would be required to submit treaties to the Senate for approval. In James Wilson's words, collaboration would be in "the spirit of an executive council."[176] Thus Washington started by seeking the advice of the Senate on negotiating treaties. But the Senators were afraid of this arrangement. They suspected that the President wanted "to tread on the necks of the Senate."[177] Thus, they discussed treaties by themselves, leaving the President to seek his own counsel. It wasn't very long before the President himself preferred such an arrangement. For awhile, however, the President continued to submit to the Senate the names of those who were to negotiate treaties—called commissioners—for the Senate's approval. But even this practice ended after 1815 when the President took full control of negotiating treaties while the Senate reserved the right to approve them, modify them, or reject them.

As a result, the treaty making process is traditionally viewed as two separate functions: the negotiation of treaties by the President and their ratification by the Senate. This arrangement was solidified with the establishment in 1816 of the Senate Committee on Foreign Relations, which ever since has acted in the ratification process. Just as the President is free to negotiate or not, so is the Senate free to consent or not to consent. Indeed, they may even consent in part. If the Senate consents conditionally, it may do so by amendments which become binding: the reservations the Senate adopts to the treaty limit the U.S. obligations under that treaty. This may or may not be acceptable to the other nations which are parties to the treaty or international accord or convention.

Sometimes the President balks at the Senate's advice and refuses to proceed further with the treaty. From 1789 to 1929, while the President proclaimed some 900 treaties, 200 were either rejected by the Senate or so altered by it that either the President or other countries refused to accept them.[178]

The Senate learned to enjoy its spoiler role. From 1871 to 1898 it ratified no important treaties at all. And when it came time for the ratification of the Treaty of Paris with Spain, it squeaked through the Senate with only two votes to spare. This was despite President McKinley's appointment of senators to the negotiating commission which produced the treaty. The Senate's record on treaty approvals became so notorious that Woodrow Wilson once quipped that the treaty making power had become the "treaty-marring" power.[179]

Treaties may be terminated not only by their own provisions but by a mere act of Congress. In addition, they may be denounced by the President alone or by the President and the Senate together. Of course, such actions would leave the continuing significance of the treaty, if any, a matter to be determined under international law.[180]

Recently, the hottest part of the debate between Congress and the President over treaties is not how to get *out* of international argreements, but how the President gets into them. Frequently, in recent years, Presidents negotiate agreements with other governments which are not referred to the Senate for advice and consent. There are two kinds of such agreements: those the President is authorized by an act of Congress or treaty to make, and those which the President or his subordinates negotiate under his power as Commander-in-Chief of the Armed Forces and chief diplomat. The first sort of agreements are generally non-controversial. In 1792, the Congress authorized the Postmaster General to enter into postal conventions. They have been entered into repeatedly since then. In the foreign trade field, acts of Congress delegating to the President the power to negotiate trade and customs duty agreements are numerous,[181] and the President's powers in this area generally are not in dispute.

"Executive agreements" made by the President with the governments of other nations without either the advice and consent of the U.S. Senate or an act of Congress are more controversial. The line between such agreements and treaties—which must be submitted to the Senate—is not clear; nor has it ever been. As early as 1817, British Minister Bagot and President Monroe's Secretary of State Richard Rush exchanged notes limiting naval forces on the Great Lakes. Not until one year later was this agreement submitted to the Senate, which promptly ratified it. In submitting it Monroe asked the Senate a crucial question. Is this "such an arrangement as the Executive is competent to enter into by the powers vested in it by the Constitution, or is such an one as required the advice and consent of the Senate?"[182] Monroe never got an answer—and neither did we. Similiar questions arose with the 1898 agreement between the United States and Spain which ceded Cuba and Puerto Rico to us; the protocol for ending the Boxer Rebellion in 1901; the World War One Armistice of November 11, 1918, and the controversial "Yalta" and "Potsdam" agreements[183] near the close of World War Two, as well as a host of more recent military assistance agreements, not all of which are even made public.

In 1905, the Senate refused to ratify a treaty which Theodore Roosevelt had negotiated with Santo Domingo. The treaty would have placed certain customs houses under United States control. The President, in that style which made him famous, simply changed this proposed "treaty" into an "agreement" and proceeded to carry out its terms. A year or so later, the Senate, not wanting to be left out, ratified his agreement and thereby converted it back into a "treaty."

In that same year, Roosevelt made a secret agreement with Japan which put the seal of American approval on the Japanese military protectorate in Korea. No one found out about this one until a historian unearthed it in Roosevelt's papers some twenty years later. And Roosevelt didn't mince any words in his executive agreements. When the Russo-Japanese war broke out, "I notified Germany and France in the most polite and discreet fashion that, in the event of a combination against Japan to try to do what Russia, Germany, and France did to her in 1894, I should promptly side with Japan . . . to whatever length was necessary on her behalf."[184] Where this left the Constitution and the Congress is not altogether clear.

This ratification issue arose in another context during the Senate's consideration of the Sinai agreements negotiated by the Executive with Israel in 1975. According to the State Department, this agreement didn't have to be sent to the Senate in treaty form because "the President has the discretion to choose whether to conclude any particular agreement as a treaty or as an executive agreement."[185]

Over the years, the Supreme Court has tended to side with the President's views on executive agreements. In the *Belmont* case, for instance, the Court held that if an "executive agreement" is within the power of the President, it is law of the land which the courts must give effect to not withstanding any state law or judicial policy to the contrary.[186]

The Office of Legislative Counsel of the Senate has taken a totally different approach. In its view, matters of "exceptional national importance must be submitted as treaties . . . " In the legal Counsel's view, if the President could decide in each case whether or not to submit the agreement to the Senate, it would make a mockery out of the constitutional provision requiring the Senate to ratify treaties, because there might never be any treaties to ratify. Any smart President would simply conclude all international agreements as executive agreements and not send them to the Senate.

Where the truth lies in this debate is not clear. "By far the greatest proportion (about 86 percent) of executive agreements are authorized by statute. Only approximately 2 to 3 percent are authorized solely by . . . the President." [187] Certainly, some agreements must be presented to the Senate or the Constitutional provisions relating to treaties would be a nullity. Yet it should be obvious that many agreements with other nations today simply are kept secret. The continuing validity of such agreements, however, is placed into great doubt when the U.S. Presidency changes hands.

But the Senate's remedy of binding the President to a standard of "importance" in choosing an agreement or a treaty and limiting his flexibility in delicate foreign transactions has problems as well. Unfortunately, neither the Constitutional debates, the Constitution, nor the courts give us much guidance on this issue. It apparently will be settled as so many other questions are—by which side has the most persuasive facts in a given case; and the most important fact may be raw political power.

Sometimes, however, it is the Congress which enters the field of foreign affairs without the President. In 1845, Texas was annexed by a joint Congressional resolution. A half century later this example was followed by the annexation of Hawaii.

In practice, the President and a mere *majority* of both houses of Congress can pretty well do as they wish in such matters regardless of the feelings of the Constitutionally required two-thirds of the members of the Senate.

EXHIBIT M — A PRESIDENTIAL PROCLAMATION

PROCLAMATION 2667

Policy of the United States with Respect to the Natural Resources of the Subsoil and the Sea Bed of the Continental Shelf.*

WHEREAS the Government of the United States of America aware of the long range world-wide need for new sources of petroleum and other minerals, holds the view that efforts to discover and make available new suppliers of these resources should be encouraged; and

WHEREAS its competent experts are of the opinion that such resources underlie many parts of the continental shelf off the coasts of the United States of America, and that with modern technological progress their utilization is already practicable or will become so at an early date; and

WHEREAS recognized jurisdiction over these resources is required in the interest of their conservation and prudent utilization when and as development is undertaken; and

(PORTION OMITTED.)

NOW, THEREFORE, I, HARRY S. TRUMAN, President of the United States of America, do hereby proclaim the following policy of the United States with respect to the natural resources of the subsoil and sea bed of the continental shelf.

Having concern for the urgency of conserving and prudently utilizing its natural resources, the Government of the United States regards the natural resources of the subsoil and sea bed of the continental shelf beneath the high seas but contiguous to the coasts of the United States as appertaining to the United States, subject to its jurisdiction and control. In cases where the continental shelf extends to the shores of another State, or is shared with an adjacent State, the boundary shall be determined by the United States and the State concerned in accordance with equitable principles. The character as high seas of the waters above the continental shelf and the right to their free and unimpeded navigation are in no way thus affected.

IN WITNESS WHEREOF, I have hereunto set my hand and caused the seal of the United States of America to be affixed.

DONE at the City of Washington this 28th day of September, in the year of our Lord nineteen hundred and forty-five, and of the Independence of the United States of America the one hundred and seventieth.

HARRY S. TRUMAN

By the President:

DEAN ACHESON,

Acting Secretary of State.

*See Executive Order 9633, 3 C.F.R. 1943-1948.

3. Presidential Appointments.

"... and he shall nominate, and, by and with the advice and consent of the Senate, shall appoint, ambassadors, other public ministers and counsuls, judges of the Supreme Court, and all other officers of the United States, whose appointments are not herein otherwise provided for, and which shall be established by law; but the Congress may by law vest the appointment of such inferior officers, as they think proper, in the President alone, the the courts of law, or in the heads of departments." —Article II, Section II, The Constitution.

Obviously this language puts the President squarely into the business of nominating officers of the United States who must be confirmed by the Senate. But as we know from the confirmation experiences of Special Prosecutors Archibald Cox as well as Leon Jaworski during the Watergate investigation of President Nixon, this language is not as simple as it looks. Except for the President and the Vice President, civil officers of the United States are appointed and fall into two classes. Either they are "Presidential officers" or "inferior officers." Presidential officers are nominated by the President, confirmed by the Senate and commissioned by the President. Because the offices of "ambassador," "public minister" and "counsul" were recognized by the "Law of Nations." [i.e.—"natural" or international law] it was first thought that the President could nominate them himself as necessary. But since 1855 the Congress has asserted its right to review and confirm such appointments. There is a class of personal agents to the President, including members of the White House staff, who are appointed without Senate confirmation. The Director of the Bureau of the Budget used to be in this class by virtue of the Budget and Accounting Act. But this Act has since been amended to require confirmation by the Senate of the head of the Agency which replaced the Budget Bureau, the Office of Management and Budget.

Congress can create, under the "necessary and proper clause" of the Constitution, any offices it wishes. It may also stipulate what qualifications appointees shall have, but in doing so the Congress must leave at least some discretion to the President. Otherwise Congress would infringe on the President's executive powers. This principle was recognized in the Civil Service Act of 1883, which allows an executive branch appointing officer to select from among candidates who are qualified on the basis of fitness tests prescribed by Congress. Congress has the power to regulate the conduct of civil officers and even control their outside political activity under the Hatch Act.

As to removal of officers, if an officer is an agent of the President, working within the excerise of his powers, he is removable at the will of the President, not of the Congress. The power of removal is based on the President's duty to "take care that the laws be faithfully executed."

4. Confidentiality and Executive Privilege.

> *"A popular Government, without popular information or the means of acquiring it, is but a Prologue to a Farce or a Tragedy; or perhaps both."*—James Madison to W.J. Barry, Aug. 4, 1822.

It didn't take long for Congress to figure out that access to information from the Executive Branch was the key to congressional control. Indeed, the Constitution itself required the President "from time to time [to] give to the Congress Information of the State of the Union." Nor was this duty restricted to the annual presidential trek to Capitol Hill to give a speech. Mr. Justice Story in his *Commentaries* stated that the Constitution required "the President to lay before Congress all facts and information which may assist their deliberation."

Information is the key to power both in the international and the domestic spheres. "The management of foreign relations," James Madison had stated, "appears to be the most susceptible of abuse of all the trusts committed to a Government." This was because foreign relations could be "concealed or disclosed, or disclosed in such parts and at such times as will best suit particular views."[188] The Executive's natural desire to keep things under his hat was inevitably in conflict with the assumption, inherited from the British experience, that the Congress was "a grand inquest" and had the right to fully inform itself on all public matters.

The information issue first arose in 1792 when the House of Representatives, investigating General St. Clair's fiasco against the Indians in the Northwest Territories, asked the President for "such persons, papers and records as may be necessary to its inquiry." President George Washington took this request seriously because he knew it would set a far-reaching precedent. He called his Cabinet into session. He didn't object to the Congress being an "inquest," he told his Cabinet, and so Congress was recognized as being generally entitled to some papers, at least those "as the public good would permit." But there were times when certain matters were to remain secret. Thus the President "ought to refuse those, the disclosure of which would injure the public: consequently they were to exercise discretion."[189] In this case, after reviewing the papers, Washington decided to give them all to the House. And he did more. He sent along his Secretaries of War and the Treasury to answer questions. Thus, the precedent for giving up information was publically established. And the reservations Washington had made to his Cabinet were not communicated either to the Congress or the public, and thus had no immediate value as precedent.

Nevertheless, Washington's actions have often been misinterpreted. Richard Nixon, who never hesitated to cite a precedent expanding his own power, once declared, "The doctrine of Executive privilege is well established. It was first invoked by President Washington, and it has been recognized and utilized by our Presidents for almost 200 years since that time."[190]

The next time the confidentiality issue arose it split the Founding Fathers. In 1796, the House asked for copies of diplomatic instructions and other information relating to the Jay Treaty with England. Washington turned the House down flat. He pointed out that generally he didn't wish to withhold information from the Congress. However, in this case, he had already sent all of the relevant papers to the Senate, and the House simply had no valid interest in the materials because it was specifically excluded from the treaty-making power by the Constitution. These materials were irrelevant to the House, said Washington, except for impeachment purposes. And impeachment was not in issue here.

James Madison took to the floor of the House and defended his political opponent Washington. Madison conceded that the President had "a right, under a due responsibility... to withold information, when of a nature that did not permit a disclosure at the time." But John Adams (who was Washington's own Vice President) disagreed, at least in a letter to his wife. "I cannot deny the right of the House to ask for papers" wrote Adams, "... my ideas are very high of the rights and powers of the House of Representatives."[191]

If Washington set a precedent here—that the House couldn't get treaty papers because the Constitution barred it from the treaty power—that precedent didn't stand for long. Two years later President John Adams sent the House papers relating to negotiations with France. And so it continued through the early Presidents. They generally agreed that the Congress was a grand inquest and had the right to the necessary information to perform their functions as the peoples' representatives.

One by one however, Presidents added new grounds for witholding information from the Congress. In 1807, Jefferson witheld information relating to the Burr conspiracy on the grounds that some of the materials requested were "a mixture of rumors, conjectures, and suspicions... and that much of it had come to him ... under the restriction of private confidence." He thus added an exception for the protection of personal privacy and confidential informants. The Congress may have seen this objection coming because their request had meekly exempted anything that Jefferson might "deem the public welfare to require not to be disclosed."[192] Thus, the President was merely carrying out the intent of Congress in making his denial.

President Jackson's experience was different however. In 1833, the Senate asked Jackson for a copy of a paper he had read to his cabinet during discussions on the Bank of the United States. Jackson told them to get lost. "I have yet to learn," he told the Senate, "under what constitutional authority that branch of the Legislature has a right to require of me an account of any communication, either verbally or in writing, made to the heads of Departments acting as a Cabinet council. As well might I be required to detail to the Senate the free and private conversations I have held with those officers on any subject relating to their duties and my own."[193]

Jackson thus added still another reason for non-disclosure–confidentiality in the personal exchanges with Executive Branch officials.

But the Senate struck again. In 1835, they asked for more information. Jackson replied in so many words that he was being harassed:

> "This is another of those calls for information made upon me by the Senate," he shot back, "which have, in my judgment either related to the subject exclusively belonging to the executive department or otherwise encroached upon the constitutional powers of the Executive. . . . Their continued repetition imposes upon me, as the representative and trustee of the American people, the painful but imperious duty of resisting to the utmost any further encroachment of the rights of the Executive."[194]

Later Presidents continued to add to the laundry list of why information couldn't be handed over to the Congress. Tyler told the Congress that matters currently in private litigation and involved in ongoing investigations were his, not theirs. And Polk resisted the Congress' attempt to obtain information relating to foreign intelligence operations.

In 1954, at the height of the Army-McCarthy loyalty hearings, President Dwight D. Eisenhower sent a letter to the Secretary of Defense directing employees of that Department not to testify about any conversations or communications among themselves, or to produce any documents that could be interpreted as rendering internal advice within the Department.[195] In 1958, Attorney General William P. Rogers presented a statement to the Senate Subcommittee on Constitutional Rights which argued that the Executive had almost unlimited discretion to withold information from the Congress.[196]

John Kennedy apparently invoked executive privilege only once. In 1962, a Senate committee demanded to know which of Secretary of Defense McNamara's subordinates had deleted war-like passages from speeches by admirals and generals. Kennedy turned the Committee down, saying that McNamara had called his own shots and it would not be possible to run the Department of Defense if the Secretary's subordinates were continually answerable to the Congress. When Chairman Stennis of the Senate Armed Service Committee took up the matter he concurred by saying, "The chair sustains the [Secretary's] plea . . ."[197]

In further congressional forays for information from the Executive, Kennedy laid down a position that "each case must be judged on its own merits." He rejected any broad claim to executive privilege. Some on the Hill were not convinced, however. "The powerful genie of executive privilege is momentarily confined but can be uncorked by future Presidents," prophesied Congressman John Moss.[198] Moss was right. With the Nixon Administration the cork came out of the bottle. To perfect his plan of expanding the power of the Presidency in all directions it was essential that Nixon control the flow of information reaching the Congress. During his first term Nixon invoked executive privilege four times. Members of his Administration rejected formal congressional requests for testimony or documents an additional 15 times. And members of the White House staff refused to testify eight times.[199] In addition, footdragging and the threat of refusal to cooperate were even a greater impediment to the Congress. In Senator Symington's words:

> "More often than not it has been the implied threat of executive privilege, rather than its actual exercise, that has hovered over negotiations to obtain the release of information, even in executive session; information which we considered so crucial to the Senatorial responsibility that it belonged to the Committee as a matter of right; and therefore information which should have been volunteered."[200]

To justify his program of denying information to the Congress, Nixon invoked the Eisenhower doctrine that the President had "uncontrolled discretion" to keep executive information from the Congress. Thus, Attorney General Kleindienst could tell the Ervin subcommittee in 1973 that it was the "constitutional authority of the President in his discretion" to withold information in his possession "or in the possession of the Executive Branch" if he believed that disclosure would impair the proper exercise of the President's constitutional functions. When incredulous Senators asked whether this meant that the Congress could not compel testimony from any of the millions of Federal employees in the Executive Branch over the President's objection, Kleindienst replied that that was exactly what he was saying.[201]

The Nixon doctrine of executive privilege was all the more potent because of the way he ran the Executive Branch. First, Nixon put the power to run the Administration in personal White House assistants, such as Assistants to the President John Erlichman. Then, he wrapped the blanket of executive privilege around his entire White House staff and thus prevented the Congress from getting certain information. Nixon did this despite the admission from his counsel, John Dean, that "no recent President has ever claimed 'blanket immunity' that would prevent his assistants from testifying before Congress on any subject."[202] Under previous administrations, when the State Department or any other Department had a major role in setting policy, the Congress could call up the Cabinet officer concerned and get much of what they wanted. But when there was no one to testify except White House officials covered with a blanket of executive privilege, the Congress was stymied.

And Nixon continued to extend Executive privilege. In 1973, he announced that not only present but also former White House employees were entitled to executive privilege.[203] Later that year, Nixon extended executive privilege to informational requests from Federal grand juries and the Federal Bureau of Investigation.

Next, he wrapped all "presidential papers" in executive privilege. Presidential papers were defined as "all documents, produced or received by the President or any member of the White House staff in connection with his official duties."[204]

Of course, Presidents may protect themselves and their

agents from attack, either by assuming their defense in litigation or by refusing to hand over papers to Congress in certain limited circumstances.[205] But as the celebrated case of *United States v. Nixon*[206] held, neither the doctrine of separation of powers nor the general need for high-level confidentiality sustains an unqualified executive privilege, at least in regard to criminal acts. As the Supreme Court unanimously stated in the Nixon case, "the generalized assertion of privilege must yield to the demonstrated, specific need for evidence in a pending criminal trial."[207] The extent of executive privilege from congressional subpoenas, however, is yet to be determined. In addition, the Supreme Court has left open the question as to whether the Judicial Branch would ever order military or state secrets to be revealed by the President. Instead, in *United States v. Nixon* the Court cryptically offered the dicta that: "It is . . . necessary in the public interest to afford presidential confidentiality the greatest protection consistent with the fair administration of justice."[208]

Nixon's need for secrecy began to sow the seeds of its own destruction. In the Spring of 1969, Nixon exploded with rage when he learned of leaks to the *New York Times* about secret B-52 bomber raids on Cambodia in furtherance of the war in Vietnam. Apparently these leaks didn't come as any surprise to the Russians, the Chinese or the Cambodians, but Nixon may have been concerned about their impact on the anti-war movement. Nixon complained that these leaks were endangering national security (despite statements to the contrary by the State Department and the Department of Defense) and ordered wiretaps on the telephones of between ten and twenty members of the National Security Council staff and four newspapermen. The infamous political "emenies list" of 1971 followed. With the list came a memorandum by Presidential Counsel John Dean detailing "how we can use the available Federal machinery to screw our political enemies."[209]

Next came a Nixon interagency committee to develop schemes for better domestic intelligence operations. In July 1970, Nixon issued a memorandum which authorized surreptitious entry—breaking and entering—for the purpose of seeking intelligence information. Nixon aide Tom C. Huston, while supporting and proposing an extremely harsh "internal security" program, specifically warned the President that such tactics were illegal, but the President nevertheless proceeded. After the illicit publication of the Pentagon Papers in 1971, Nixon established the "plumbers" operation in the White House to plug further leaks. The plumbers instigated the break-in of the office of Daniel Ellsberg's psychiatrist, and when other excesses such as the break-in of the Democratic National Committee produced Watergate, the whole house of cards began to fall.

With its fall, not only the Constitution but the Congress and the judiciary were made stronger. And many of the abuses carried out in the name of secrecy were stopped. But it was a close call.

Nixon's actions were an illustration of "watch what I do, not what I say." On the surface, he made some gestures of sharing information with Congress. In 1969 he issued a memorandum to all agencies ordering them to comply "to the fullest extent possible with Congressional requests for information" and establishing a formal procedure for invoking executive privilege. Under the procedure, the agency head wishing to invoke the privilege would consult with the Attorney General. If they agreed that the privilege should not be asserted, that was to be the end of the matter. If either believed it should be asserted, the matter would be referred to the White House Counsel's Office, which would relay the request to the President. But the procedure "was no better or worse than the decision-making pyramid."[210] This procedure does reduce the temptation for an agency head to arbitrarly refuse information to the Congress.

5. Presidential Messages

"He shall from time to time give to the Congress information of the state of the Union, and recommend to their consideration such measures as he shall judge necessary and expedient."—Article II, section II. Constitution.

Often, the President has been seen by a wary Congress as an intruder on the congressional turf. The Constitution,

EXHIBIT N -- FROM A PRESIDENTIAL MESSAGE

To the Congress of the United States:

At the dawn of the twentieth Century, almost as a voice in the wilderness he loved, President Theodore Roosevelt proclaimed an environmental ethic for America. He said:

> *I recognize the right and duty of this generation to develop and use our natural resources; but I do not recognize the right to waste them, or to rob by wasteful use, the generations that come after us.*

At the dawn of the 1970's there was still no more significant challenge facing Americans than the task of wisely conserving our natural resources and leaving the Nation a cleaner and healthier place for our children and grandchildren.

(SEVERAL PAGES OMITTED)

I proposed a new type of law for pollution control purposes—a charge on harmful sulfur oxides emissions. This proposal embodies the principle that the price of goods should be made to include the costs of producing and disposing of them without harm to the environment. I also proposed a law that would employ our tax structure to discourage potentially harmful development in our precious coastal wetlands.

I have asked for a new and more effective Federal law to protect endangered species of wildlife—by covering species likely to become endangered as well as those more immediately threatened, and by imposing Federal penalties for taking of such species.

These proposals, and others I have put forward, are vital to all Americans in the years to come. But the critical final steps have yet to be taken. The Nation needs these laws, and they should be enacted this year. The Congress has a splendid opportunity to leave an historic record of environmental achievement, an opportunity which it must seize. The time for deliberation has passed. *It is now time for action.*

(PORTION OMITTED)

I am reminded of Benjamin Franklin's remark at the Constitutional Convention in Philadelphia, when he pointed to the golden half-sun engraved on the back of General Washington's chair: "Now at length I have the happiness to know that it is a rising and not a setting sun."

Richard Nixon

THE WHITE HOUSE, *August 1972.*

however, clearly gives the President the right to transmit information to the Congress with his recommendations any time he pleases. Combined today with the power of mass media, it is one of the most important aspects of the President's legislative power.
was well used.

The President's State of the Union Address has been seen in various ways by various Presidents. George Washington considered it something like the formal ceremonial speech of the English Monarch to the Parliament. Recently, such speeches have been mood pieces, setting the tone for the administration while the details are left for individual messages to Congress. This constitutional duty to keep the Congress posted from time to time is, in the words of Richard Neustadt,

> "...a handy and official guide to the wants of its [Congress'] biggest customer; an advance formulation of main issues at each session; a work-load ready-to-hand for every legislative committee; an indication, more or less of what may risk the veto; a borrowing of presidential prestige for most major bills."[212]

6 • Convening and Adjourning Congress

> "[the President] *may, on extraordinary occasions, convene both houses, or either of them, and in case of disagreement between them, with respect to the time of adjournment, he may adjourn them to such time as he shall think proper ...*"—Article II, section III, the Constitution.

Presidents have occasionally called the Congress back into session. Sometimes this was because there was urgent work to be done, and sometimes it was just to score political points by blaming the Congress for inaction. The Senate has also been summoned by itself "for the consideration of nominations and treaties."[214] But the President's power to adjourn the houses of Congress has never been used.

But one old statute dealing with this constitutional power gives the President the power to convene the Congress in a place other than Washington, D.C. in cases of "contagious sickness" or other circumstances.[215]

7. Faithful Executive of the Laws

"[the President] *shall take care that the laws be faithfully executed*... "—Article II, section III, Constitution.

This final constitutional clause dealing with the President's legislative powers spells out his duty to "take care" that others in the Executive Branch faithfully execute the laws. Without proper execution, legislation is meaningless.[216] And as the Supreme Court held in the *Neagle* case,[217] the President may execute even non-existent laws. *Neagle* takes us back to the days of the wild and wooley West. U.S. Supreme Court Justice Field was in California "riding the Circuit"—sitting as a Circuit Court Judge in the days when Supreme Court Justices used to perform such menial tasks—when a man named Terry, who had previously threatened to kill him, assaulted him. Deputy United States Marshal Neagle, who was assigned to protect the Justice, killed Terry. California officials locked up Neagle on a state murder charge. Neagle was promptly released by the Circuit Court on a Federal writ of *habeas corpus* on the grounds that he was in custody for an act done pursuant to the laws of the United States. But the state sheriff who arrested Neagle appealed to the Supreme Court.

On appeal, the Sheriff argued that there was no Federal law authorizing U.S. Marshal-protection for the justice. Thus, the act could not have been done pursuant to the laws of the United States. The Supreme Court crawled out of this legal box by declaring that a law was present even though there wasn't one. They said that "the law of the United States," which was the basis for the *habeas* action included not just statutes and treaties but all "rights, duties and obligations growing out of the Constitution itself, our international relations, and all the protection *implied* by the nature of our government under the Constitution ..."[218]. In short, the President not only enforces laws that are on the books, but even those that aren't.

PART FOUR: Statutory and Other Legal Support for the President's Role in Legislation

In addition to the vast powers that the Constitution gives the President, Congress has expanded the President's legislative powers by enacting many statutes. Two of the most important are the Budget and Accounting Act of 1921,[219] which established the Bureau of the Budget (now called the Office of Management and Budget), and the Reorganization Act of 1939,[220] which created the Executive Office of the President—the White House's own bureaucracy.

The Budget and Accounting Act revolutionized the way the federal government prepared its work plan—the annual budget. But it also gave the President the tools with which to overwhelm Congress. For many years after the passage of this Act, the Executive Branch grew in legislative power, initiating much of the legislation itself. And Congress, instead of proposing and passing the laws, fell into the role of primarily being a source of legislative oversight and/or obstruction. This state of affairs continued unabated at least until the partial awakening of Congress from the abuses of legal power during the Nixon Administration. One backlash was the passage by Congress of the Budget and Impoundment Control Act of 1974;[221] its purpose was to reassert the intended role of Congress in bugetary matters.

To see these important acts in perspective, it is necessary to know what preceeded them and how the federal government previously had planned its legislative programs and the annual budget.

A. Development of the Budget Bureau and Early Budgetary Procedures

To aid analysis, five major periods in United States budgetary history can be identified prior to the passage of the Budget and Impoundment Control Act of 1974.

1. *The Articles of Confederation: 1776-1789.* This first working agreement among the thirteen American colonies which had declared their independence from Great Britain was something more than a mere multilateral treaty among independent states, and something less than the complete basis for a national government. Proposed to the Continental Congress on July 12, 1776, the Articles were recommended for adoptation on November 17, 1777. The last of the thirteen self-declared states ratified the articles in 1781, and the first Congress under the Articles was convened on March 2, 1781. They were in effect until replaced by the Constitution on March 4, 1789.

Under these "Articles of Confederation and perpetual union between the states" there was no provision for an independent executive department, although the exigencies of the Revolutionary War (which lasted until 1783) centralized a few such powers in the military command of General George Washington. The sole organ of national government was a Congress of a single chamber comprised of representatives of the thirteen states. Each state had one vote, and the agreement of nine states was required to pass important legislation. The Congress could not impose taxes (it depended on contributions from the states), and was powerless to prevent trade "wars" of retaliatory tariffs among the states. Congress resorted to the printing press to finance its bills, particularly during the Revolutionary War, and printed some $40 million in paper money which was later virtually entirely repudiated. It also borrowed several millions from the French and the Dutch governments from 1778 to 1783, and was unable even to pay the interest. Congress could not even negotiate binding treaties—commercial or otherwise. In short, there was little national government of any sort.

There was agitation at least from 1780 for a stronger national government, and this was almost accomplished in 1781 when all of the states except Rhode Island agreed to give the national government tariff powers. But the Rhode Island veto set the national budgetary system back for eight years, until 1789, when this and more sweeping powers were granted to a national government under fundamentally the same basic Constitution in use today.

2. *The Constitutional Period to 1921.* After the Constitution went into effect in 1789, a customs service was adopted and Treasury Department formed which was patterned on the British concept of the Exchequer.

It became the duty of the Secretary of the Treasury to "prepare and report estimates of the public revenue and public expenditures."[222] In 1800, legislation codified this process by providing that the Secretary of the Treasury should lay before the Congress at the commencement of every session a report:

> "... on the subject of finance, containing estimates of the public revenues and public expenditures, and plans for improving and increasing the revenues from time to time ..."[223]

There is no evidence, however, that this procedure actually was ever followed, apparently because of jealousy and hostility between the Legislative and Executive Branches. Finally, in 1884, Congress forced it to be followed by providing that estimates of appropriations and deficiencies "shall be transmitted to the Congress [only] through the Secretary of the Treasury and in no other manner."[224]

The country rocked along under this relatively primitive procedure with amazingly few difficulties, apparently because receipt's were so often in line with expenditures. Up until the 20th century, total receipts of the Federal government (mostly customs revenues) amounted to only $15 billion, while total expenditures came to a little more than $16 billion; the national debt was $1.4 billion.[226] Occasionally, however, problems developed, some of which would cause modern Congressional watchdogs to hit the panic button. President Lincoln, for instance, once directed the Secretary of the Treasury to advance, without requiring security, $2 million of public money to two gentlemen to be used by them in requisitioning materials necessary for the "defense of the government." According to one scholar, this controversial act was necessary under a "law higher than the statutes."[227]

3. *First Years of the Bureau of the Budget: 1921-1932.* With the passage of the Budget and Accounting Act of 1921, preparation of the budget and certain important management fuctions were given to the Bureau of the Budget. The Bureau was organized as a part of the Treasury Department, but reported directly to the President, who was directed to submit the budget in whole to the Congress.

This important period began in 1911 when President Taft's Commission on Economy and Efficiency issued a report entitled "The Need for a National Budget." The President forwarded this report to the Congress and urged its enactment in a message which stated:

> "Notwithstanding the magnitude and complexity of the business which is each year conducted by the executive branch and financed by the Congress . . . there is at present no provision for reporting revenues, expenditures, and estimates for appropriations in such manner that the Executive, before submitting estimates, and each Member of Congress, and the people, after estimates have been submitted, may know what has been done by the Government or what the Government proposes to do."[228]

This message contained six recommendations, including the submission of a budget each year to the Congress by the President; a budgetary message setting forth the significance of the proposals and a summary of expenditures, estimates and changes of law which would encourage economy and efficiency.

The next year, 1912, President Taft went down to defeat, but his recommendations survived and gradually won support. The Chamber of Commerce found by a referendum that the majority of its members favored this change, and public groups sprang to its assistance. By 1919, the national debt had risen rapidly—to $25.5 billion—and President Wilson called for the adoption of a budgeting system in his annual message to Congress. Congress responded in 1920 by legislating most of what he had requested. Yet Wilson then vetoed it on the grounds that its provision for a Comptroller General, who was independent of the Executive and beyond the President's power of removal, was an unconstitutional limitation on the Presidency.

In 1921, however, a similar bill was passed and President Harding signed it into law; the Budget and Accounting Act of 1921 was born. This Act provided for the preparation of the annual federal budget and established management duties within the Bureau of the Budget. BOB was placed in the Treasury Department but reported directly to the President. The House committee report on this legislation attempted to make it clear that Congress was not surrendering its authority over appropriations:

> "It will doubtless be claimed by some that this is an Executive budget and that the duty of making appropriations is a legislative rather than Executive initiation of the budget, but the President's responsibility ends when he has prepared the budget and transmitted it to the Congress. To that extent and to that extent alone does the plan provide for an Executive budget, but the proposed law does not change in the slightest degree the duty of Congress to make the minutest examination of the budget and to adopt the budget only to the extent that it is found to be economical. If the estimates contained in the President's budget are too large, it will be the duty of Congress to reduce them. If in the opinion of Congress the estimates of expenditures are not sufficient, it will be within the power of Congress to increase them."[229]

In fact, however, the ball had been moved from the Congressional to the Executive court. That same year, General Charles G. Dawes was appointed by President Harding to be the first Director of the Bureau of the Budget. The immediate impact of the Bureau on the Federal establishment is shown by General Dawes' first report to the Cabinet:

"I am glad to say that the Secretary of the Treasury walked upstairs to my office—one of his subordinate bureau chiefs—because he regarded it as necessary in connection with a call from me for information needed by the President of the United States. That will be an historic walk in the annals of the Budget Bureau."[230]

4. The Early Years Under Franklin D. Roosevelt The fourth chapter in our budget history, one of experimentation and budget deficits, runs from the start of the Roosevelt era in the Great Depression through 1939. The Budget Bureau staff remained small, numbering about forty, but new budget concepts were being developed, and many more responsibilities were being assigned to the Bureau. In 1933, for instance, the Bureau's budgetary functions were increased by an Executive Order that gave it authority to make quarterly financial apportionments to the agencies of the federal government. This power to apportion is central to the impoundment controversy discussed later in this volume. In 1936, the Bureau was directed to assist the President in the consideration, clearance, and preparation of Executive Orders and proclamations. These powers, marked the beginning of "legislative clearance"—the heart of the President's formal machinery for the control of what is legislated.

5. *Establishment of the Executive Office of the President: the Reorganization Act of 1939.* Beginning in 1937, there were developments which were to open a new chapter in the Budget Bureau's history and lead to the passage of the Reorganization Act of 1939, which established the Executive Office of the President and placed the Bureau of the Budget within it to occupy a key position of federal control. In 1937, Chairman Louis Brownlow of the President's Committee on Administration Management submitted a report to President Roosevelt who summarized it in a message to Congress that same year. This message said in part:

"To bring our administrative management up to date, the Committee presents an integrated program, which you will find set out in its report. It includes these major recommendations:

"1. Expand the White House staff so that the President may have a sufficient group of able assistants in his own office to keep him in closer and easier touch with the widespread affairs of administration, and the make the speedier clearance of the knowledge needed for Executive decision.

"2. Strengthen and develop the managerial agencies of the Government ...

"3. Overhaul the 100 independent agencies, administrations, authorities, boards, and commissions ..."[231]

The Brownlow Committee's proposals constituted a tremendous expansion in the role of the President's power. They were discussed for two years by the Congress, and incorporated in the Reorganization Act of 1939. Later that year, by Executive Order, the President defined the functions of the newly established Executive Office of the President and assigned the following duties, among others, to the Bureau of the Budget:

" ... to assist the President in the preparation of the budget and the formulation of the fiscal program of the government;

"... to advise the executive departments and agencies of the government with respect to improved administrative organization and practice;

" ... to aid the President by clearing and coordinating departmental advice on proposed legislation and by making recommendations as to Presidential action on legislative enactments, in accordance with past practice;

" ... to assist in the consideration and clearance and, where necessary, in the preparation of proposed executive orders and proclamations ..."[232]

And so the Bureau of the Budget arrived at maturity. With the approach of the Second World War, the Bureau staff was expanded to approximately 600 under Director Harold D. Smith. Five divisions were formed:

- *Estimates,* which assisted in budget preparation and apportionment;
- *Administrative Management,* which was responsible for organization and management studies;
- *Fiscal,* which advised on economic aspects and the Budget Message;
- *Statistical Standards,* which coordinated the far-flung statistical programs of the Executive Branch; and finally,
- *Legislative Reference,* which was responsible for clearing and coordinating Executive Branch legislation.

But the Bureau's increased responsibilities did not terminate with the end of the War. Presidents Harry S. Truman and Dwight D. Eisenhower were both budget-minded men. Despite the sharp drops in overall federal expenditures which occurred in 1947 and 1948 due to lessened military expenses, a tight rein was maintained on budget increases in other federal operations. The late forties and fifties saw the Bureau take over many new responsibilities, for the die had been cast. The Budget Bureau, reporting only to the President, was firmly in charge of legislation for the Executive Branch, and could force its policies on reluctant agencies by holding the reins on their budget.

The Bureau of the Budget wasn't the only agency established in the Executive Office of the President (EOP). In addition to BOB, the Executive Office also included the White House Office; the Council of Economic Advisors and the National Security Council were placed there by 1947. In the 1970's ten offices and councils were attached to the Executive Office.

> "These agencies cost $100 million to operate in 1973, a figure which exceeds annual expenditures for the entire federal government during much of the nineteenth century. President Nixon had noted the expansion of the EOP from 570 employees in 1939 to 4216 staff members in 1973. This is a far cry from the lone presidential assistant who advised Woodrow Wilson or the two presidential aides assigned to assist Herbert Hoover."[233]

B. The History of Legislative Clearance

The President's legislative power in the Executive Branch evolved largely during the last half century. It developed in a pattern that parallels the President's increased powers in other spheres. In regard to legislation, that power is coordinated through the Office of Management and Budget (OMB), and the process is called legislative clearance. This is the power of the President, acting through the Legislative Reference Division of the OMB, to control legislative proposals, Executive Orders, Proclamations and other legislative and quasi-legislative materials within the Executive Branch. It is also the President's major tool for control of legislation in Congress. No bill can leave the Executive Branch without being "cleared" by the President—that is, in practice, by OMB. And no agency's comments on any bill can be transmitted to Congress unless the President clears them. Neither are legislative proposals generally presented to the President until he has the views of every key agency on the proposed legislation in front of him and the summary views of OMB on top. This is legislative clearance as it is designed to work, but it is an over-simplified view. Things do not always work so smoothly. Nevertheless it is reasonably close to the true state of affairs. OMB's legislative clearance has been called:

> ". . . the only clearing house that operates regularly between the multitudinous departments and bureaus . . . sometimes the only possible way to get government agencies working together . . ." [234]

Not that legislative clearance is the only way to coordinate legislation. The continued power of White House super staff, such as the National Security Council and the Domestic Council may sometimes make legislative clearance look like a seldom-used second string. But it is not. It is still the mechanism which Presidential advisors lean upon most heavily to control legislation. This resilient system has survived many Presidential transitions, from Herbert Hoover to Roosevelt and from Lyndon Johnson to Richard Nixon. Where did it come from?

1. The Bumpy Beginnings—Financial Clearance in the 1920's

In 1921 the Budget and Accounting Act rearranged both ends of Pennsylvania Avenue. Down in the Executive Branch it took away the agencies' powers to decide for themselves what appropriations they wished from the Congress. Now the President and only the President was to make that decision. And the Congress gave him a whole new agency to help him—the Budget Bureau. On Capitol Hill only one committee in the House of Representatives was to receive and act on appropriations—the House Appropriations Committee. The other seven committees that had handled appropriations bills would no longer do so. And the Senate was to follow suit in 1922 with a similiar change in its rules. The Budget Bureau and these congressional committees had a common goal: to close off all other exits and force financial legislation to be channeled through their system alone. End runs were caught and cancelled. Legislative clearance began to operate.

You can't say that this change was the result of a power-grabbing President. The idea apparently didn't even come from the White House—it came from the Congress. In 1921, Chairman Madden of the House Appropriations Committee became enraged when two appropriations bills came to the Hill but were referred to another Committee. He wrote the Budget Director insisting that all such bills come "through the Bureau of the Budget . . ."[235]

The President responded with what has become a trademark of OMB operations ever since. He issued a Budget Circular. The history of OMB is the history of budget circulars. This first one was inexplicably called Budget Circular Number 49. In it the President let the departments have it broadside. All executive branch proposals for legislation which might require appropriations "or create a charge upon the public treasury"[236] were to be sent to the Congress with a letter from BOB giving the Congress the President's "advice" on the legislation.

Because the BOB instructions set up a roadblock between the agencies and the President—not to mention between the agencies and the Congress—the agencies' reaction was predictable. They didn't like it. The rest of the Hoover Administration's history of legislative clearance is of weaving and dodging their complaints.

There were some clearance powers the President could have asked for but didn't. One was to stop wayward agency views in regard to proposed legislation *originating* in Congress from going to the Congress. The President didn't do that and Presidents still don't, for the most part. What the President can do is to study the agency's views and add in a paragraph with his own views. And the President's views carry the implicit warning: "If you side with the agency against my wishes, you run the risk of a veto if such legislation ever passes Congress."

The other thing that Hoover did was to allow agencies to provide a "technical drafting service" when asked to do so by the Hill. If a congressman wishes a bill drafted by an agency, the agency can draft it without clearance. But no agency policy position can be taken on such a bill without OMB clearance. Hoover didn't have to let the agencies get away with this. But he did. And now it is tradition.

By 1924 legislative clearance procedures were running fairly smoothly. The Bureau of the Budget had been organized and staffed. And just in the nick of time. For on to the scene charged Calvin Coolidge, the greatest evangelistic budget-cutter ever seen. For him, budget balancing and economy were not just good practice, they were an indispensable part of a moral code. "I am for economy and after that I am for more economy," said Coolidge.[237] Straight-laced Mr. Coolidge generated a lot of jokes during his reign. One that made the vaudeville circuit in many variations ran something like this:

"I hear Calvin Coolidge just died!"

"Oh really, how can you tell?"

But no one joked about Coolidge's belief in government economy. In 1924 Coolidge's Budget Director General Lord saturated key departments with letters of warning, complaint and outrage over failure to comply with legislative clearance. In Lord's view the price tag on proposed legislation determined its success. Agency reports asking for too much money were frequently denied or found to be "in conflict" with the President's program. Agency reports saying that a proposal was "unnecessary" were quickly cleared to the Hill. When BOB got two conflicting agency reports, one saying "yes" and one saying "no" to a program, the no's usually won. Clearance was in full swing, but bills were judged on their costs. This was financial rather than policy clearance. In non-financial policy questions, the Bureau took a back seat as clearance procedures didn't apply.[238]

When Herbert Hoover took over the Presidency in 1929, he examined legislative clearance and simplified it. "Why clear everything," he apparently concluded, "when the Congress pays so litte attention to most of it." Under Hoover, no bills were cleared until Congress expressed an interest in them. To further cut the volume of agency reports he received, clearance was not required on unfavorable agency reports or reports on private bills. Hoover's motive may have been less ideal policy than simple practicality. Because he cleared all bills personally, he may have had an interest in cutting his own work load. As the Great Depression came and grew, Hoover had more reason to use the clearance process to balance the budget by stiffling costly legislation. And he did just that. Nevertheless, his cost-cutting program was so unsuccessful that in the heat of a political campaign Mr. Hoover was actually accused of being a big spender by the man who replaced him and so vastly expanded the U.S. Government—Franklin D. Roosevelt.

2. Roosevelt and Budget Bureau Revolution

In 1933 Franklin Roosevelt blew into town. He threw the Hoover appointees out and took over. Programs for dealing with the Depression suddenly were generated all over town. Many were contradictory. And some might have been downright destructive. A battle raged in FDR's Administration between those who wanted to fulfill his campaign promises of a balanced budget and those who favored massive government spending to prime the economic pump. In the confusion that followed, the procedures of legislative clearance were temporarily forgotten. In fact, few in Roosevelt's Administration had even heard of it. But things were to change, and drastically. The confusion of conflicting agency programs came to Roosevelt's attention and he was determined to put a stop to it. In 1934, during a National Emergency Council Meeting Roosevelt told the Group that he had been: "... quite horrified—not once but half a dozen times—by reading in the paper that some department or agency was after this, that, or the other without my knowledge."[239]

The remedy, he explained, was for legislation to be cleared by the Administration. To carry this out, another BOB Circular was drafted to require all agencies to clear proposals for legislation and views on pending legislation through BOB. The kicker was that it applied to both appropriations and non-appropriations bills. For a time, policy matters not involving appropriations were to be cleared by the President through his Emergency Council Staff. But this was soon to give way to BOB clearance alone when the Council faded out of existence.

Roosevelt's clearance system was designed not only to protect the President from the agencies but also to protect agencies from each other. He wanted the Congress to know where he stood on legislation without it being confused by voluminous agency proposals. As Roosevelt put it:

> "Obviously I have to confine myself to what the newspapers called last year 'The comparatively small list of *must* legislation.' If I make every bill that the Government is interested in *must* legislation, it is going to complicate things ... very much ..."[240]

FDR made it clear that in his view there were three kinds of legislation. The bad stuff that "I could not give approval to—[clearance] will eliminate that." Second was "the type of legislation which we are perfectly willing to have the department or agency press for, but . . . I do not want to put it in the category of major Administration bills."[241] This could be called the "I don't mind if you do but don't look to me for help legislation." And finally there was what Roosevelt called "must legislation," which was at the heart of FDR's personal legislative program. If legislation required clearance—coupled with BOB "advice" as to how the President felt about it and how it ranked in those three categories—the President would be protected from his agencies. No matter what the agency told the Hill in private, it was only the White House that could deliver on the promise by signing the bill. And everyone would know where both the agency and the President stood on the proposed legislation. On the other hand, agencies would be protected from themselves by legislative clearance because it would prevent them from ". . . stepping on each others' toes . . ."[242] with conflicting views. And there was one final aspect to legislative clearance. It would generate new ideas, at least in theory. In Roosevelt's words it would "give somebody else outside the department itself the opportunity to have happy thoughts."[243]

On paper the system looked excellent. But it wasn't used much except for minor legislation. From 1935 to 1936 clearance "was restricted almost entirely to minor department bills. . ."[244] The big bills and matters personally discussed with the President escaped this process.

Over the next few years however, things began to change. Legislative clearance caught on, and a much higher percentage of proposed legislation became subject to it. There appear to be at least three causes for this change. First, the National Emergency Council (NEC) fell into disuse, and BOB filled the power and legislative policy gap created by its decline. Second, the creative stream of New Deal programs slowed down, making more legislation routine and thus subject to clearance. Finally, the legislative clearance process attached itself to the enrolled bill process (i.e.—not only to legislative proposals generated within the Executive Branch but also to bills passed by both houses of Congress and ready for the President's signature or veto).

The Brownlow Committee, which was charged with reorganizing the President's staff, reported in 1937 that the NEC's functions should be given to BOB, and that BOB should be made a part of the President's own office. This was no suprise; the report merely stated what already had been taking place informally.

In 1937, with the Brownlow Report in hand, Director Bell did something that we've seen before. He issued another BOB circular. This time it was Circular Number 344, which kicked the NEC out of the clearance process altogether. Bell then increased his legislative clearance staff and reorganized it as a separate entity called the Division of Coordination. This was the predecessor of the Legislative Reference Division of OMB.

The change in Roosevelt's handling of enrolled bills shows just how rapidly BOB was building its clearance power. Around 1937, BOB began requesting the views of all agencies on private bills which had passed the Congress and provided for expenditures. BOB then took these views, consolidated them, attached a discussion memo, and sent them to the President's desk with the bills attached. The White House staff liked the process. It saved them valuable time in analysis. As a result, they requested that BOB handle certain other bills in the same way. By 1939 all bills were run through the BOB in this way. This evolution is a good example of the "ratchet effect" of bureaucratic power: when a system is formalized to use power, it rises but rarely falls. We will see this time and again in BOB's development.

But there still were technical problems to be overcome in the enrolled bill process. The first was that in the days before inexpensive copying processes, there was just one enrolled bill—the official copy from the Congress for the President's signature. Passing this priceless treasure from agency to agency to get views was sometimes impossible and always cumbersome. In 1938, however, the Public

Printer caved in to BOB requests that multiple copies of the enrolled bill be made. These copies were sent to BOB the same time that the official copy of the enrolled bill went back to the Congress for signature by the Speaker and the Vice President. Now BOB could really get rolling. And they issued a new circular to announce some new routines.

Circular 346, issued in 1939, "by the direction of the President" officially designated BOB as the indispensable agent of the President in handling all enrolled bills. BOB requests for agency views were to be given absolute priority. Replies were to be at BOB within 48 hours of their request, and were to include a factual summary of the bill, and a recommendation for Presidential approval or veto. Any veto recommendation was to include a proposed veto message or (for use with pocket vetoes) a memorandum of disapproval. The current system had come of age.

FDR loved it. The veto power was only potent when it was used. And FDR loved to use it. "If the decision is close, I want to veto." he once remarked to his Cabinet.[245] And veto he did. In 1939 he vetoed sixteeen bills which the Bureau had recommended that he approve. "The Budget Bureau is getting too soft; tell them to stiffen up," he said.[246] And Roosevelt even called on occasion for "something I can veto," as a "reminder" to department heads and congressmen alike that he was the President.[247]

Because BOB input into the enrolled bill process was institutional not personal to the President, FDR added a "final political filter." In 1943, "Judge" Samuel I. Rosenman, a Special Counsel to the President, was assigned to review the BOB enrolled bill package before it went to the President. Ever since, (with a few exceptions) the President's legal advisors (including some distinguished alumni of the White House bureauracy) have continued to play the same role. In 1946, for instance, Clark M. Clifford took over as Special Counsel and performed this function among others; his role as an advisor to several Presidents continued.

The legislative clearance process placed great emphasis on agency comments. Rarely were face-to-face meetings called on enrolled bills. And BOB's priorities governed. In their view, nothing was more important than processing enrolled bills. If agency views on pending or proposed legislation were held up in the meantime, then so be it. If an agency took the chance of running to the Hill without getting clearance first, then they also took the chance of a veto when the bill came to the President.

3. The Truman Experience—Policy Clearance

During World War II, winning the war was obviously more important than coming up with new agency proposals on the domestic scene. BOB placed emphasis on clearing enrolled bills, while legislation still pending in Congress received less attention. The Office of War Mobilization and Reconversion (OWMR) took control in many legislative areas, and the result was to down-grade the role of BOB as coordinator. For the most part, BOB personnel took the change as a necessary evil. But when the war was over and OWMR kept a hand in legislation, BOB personnel were unhappy and nervous.

The situation was to grow worse for BOB before it became better. For two years after Roosevelt's death in 1945, there was great confusion in the President's staff as the country moved from war to peace. Most of what BOB did was unknown to Truman's associates, and Truman's OWMR Directors were much closer to him than the hold-over Budget Directors, Smith and Appleby. By mid-1946, OWMR appeared in control. In addition a whole new staff agency, the Council of Economic Advisors, had just been authorized and their undefined mandate muddied the waters considerably.

In just two years, however, BOB was back on top as the prime source of Presidential staff work for the Administration's legislative program. Professor Richard E. Neustadt has identified three factors which contributed to this return to power: The demise of other Presidential staff groups, the reappearance of the legislative process as a key government proccupation, and finally the dynamic personality of James E. Webb, Truman's new Director of the Budget.[248]

Times were certainly ripe for BOB's resurgence. The Congress was saying "no" to Truman in the post-war period; his legislation was being turned down right and left. Thus, Truman's legislative proposals had to be pragmatic, well-supported, and pursuasive. It was a time for record-building: Truman's record versus Congress'. Even if Truman's proposals were shot down by the Congress, there might be another time, and they had to be good. Webb knew this and sought to make BOB the right hand of the Presidency. He largely succeeded. Aides were detailed to the President's offices when needed, and subordinates became accessible to the White House staff. More important, the negative bias of BOB's legislative coordination was turned into a positive bias. New programs had to be developed to solve old problems. And BOB had the expertise to know how to solve them without the tunnel vision sometimes found in individual agencies.

But there was one problem in BOB's handling of legislation. When hearings were called on short notice, agencies tended to bypass BOB's clearance requirements because BOB took too long. To make BOB's role unassailable, BOB had to catch up with the Hill and the departments by scheduling its work so that agencies would have time to clear all legislation. BOB's contacts with congressional committees over this period were helpful in educating BOB on what legislation needed to be moved quickly. And BOB responded by moving that legislation quickly. This dialogue between BOB and Congress was a two-way street. The committee staffs soon also learned what was important to the Truman Administration. This new and close relationship with congressional committees provided another thread in the fabric of power that OMB was weaving. Knowledge is power. An early warning of a committee meeting, of upcoming hearings, or a change in the legislative picture is vital to guiding the President's legislative program. And BOB was building up the personal relationships to bring the President in adequate time the knowledge he needed.

As a part of its emphasis on the positive side of legislative clearance, BOB soon began using "working teams" to draft legislation. These teams were staffed with personnel from both the Executive Branch departments and agencies and the Executive Office of the President. But more often than not, BOB played the role of initiator, moderator and key coordinator on these teams. Many of Truman's Fair Deal programs, such as the Housing Act of 1949 and the Social Security Act Amendments of 1950,[249] came out of such team efforts. On lesser proposals, the Legislative Reference staff either tinkered with agency proposals on their own, or convened meetings to attempt to overcome impasses.

When Dwight D. Eisenhower took office in 1953, legislative clearance survived, thanks to sound transition planning by both outgoing and incoming Presidents. But where Truman had used clearance for developing and pushing his legislative programs, Eisenhower in his first year in office seemed to be using it to buy time to do nothing. "The key to this whole operation, said one budget aide, "is whether Ike decides to have a legislative program. We can't interpret, much less develop, something that isn't there."[250] With the reconvening of the Congress in January, 1954, however, the change was remarkable. It was evidenced by a stream of Presidential messages. The President now had a program. And thus BOB had proposed legislation to watch over and coordinate.

Indeed a glorious high point in the Bureau's power over legislative clearance came in 1954, when President Eisenhower presented his legislative program to the Congress and the people—some 65 proposals for new legislation. This was a massive affair. First, there were six weeks of well-publicized openers—"cabinet deliberations, congressional briefings, press conferences, and even a fireside chat." Then, in three separate annual messages to the Congress—the State of the Union Address, the Economic Report and the Budget Message—the President outlined his proposals. Next, there were seven supplemental messages filling in details on various proprosals. And finally, there came the host of bills, introduced in the Congress to carry out these proposals. One theme was emphasized:

> ". . . here was a comprehensive and coordinated inventory of the nation's current legislative needs, reflecting the President's own judgments, choices, and priorities in every major area of Federal action; in short, his 'legislative program,' an entity delimiting his stand across the board. And—quite explicitly—this stand was being taken, this program volunteered, in order to give Congress an agenda, Republicans a platform, and voters a yardstick for 1954."[251]

This comprehensive program is all the more surprising because in 1953, the year Eisenhower was inaugurated, there was no legislative program at all. Truman had left, and Eisenhower was left holding the bag. What happened to reverse this trend is an interesting story. A story that illustrates the influence of the Budget Bureau on legislation.

In May, 1953, the Budget Bureau sent to the printers its annual call for Executive Branch departments and agencies to submit legislative programs to the President. Roger W. Jones, Chief of the Office of Legislative Reference of the Bureau, collected almost 300 major proposals from agencies and briefed key White House aides on them. These briefings were large-scale affairs. Under the chairmanship of Assistant to the President Sherman Adams, some six to ten members of the President's staff joined in an item-by-item review around a conference table. Over a two-week period this developed into a continuing marathon session of some twelve meetings of two to three hours each.

One purpose of this exercise was educational. Few on the President's staff had been exposed to the bureaucracy's programs. And every White House aide who had any role to play in legislative policy or tactics had a stake in developing the White House's position on agency programs. Thus the conference approach was just what the doctor ordered. Jones, acting as a guide, led the new White House team on a guided tour of the last twenty years of agency programs.

Each of the 300 legislative items—organized into major groups—was systematically reviewed. Jones put the programs into context. He briefy sketched the proposals, gave their background, itemized their pros and cons, but left the policy judgments for his audience.

After the show and tell, the next steps came naturally. Key aides took up assignments to dig deeper and report on the proposals. Should they be recommended by the President? Should they be modified or should they be forgotten? Some aides checked out Jones' facts. Others sounded out agencies' attitudes, congressional and outside opinions, and determined what open issues remained in each case.[252] Then, the staff consulted the President. Certain proposals were eliminated; others assigned to staff members to study further and present informally to the President; some were referred to the Bureau of the Budget for further research; and several controversial proposals were selected for formal presentation to the Cabinet and the National Security Council. Among these latter proposals were ones in the fields of foreign aid, tax increases, and Social Security changes.

Presenting proposals to the Cabinet in an elaborate manner was a real Eisenhower characteristic. Each Cabinet officer was asked to prepare a full-scale visual presentation making the case for his own program. Next, the Cabinet members were required to come to "try-outs" before LRD Chief Jones and members of the White House staff. The Cabinet members were subject to a full critique after this rehearsal. Finally, when the staff felt the show was up to snuff, the President was informed and the Cabinet member then performed at a full-scale Cabinet meeting. Discussion followed, and participation in the program was invited. Seven of these episodes were held at the end of November and early December 1953, and in each case President Eisenhower chaired the show.

By today's standards, this whole process seems unbelievably formal. But some positive things can be said about it. First, it educated the White House staff—which is no mean accomplishment in any Administration. Second, it educated the President. Also extremely helpful. Third, it focused the whole Administration on a comprehensive legislative program. And finally, it prepared Cabinet officers to "sell" their program as they would have to before the Congress.

By the end of November 1953, it became clear that as a result of this prosess the President would have his own legislative program, if only because the process once set in motion couldn't easily be stopped. There was another reason for proceeding with a comprehensive legislative program. The President needed an issue to counteract his struggle inside the Republican Party over McCarthyism. Eisenhower made it clear in the coming weeks that his legislative program, not the political activities of Republican Senator Joseph McCarthy was to be the major issue in the 1954 election. The legislative program came as a godsend to divert the party from the McCarthy struggle.

Once the policy decisions had been made, the propaganda for the legislative program was cranked up. First, in the early weeks of December 1953, Eisenhower formally unveiled his program to the Republican Congressional leadership. This was done through the unprecedented mechanism of fully-staged White House briefings. Eisenhower presided over three days of eight-hour briefings covering the full scope of his legislative program. The Vice-President, the Speaker of the House and the major Congressional leaders were there through the whole thing, as were most of the Cabinet and the White House policy makers. Committee chairmen were scheduled to shuttle in and out to comment and participate on issues within their committee's realms. High-ranking Departmental personnel below Cabinet rank were also there. The publicity was handled with some skill. Eisenhower issued communiques on the meetings each afternoon, but kept them in general terms so as not to upstage his State of the Union Address. Those who moved in and out of the White House also avoided detailed comment to the press, but kept the public's interest up by revealing a few tibits. Headlines, in any event, always went to Eisenhower.

The briefings were well coordinated. They avoided specifics, using the excuse that the precise language of the proposals was still in the drafting stages. But the impact was clear to those who attended:

> "Most of the people from the Hill were dazzled, very much enthused," reported an executive observer of these gatherings. Some of them discovered things they hadn't known about the President ... he was fast on his feet, and on top of the issues ... very quick and very shrewd ... a lot of people realized that for the first time. And then it turned out that his program had real substance and real salability ... something they could really use ... packaged and ready ... a very great attraction and they weren't prepared for it ... they were bowled over by it ..."[253]

Once the meetings were over it was time for the legislative drafters to move. It was less than three weeks until the State of the Union Address. The White House generally handled the State of the Union Message under the direction of Bryce Harlow, a "speech and message" coordinator who later also worked in the Nixon Administration. While the main themes of the address were being worked out by Harlow, the legislative proposals in the message was being drafted by the departments and agencies concerned under the coordination of the Budget Bureau. The Budget Bureau's Office of Legislative Reference rode herd on the agencies, coordinating the work flow, ironing out differences between agencies, and sending the drafts over to the White House for final approval.[254]

In the five weeks before the State of the Union Address, a steady stream of press releases and stories concerning the program had poured out of the White House. These stories were played up with all the fanfare usually reserved for international conferences. When those meetings were concluded, Eisenhower retreated to Georgia for last-minute polishing of the Address. Press stories continued almost daily on his high-level conferences and decision-making. Cabinet officials were flown back and forth from Washington. In early January, the President took to the airwaves with a radio and television address plugging his program and urging everyone to watch his State of the Union Address. Then, the President met with the minority leadership on the Hill for a courtesy preview of his recommendations. This gave the press one last crack at a preview story on his Address. Then, two days later, the President gave his address to the Congress with full television and radio coverage. For the next three Mondays and Thursdays, seven of his supplemental messages went to the Hill. These were spaced for optimum press exposure. And they undoubtedly created the impression that a vast Executive creation was blossoming. And it was.[255]

And so the pattern of renewal of legislative involvement which we saw before in BOB was reborn in the Eisenhower Administration. And this pattern has continued, pretty much unchanged through the turbulance of the 1960s and the 1970s. There were some downfalls, to be sure and the legislative clearance system today is under continued challenge from new offices and groups, and the super staff in the Executive Office. But it has shown great resilience to the attacks levied upon it. What are some of the secrets of this durability?

Part of the answer can be seen in the personalities who wished to make the system work. Persons such as FDR, Webb, and Roger Jones (the head of Legislative Reference Bureau through the late 1940s and early 1950s). Another reason is that the clearance function was lodged in the Budget Bureau. And its preparation of the annual federal budget was as regular a function as the rising and setting of the sun. This made BOB (now OMB) the reliable, logical choice to handle both legislation and the money to implement the legislation. The more visibility that the other mission-oriented offices such as NEC and OWMR got, the more vulnerable they were to being shot down by agency infighting. As Neustadt points out, "nothing is so vulnerable as the high policy performer dangling loose, a ready target and potential sacrifice at every turn in presidential circumstances."[256]

Then too, for the agency that has a weak proposal, the clearance process may be a friend. Favorable or non-committal views from other agencies often mean favorable views by OMB, and in turn by the Administration. This results in agency support for clearance. Of course, clearance also may be a foe to a proposal if another agency opposes it. In any event, the clearance process takes some of the venom out of the system and provides a regular route for accomodation and appeal if necessary.[257]

Not that agencies have always used the clearance system. When an agency knows that it is riding a wave of public support and the committees are begging for legislation from it, few agencies can resist the temptation of informally sending a staff member to help a committee draft legislation without OMB's blessing. But for the bulk of measures that are not on the President's "must" list, agencies need some means of getting Administration support. And the Hill needs some assurance that the agency is pushing a bill which is acceptable to the government as a whole, not just to the narrow constituency of one agency. Last but not least, most legislation needs money to implement it. That means that the President must sign an authorization bill, sign an appropriations bill, and be willing to allocate funds for it in the usual budget cycle. Thus, while an agency can bypass OMB, it does so at at considerable risk over the long-run.

And so legislative clearance works most of the time with good results. And when the going gets rough and OMB has misjudged the sentiment of the Administration or the Hill, it is considered OMB's mistake and the President can use OMB as a lightning rod or a whipping boy. Basically, the system as developed over the last half century has made sense, and so it has survived and flourished.

C. The OMB Today—The Mechanics of Legislative Clearance

OMB's processing of departmental and agency reports usually involves six steps.[258] These are similar to those which OMB uses for virtually all of its legislative clearance functions from clearing proposed legislation to processing enrolled bills. Thus, it is useful to examine them in some detail. However, not all of them are always followed. There is considerable flexibility in the system. The White House or other interests may demand specialized handling of certain legislative matters.

1. Initial Processing

The first thing done to a proposed agency report on pending legislation or any other legislative item (a draft bill, a request from a congressional committee for an OMB report, a proposed agency report or an enrolled bill) is to log it in so that the Legislative Reference Division (LRD) of OMB can keep track of it. When a draft agency report arrives at OMB, it is date-stamped and sent to a records unit to be assigned to the appropriate staff member in the Legislative Reference Division and to the "lead division" within OMB. Any existing OMB file on the matter will be ordered and attached by the records unit. A master record card is also made which shows the complete history of the legislation so far as OMB's handling is concerned.

2. Initial Review

One of the approximately fifteen OMB Legislative Reference Division staff members who receives the legislative item then makes a preliminary review of the matter to determine whether it requires special handling. Some of the LRD staff keep their own control cards or "tickler" files to indicate which reports have been received on proposed legislation so that they can remind slower agencies to get their reports in for clearance. Sometimes, particularly on the first incoming report, the LRD staff will call the congressional committee which has required the reports to determine which agencies were asked to report. If essential agencies have been left out, the OMB staffer might ask (either by phone or by letter) these other agencies also to report on the proposed legislation. The LRD staff member may also inform the staff of the congressional committee involved so that it can send out a formal committee request asking the Executive Branch agency to report to the committee as well. OMB may ask views of as many as fifty agencies. Sometimes, however, LRD staff of OMB may ask to know how other agencies feel about the legislation, but will purposefully not tell the Hill that additional agency views are being sought. In that way OMB will know more about agency positions than the Hill. This can be valuable in a situation where OMB wishes to know whether an agency agrees with OMB. And keeping any internal disagreements within the Executive Branch rather than telling Congress about them can also be an advantage. Any additional agency views will usually be requested within 30 days.

3. Preliminary Action Within OMB

Once the LRD attorney has reviewed the incoming agency report he sends it to the appropriate OMB division or office for review. There they examine the agency's position in light of the President's budgetary and other policies. In the process of this review the division or office personnel might inform LRD staff of additional agency comments that are necessary, and ask LRD to request views from other agencies if they were overlooked. The reviewer will also tell LRD staff whether other divisions of OMB or the White House or the Executive Office staff should be consulted. Then, the reviewer considers and compiles any cost or employment information required.

4. Analysis By OMB.

One of the approximately 200 budget examiners in OMB's four program divisions then makes his or her full analysis of the facts and issues involved in the case in order to recommend appropriate action. Some of the factors to be considered in this review include the type of legislation involved, its relationship to ongoing programs and policies, particularly the programs of the President, its organizational, budgetary, or management implications, jurisdictional questions, timing of congressional or other action, precedents which might be established, and any legal or constitutional issues which might need to be tackled. Sometimes, it is necessary for interagency meetings to be conducted to harmonize conflicting views or to develop further information. If meetings are held, LRD staff are advised of them and participate. And sometimes where there is a major battle among agencies meetings are chaired by an OMB associate director or White House staff.

When OMB officials deal with an issue on which the President has already spoken, clearance is easy. OMB just tells the agencies, "OK, that's it, the decision's been made." If OMB shoots down an agency's proposal, however, there is a great temptation for the agency to go running to a friend on the Hill and get the bill introduced anyway, without OMB clearance.

5. Recommendation for OMB Action

The responsible office or division handling the case then makes its recommendation. If the matter is unusually complex or subject to misinterpretation or other special circumstances are involved, a "letter of advice" is prepared to send to the agencies involved.[259] Generally, however, OMB advice is transmitted to agencies by telephone if it is "no objection advice" on routine legislation (see the discussion of different types of advice later in this chapter).

Sometimes OMB rewrites agency reports or proposed testimony. But more often it asks the agencies to handle this job. Timing is important in the legislative game, and often agencies purposefully submit their reports or testimony at the last minute so that OMB won't have time to change them. The agencies know that OMB will rarely exercise its powers to prohibit an agency from showing up at an already scheduled congressional hearing. Nor is it likely that OMB will delete words in testimony which has already been delivered to congressional committee staff.

Letters giving OMB's advice to agencies or to the Congress generally state the purpose of the legislation, the agency's views, and sometimes include the reasoning supporting OMB's position.

Often, the division's advice to LRD is just initialed or written on the corner of the incoming agency report, or a memo from the division to LRD may be prepared. Such advice might be "no objection," "OK provided that the dollar amount is lowered to x dollars," or other similiar language. Once the first office or division handling the legislative matter has signed off on it, it is transmitted through any other office or division for concurrences and finally to the appropriate LRD staff member.

6. Final Review, Signature, and Transmittal of Advice

The LRD staffer looks over the recommended advice, negotiates any remaining inter-agency disagreements and discusses any unresolved policy differences with OMB's Assistant Director for Legislation. The Assistant Director then contacts White House or other staff as necessary to work out any remaining problems. Once these are resolved and the OMB position is finalized the Assistant Director may sign an advice letter to the agencies concerned or to the Congress. In some cases the OMB Director or Deputy Director may sign the advice letter. In the usual case, advice to agencies is transmitted by telephone. They are told their legislation is, in OMB parlance "cleared." Reports are then sent to the Hill by the agencies which prepared them. This completes the legislative clearance process for agency reports. Similiar steps are followed for agencies' proposed congressional testimony and draft bills.

D. Types of OMB Advice

The key to any agency report is found in its final paragraph where OMB's "advice" is be found. Agencies are required to put this "advice"—or clearance language—in every report or letter transmitting views on legislation. "Advice" is a brief statement, required by OMB's Circular A-19, stating the relationship between the agencies' views on the legislation and the President's legislative program. "Advice" takes several set forms. But even these vary depending on the circumstances. (See Exhibit G for samples of OMB advice to agencies.)

When the proposed legislation carries out an item in the President's legislative program and is sufficiently important to warrant the President's personal support it will read:

> "The Office of Management advises that this legislation is in accord with the program of the President."

This is the strongest endorsement presidential legislation usually gets. Only slightly less enthusiastic is:

> "The Office of Management and Budget advises that this legislation is in accord with [or consistent with] the administration's objectives."

Either of these forms may be used in the negative. Advice is used not only for agency reports but also for agency testimony and draft bills. The advice forms above are only used in those rare cases of key Presidential legislation. All other legislation falls into a second category with a "no objection" advice paragraph attached to it:

> "The Office of Management and Budget has advised that there is no objection to the submission of this report from the standpoint of the administration's program."

No objection advice doesn't indicate anything regarding ultimate Presidential approval or disapproval should the bill later pass the Congress. It does indicate that the matter is more within the interest of an individual agency than the White House. But such clearance does set up two presumptions. First, if all agency views are favorable no major objections are known at the time of the clearance and agencies will recommend that the President sign the legislation if it passes. Second, is the converse. If all agency reports are opposed to the legislation the presumption is that the agencies may recommend a Presidential veto should the legislation pass Congress.

What does it mean if OMB clears conflicting reports with no-objection language? It means that there would be no objection to the bill if the Congress passed it. Or it means that the Administration's position is being reserved pending resolution of the agencies' differences.

Agency reports usually spell out their position on the legislation. Usually an agency's position is stated in the following or similiar language:

- The Department recommends enactment of this legislation;
- The Department has no objection to the enactment of this legislation;
- The Department recommends enactment of this legislation with the above modifications;
- Whether this legislation should be enacted involves policy considerations as to which the Department makes no recommendations;
- Whether this legislation should be enacted involves questions as to which the Department defers to the Department of . . . .

In other cases of conflicting views, OMB may withold its advice. Sometimes, an agency feels that it must make its position known to the Congress even though OMB disagrees with it. In this situation, the OMB advice paragraph may say something like:

> "The Office of Management and Budget does not concur with the position of the Department of . . . in this matter but favors enactment of this legislation." (Reasons may be included)

E. The Status of the OMB Today

Since 1939, OMB has been a part of the Executive Office of the President. The President appoints the Director, who is responsible to the President and the President alone. The Director holds Cabinet rank and is invited to attend Cabinet meetings, although technically, he is not a member of the Cabinet. He is totally independent of all other agencies of the Executive Branch and all other branches of the government.

Until 1974, when the Congress reacted to the growing exercise of the impoundment power of the President by requiring Senate confirmation of the OMB Director and Deputy Director,[260] both had been appointed by the President without the burden of Senate confirmation. In the past, Senate confirmation had been avoided because the President had convinced the Senate that the OMB Director was a personal assistant, just like his White House staff, and should not have to be confirmed. All this has changed, however, and it would not be surprising if even more White House officials are required to jump through the Senate's confirmation hoop before entering service.

There has never been any question that the Director is powerless without the confidence of the President. One well-worn statement on the Bureau's role in the Executive Office is contained in a report by a subcommittee of the Senate Committee on Government Operations in 1961:

> "The Budget Bureau will never win a bureaucratic popularity contest. The total program requests of the operating departments always far exceed any budget a President can prudently approve. The Bureau must often be a no-sayer and help the Chief Executive trim agency programs to fit the Presidential cloth. Hence, its reputation, even if undeserved, as the villain of the executive branch.
>
> "Each President must decide how he wants to use the Bureau.
>
> "A President can employ the Bureau mainly to keep a lid on expenditures. The Bureau, in such cases, is told to 'hold the line' but may be given little guidance concerning the Chief Executive's priorities and program goals.
>
> "A President, however, can employ the Bureau differently. He can use it as his 'lengthened shadow' across the whole front of fiscal policy and program management. The Director of this kind of Budget Bureau sits in the innermost policy councils of the Presidency. Program planning and budgeting are seen as but different

aspects of one process, which starts with the formulation of policy objectives and ends with costed and time-phased programs for action. The President regards the Bureau as his strong right arm in executive mangement.

"A President will do well to use the Bureau of the Budget in this way."[261]

Sometimes, OMB, which tells the rest of the Executive Branch how to get organized, has had trouble organizing itself. For many years, the Budget Bureau was in a difficult position. It was an agency staffed with non-political civil servants working closely with the political White House. This was always a delicate situation. By and large, Bureau employees accomplished it well, although some quick direction changes were necessary when there were major changes at the top, such as from the Eisenhower Administration to the Kennedy Administration. The Bureau has always been proud of its employees' professionalism. One Bureau official speaking at a staff orientation conference put it this way:

"The one thing that a staff member of the Bureau never loses sight of is his service to the Presidency. It does not matter to us, professionally speaking, who occupies that office. We are working for the institution."[262]

To maintain their independence, the Bureau's leaders used their heads. And they were loyal. In that same staff orientation a Bureau official put it this way:

"The Bureau's staff member must be humble, self-effacing, and quietly loyal . . . He is a team player, not a brilliant break-away runner.

* * *

"This means, of course, that the Bureau's staff member must develop his instinct for self-preservation to the highest possible point. He cannot afford to make many mistakes."[263]

Unfortunately, these words were to be prophetic. With the coming of the Nixon Administration, the Budget Bureau failed to convince the new President that it was loyal or politically responsive enough for Nixon-style government. It wasn't that the Bureau didn't try. The Bureau had used all of its tools to survive the Nixon transition. Tools that had worked in the past. One of these tools was to keep a shoe box or two through the Presidential campaigns. These shoe boxes were filled with file cards listing statements by the candidates on major issues. By the time the campaign winner took office, he usually hadn't had time to consolidate his remarks, much less plan his Presidential programs. But the Bureau was ready for him. They knew what he had said and were prepared with options to meet his campaign pledges the day he arrived.

The Bureau, which has had its ways of "Getting there first with the mostest", is at its best when a new President arrives on the scene. While the new man and his staff are still trying to figure out the names of the agencies, the Bureau can tell them what to look out for in them. And the Bureau has the backgrond and expertise to handle problems of coordination among agencies which can't be neatly compartmentalized.

At any rate, the Bureau, whether because of insufficient flexibility or because the President was too demanding, ran into a new situation with Nixon. The Bureau was too uncontrollable for the new President.

"Responsiveness" was the name of the game. To remedy this problem, in 1970, President Nixon added a layer of political intimates at the top of the Bureau's divisions and renamed the whole operation the Office of Management and Budget. The basic structure of the Bureau, however, remained—and still—remains. The five divisions with government-wide management responsibilities have stayed the same, ranging from a Statistical Policy Division to the Legislative Reference Division. These management divisions surround a core of eight program and budget divisions. The core divisions consist of budget examiners and others who are trained in analyzing agency programs. Examiners, at the direction of the President, set agency priorities and allocate funds for the programs as OMB sees fit. With both access to the President and brains, OMB has maintained its power.

E: Other Sources of the President's Legislative Powers

"... Executive legislation is law. It can collect money from those who would be liable under a statute; it can cause people to be put in jail; it can cause some people to be shot. Any theory that cannot accomodate these facts has, on this ground alone, outlived its usefulness."—Glendon A. Schubert, Jr., *The Presidency in the Courts,* 1957, p. 311.

"With all its defects, delays, and inconveniences, men have discovered no technique for long preserving free government except that the Executive be under the law, and that the law be made by parliamentary deliberations."—Mr. Justice Jackson, concurring in *Youngstown Sheet and Tube v. Sawyer,* 343 U.S. 579, 655 (1952).

Although the statutory sources of the President's legislative power are important, there are many other sources as well. These range from the sources listed in the Constitution, such as the veto power, to more nebulous powers such as the power to persuade. One of the most neglected powers, however, is the growing power of Executive Orders—or as some call them—Presidential legislation.

1. The Scope of Executive Orders and Proclamation

The definition of an Executive Order is broad, and vague with unknown limits. That is one of the problems with Executive Orders. An Executive Order is any written order promulgated by the President under any of a number of usual formats.

Beginning in 1789, with George Washington, Presidents have issued Executive Orders. Often a President would write "Approved," or "Let it be done," at the end of a recommendation drawn up by a Cabinet member. Sometimes an Executive Order was signed by a secretary at the order of the President. One example is Executive Order 113 of 1899, which was signed by J.A. Porter, secretary to President McKinley. This directed the flag to be flown at half-mast during the removal of the remains of John A. Rawlins to Arlington National Cemetery.

President Millard Fillmore wrote an Executive Order on the border of a large colored map, showing a "Proposed Method of Laying Out the Public Grounds at Washington." The notes approved portions of the plan. Other Orders have been signed by the Secretary of State in the absence of the President and Vice President, such as Executive Order No. 7 of July 28, 1868 signed by Secretary of State William H. Seward, which ordered the publication of the 14th Amendment to the Constitution. Some have been signed by other Cabinet officers. Because of the informality with which Executive Orders were treated for many years, no one is sure just how many have been issued.[264] Former Secretary of the Interior Harold L. Ickes once estimated their number at 15,000, while others have placed the figure as high as 60,000. Because many are secret, such as the Orders to bomb Cambodia from 1969-1970, the number of Executive Orders and their content may never be fully documented.

Executive Orders cover every aspect of life. The hundreds of Orders relating to the Panama Canal Zone alone provide some interesting titles:

> Order of January 27, 1908, providing for fines to prevent Chinese escaping on the Canal Zone;
>
> Order of February 6, 1908, establishing jury trials in the Canal Zone;
>
> Order of September 8, 1908, prohibiting hunting by night with artificial light or with spring guns in the Canal Zone;
>
> Order of January 16, 1911, authorizing the use of French dump cars without safety appliances for dumping gravel.

The scope of Executive Orders is as great as the government's reach. And when a Presidential act is a "Proclamation" and when it is an Executive Order is sometimes difficult to say. Are they government by fiat? The word "proclamation" suggests declarations of National Boy Scout Week and other such. But both Executive Orders and Proclamations have occasionally played very important roles in this nation's governance. The Emancipation Proclamation of 1863, which purported to free the slaves in the rebelling southern states, was (as its name suggests) no act of Congress or Constitutional amendment, but simply a Presidential Proclamation. At its foundation was no statutory authorization, but merely the general war powers of the President as Commander-in-chief of the armed forces.[265]

Under an Executive Order issued by President Nixon, the Agriculture Department got permission to audit tax returns of farmers. During the Watergate hearings, an "administratively confidential" memo written by Jerry Jones, the White House patronage chief, suggested that an Executive Order be issued circumventing Senate confirmation of Jeb Magruder to a high-paying Administration job. On another occasion, President Nixon received a letter from Patrick J. Hillings, a Washington lawyer representing the Associated Milk Producers, Inc. (AMPI). This letter noted that AMPI was working with Nixon fund-raisers to set up "appropriate channels for AMPI to contribute $2 million for your re-election." The letter continued rather pointedly that "No Presidential Proclamation has been issued" as yet to put these quotas into effect. Apparently, the message was not lost on the White House. Two weeks later, the President signed the proclamation and shortly thereafter the political contributions came pouring in. In another case, in 1973, Congressman John D. Dingell pointed out to his colleagues that the entire appropriation for former Vice President Spiro Agnew's 40-member (which served him for some time after his resignation) staff was never authorized by statute, just by Executive Order. In Dingell's view, this violated the Constitution because funds were being appropriated without an act of Congress.[266]

One Congressional source reported that the Federal Bureau of Investigation's domestic intelligence program "was never authorized by statute but was initiated under the term of an Executive Order issued by Franklin D. Roosevelt during a 'state of emergency' declared in

1939."[267] While this statement does not answer the question as to whether the Executive Order was lawful, it does show the scope of such orders.

The 1939 order wasn't the only one issued under a "state of national emergency." For some forty years, the United States has been living through various "national emergencies," which theoretically give the President the power to suspend civil rights, declare martial law and seize certain public and private institutions. Four of these Executive Orders were still on the books in the early 1970's: one proclaimed in 1933 by Franklin Roosevelt because of the financial crisis of the Depression; a Proclamation issued by President Truman at the start of the Korean War; and two imposed by President Nixon because of a 1970 postal strike and the 1971 devaluation of the dollar.[268] At least these four were public. Many Executive Orders are private, such as those dealing with national security following decisions by the National Security Council. The full impact of such orders is perhaps impossible to determine.[269]

There is no doubt that the scope of Executive Orders can be substantial. The Japanese detention Orders during World War II are one example. In February 1942, President Franklin Roosevelt issued Executive Order No. 9066. This Order gave a blank check to the Secretary of War and military commanders to issue regulations prescribing military areas from which persons might be excluded. It also subjected those persons remaining to whatever restrictions the military deemed necessary. The President acted without statutory authority. The following month Congress enacted a statute setting penal provisions for the violation of military orders in such designated zones. Apparently this legislation was designed to provide the President some authority for his actions.

On March 24, 1942, General J. L. DeWitt, commanding general of the Western Defense Command, declared a curfew for the entire Pacific coastal area of the United States. This curfew required German and Italian nationals and all persons of Japanese ancestry to be off the streets from 8:00 p.m. to 6:00 a.m. Thereafter, a series of Orders against Japanese nationals and American citizens of Japanese descent were issued. Public Proclamation No. 4 of March 27, 1942, recited the necessity of removing all such "Japanese" persons from the coastal area; two months later the commander of the Western Defense Command formally decreed the exclusion of all persons of Japanese ancestry from the area. Soon, Japanese nationals and American citizens of Japanese descent were under two contradictory orders: one that they could not leave the area unless future orders were issued; and a second order prohibiting them from the area. The only way to legally comply with these orders was to report to a number of Civil Control Stations where the Japanese and Americans of Japanese ancestry were gathered and shipped to "Relocation Centers," a euphemism for concentration camps. Japanese-Americans were detained in these camps pursuant to Executive Orders for up to four years and then resettled outside the Pacific coastal zone. This program, which separated thousands of American citizens from their homes and took away their reputations, property and jobs while subjecting them to imprisonment at the discretion of military officers, was first challenged in the Supreme Court in the case of *Hirabayashi v. United States.*[270] That case arose when an American citizen of Japanese descent was charged with violation of the military curfew and failure to report to a designated Civil Control Station. The Court ducked the question of the constitutionality of the detention program and unanimously held that the March 1943 Act of Congress authorizing the curfew Order was within the combined constitutional power of the Congress and the President. Chief Justice Stone, speaking for the Court, held that discrimination based on race was "odious to a free people whose institutions are founded upon the doctrine of equality," but that race was a relevant factor to the national welfare in a time of war and therefore the statute did not violate the due process clause of the Constitution. Justice Murphy, in a separate concurring opinion, stated the views of others on the court that the curfew order "bears a meloncholy resemblance to the treatment accorded to members of the Jewish race in Germany and other parts of Europe." Obviously, however, the Justices did not want to run the war for the President, and thus let the statute and Executive Orders stand.

The validity of the exclusion Orders came squarely before the Court in the December 1944 case of *Korematsu v. United States.*[271] In that case, the appellant was a Japanese-American who had remained in the West Coast military area in violation of the exclusion Order. Justice Black, speaking for a divided Court, reiterated the conclusion of the *Hirabayashi* case that the statute and Orders promulgated under it were constitutional even though they worked great hardships on the persons concerned. In *Ex Parte Endo,* decided the same day as *Korematsu,* the Court upheld the right of a Japanese-American girl to a writ of habeas corpus freeing her from the custody of a relocation camp. Justice William O. Douglas' opinion avoided a review of the constitutionality of the executive orders, and merely held that the War Relocation Authority had no right to subject loyal persons to confinement or conditional parole.[272]

2. The Powers of Executive Orders and Proclamations

The power of Executive Orders is awesome. Under some circumstances, such as while at war, the power presumedly cannot be limited either by international law or by the Congress. Charles Evans Hughes once said before he ascended to the Supreme Court as Chief Justice, "The power to wage war is the power to wage war successfully."[273] In practice this philosophy, which the courts have embraced, has resulted in the merging of the powers of the President and the Congress to exercise any power necessary to fight a war. That includes issuing wide-sweeping Executive Orders. As one commentator has said:

> "American Presidents have always acted beyond the scope of their explicit powers when this appeared necessary in the public interest, and many decisions of the Supreme Court have approved their authority to do so. Yet there has been no formulation of a general theory of implied presidential powers. What American Presidents have lacked has not been power, but a theoretical justification for their exercise of it."[274]

Agreement between the Congress and the President in wartime simply has placed any wartime action by the President beyond the pale of judicial review.

The controversy over the legality of Executive Orders goes back at least to President George Washington's Proclamation of Neutrality. When France declared war against Great Britain and Holland in 1793, her action precipitated a crisis of substantial proportions within the young government of the United States which was both anti-Britsh and pro-French.

President Washington's Cabinet was split on what to do. Secretary of State Thomas Jefferson was anti-British and pro-French, while Alexander Hamilton was pro-British. Washington, however, was firmly determined to keep the United States out of the war. So were Hamilton and Jefferson, but each favored a different side in the war. A fierce struggle ensued in Washington's Cabinet as to whether he should issue a proclamation (or an Executive Order) "...for the purpose of preventing interferences of the citizens of the United States in the war between France and Great Britain..." and whether the proclamation should contain a declaration of neutrality.

Jefferson opposed such a proclamation on the grounds that it would be politically wise not to take sides. This way the United States could bargain with either side as necessary. On Constitutional grounds Jefferson argued that a proclamation of neutrality was a declaration of "no war" and thus it usurped the Congressional power to determine whether the country was at war. Hamilton, on the other hand, felt it was well within the Constitutional power of the

President to issue such an Order. He saw the language in Article II of the Constitution, "the Executive power shall be vested in a President of the United States of America," as the source of such power. Hamilton argued his case in a series of articles under the pen name of Pacificus; while James Madison replied, under the name of Helvidius, that the Executive power clause of the Constitution was not a grant of power itself because we are not a government involving royal prerogatives; rather we are a government strictly limited to enumerated powers.

Washington apparently agreed with Hamilton; he issued a proclamation of neutrality in April 1793, which stated that citizens were to "... avoid all acts and proceedings whatsoever, which may in any manner tend to contravene such disposition ... " of "a conduct friendly and impartial toward the belligerent powers."[275]

But there are some limits to the powers of Executive Orders as demonstrated in the famous steel mills seizures case of *Youngstown Sheet and Tube Co. v. Sawyer.* In 1951, while the government was increasing military production for the war in Korea, the steelworkers went on strike. In response, President Truman issued an Executive Order directing the Secretary of Commerce to seize and run the steel mills. The Supreme Court struck down this Executive Order, partly on the grounds that this seizure took place outside the theatre of war, and without the blessing of Congress. But in so doing, the Court appeared to say that if the President had enjoyed the support or even the neutrality of Congress, the Executive Order would have been upheld. In Justice Jackson's words:

> "When the President acts pursuant to an express or implied authorization of Congress, his authority is at its maximum, for it includes all that he possesses in his own right plus all that Congress can delegate. In these circumstances, and in these only, may he be said (for what it may be worth) to personify the federal sovereignty. If his act is held unconstitutional under these circumstances, it usually means that the Federal Government as an undivided whole lacks powers."[276]

Sometimes, the President acted first with an Executive Order and the Congress later ratified his action by passing a law. One of the clearer examples of this procedure occurred during the Civil War. Many of President Lincoln's Proclamations issued during the first four months of his administration were outside any authority under the Constitution, at least as it had previously been interpreted. Once the war got rolling, however, the President called Congress into special session and it obligingly enacted bills of "indemnity." These bills said in part:

> "All the acts, proclamations, and orders of the President of the United States . . . respecting the army and navy of the United States . . . are hereby approved and in all respects made valid . . ."[277]

In effect, the President got an antedated blank check. The courts not only have closed their eyes to such political incest in the constitutional household, they have blessed it. Even worse, they have blessed it with a maximum of faith and a minimun of evidence. The judiciary has accepted not only remarks by an individual congressman in the *Congressional Record* as constituting an expression of the legislative will, but they have also said that even silence by Congress may constitute consent and ratification.[278] Courts are doubly reluctant to strike down a President's Executive Orders in wartime. This principle was illustrated in the cases of *Ex Parte Vallandigham and Ex Parte Milligan,* both of which arose during the Civil War. The facts were somewhat similiar, but one case came to the Supreme Court during wartime while another was decided after hostilities had ceased. That difference apparently explains their different result.

Vallandigham, a civilian, was tried and convicted by a military commission for having spoken against the Union case in 1863. Vallandigham petitioned the Supreme Court following his conviction claiming that the military courts had no jurisdiction over him. The Court sidestepped the issue on procedural grounds and stated that it had no jurisdiction to grant the writ of certiorari (bringing the case before the Supreme Court) in his case because military commissions were not "courts" from which relief could be sought under the Constitution and Judiciary Act of 1789.

On the other hand, in 1866, once the Civil War was over, the Supreme Court dealt differently with a similiar case—*Ex Parte Milligan*. Milligan, a civilian, had been sentenced to be executed following a trial by a military commission in 1864 on charges of insurrection. The sentence was approved by the President and Milligan petitioned the court of Appeals to be discharged from custody under the Habeas Corpus Act of 1863 on the grounds that he had not been indicted by a grand jury in the civilian courts. The Supreme Court held that Milligan should be discharged from custody under the terms of the Act and that the military commission had no jurisdiction to try or to sentence Milligan.

Lincoln's use of Executive Orders was unusually vigorous. While it is true that the President's position of Commander-in-Chief gains importance in periods of war, the Supreme Court has stated that even with a declaration of war by the Congress the Commander-in-Chief's powers are restricted to military affairs.

On April 25, 186l, just 13 days after the opening shots of the Civil War were heard at Fort Sumter, Lincoln addressed a letter of instructions to General Scott in Maryland, telling him to watch the activities of the Maryland State Legislature and to act to surpress insurrection including "... in the extremest necessity, the supression of the writ of habeas corpus." In May of 1861, John Merryman was arrested by federal soldiers for planning hostilities against the United States. Merryman petitioned for habeas corpus to Chief Justice of the Supreme Court Roger B. Taney. Taney concluded that the power to suspend habeas corpus was a legislative, not Executive power and that the President could not suspend the privilege or authorize a military officer to do it. Lincoln, in turn, referred the matter to Congress and defended his action in suspending the writ by asking "Are all the laws but one to go unexecuted, and the Government itself go to pieces lest that one be violated?" Even in such a case, would not the official oath (of the President) be broken if the Government should be overthrown when it was believed that disregarding the single law would tend to preserve it?" Two years later the Congress authorized the President to suspend the writ of habeas corpus in the Habeas Corpus Act of 1863. Thus, without saying so, the Congress legalized the President's actions after the fact. In addition, however, the Congress reasserted its legislative power over the suspension of habeas corpus.[279] Sometimes the Congress ratifies an Executive Order even before it is issued. The Emergency Banking Act of 1933 appeared to do this.[280] Such coziness between the Executive and the Congress has one undeniable effect: It scares the Judiciary away from declaring such acts unconstitutional.

When the President legislates and his order conflicts with an act of Congress, what happens? Can the Congress give the President the power to suspend, amend or repeal a statute? Maybe. One interesting example of this situation was a dispensation given by Thomas Jefferson. A dispensation is an exception to a law. Jefferson, it appears, expressly authorized the fitting out of a military expedition against Spain under the command of Colonel Smith in direct violation of an act of Congress. When the expedition floundered and the President failed to take responsibility it ended in court. The Circuit Court of New York quickly dispensed with the theory of dispensation saying:

> "Who holds the power of dispensation ... ? The president of the United States cannot control the statute, nor dispense with its execution ... If he could, it would render the execution of the laws dependent on his will and pleasure ... "[281]

But the issue of priority in conflicts between Acts of Congress and Executive Orders or Proclamations didn't disappear so easily. After the Civil War, President Lincoln issued his Proclamation of Unconditional Amnesty. This didn't sit too well with many congressmen because the Congress had just enacted legislation preventing Confederates from regaining their lands seized during military occupation. When it became evident that the courts were accepting this proclamation as legal evidence of loyalty (which was one of the conditions to the recovery of such property), Congress reacted by passing new rules of evidence for the Court of Claims which prevented the amnesty proclamation from being admitted in evidence in such suits. Indeed, the introduction of the pardon into evidence was deemed conclusive of guilt and disloyalty. To head off the possibility that the Supreme Court could ever thwart the Congress, the legislation also restricted the Supreme Court's jurisdiction to hear appeals from the Court of Claims in such cases. Nevertheless, the Supreme Court took jurisdiction over such a case and held that the statute was in direct conflict with the President's proclamation. In addition, the Court held that the statute was an unconstitutional attempt of the Congress to encroach on the President's powers to issue a valid executive order.[282]

There appears to be no question that the Congress can delegate to the President the power to repeal a statute. Indeed, in recent years there has been an increasing tendency for the Congress to enact statutes which are terminated either by Presidential order or concurrent resolution. This power perhaps reached its zenith in one court decision that held that only the President of the United States and not the Congress has the power to issue a proclamation declaring a national emergency and terminating it.[283]

It's really not very clear just what an Executive Order is, and how it differs from a Proclamation. Indeed, the two words have often been used interchangeably. Generally, however, Proclamations contain a preamble and a reference to the President's source of authority; gramatically, the first person is used, and the Secretary of State countersigns it and affixes the seal of the United States. On the other hand, Executive Orders usually do not have a preamble, are written in the third person, and are not countersigned.[284] One thing is clear, however; no magic words are needed for the President to issue either a Proclamation or an Executive Order.

3. The Procedures of Executive Orders and Proclamations

The use of Executive Orders grew tremedously in the early days of the New Deal. President Roosevelt, for instance, issued 674 Executive Orders in the 15 months following March 4, 1933. Because of the growing use of Executive Orders and Proclamations it became necessary to systematize the way they were handled. Perhaps the most important catalyst to this development was the bizarre "Hot Oil" case.[285] In that case the defendants were charged with criminal violations. The only problem was that the prosecutor, the defendants and the court were totally unaware of an Executive Order revoking the order under which the defendants were prosecuted. At the next session of Congress, therefore, the Congress enacted the Federal Register Act which provided for the publication of all Executive Orders and Proclamations. Under that law, unless an order or Proclamation is published, it is not effective against any person unless he had actual knowledge of it.[286]

The White House uses the legislative clearance system to keep tight reign on the issuance of Executive Orders. Under an Executive Order issued in 1962, the President regulates the issuance of all Executive Orders.[287] and they are strictly regulated, at least in form. The Executive Order regulating Executive Orders even spells out the size of the paper on which draft orders are to be submitted to the President. Proposed orders go to OMB where they may be circulated to other interested agencies. Then they are transmitted to the Attorney General for legal technical review of the language used, and finally are returned via the Office of the Federal Register to OMB to be signed by the President.

Is executive "legislation" part of the law of the land? Is it even law? The courts have done a complete turn-around on this issue. Before World War I, they generally held that Executive legislation was not law. As late as 1925, one constitutional expert (Prof. James Hart) wrote that the proper function for a presidential proclamation was to notify the public concerning existing law, but not to create law.[288] The courts concurred in this interpretation. The Selective Service Act of 1917 authorized the President to issue regulations to govern registration and the Act provided penalties for violation of such regulations. The Court of Appeals, however, squelched any notion that the Proclamation had the effect of law. Instead, said the court, the purpose of the the proclamation was merely to "give notice of the provisions of the Act."

Today, however, it is generally accepted that Executive Orders and Proclamations have "the force and effect of law." *Maryland Casualty Company v. United States.* The major legal questions remaining are whether they are properly issued with adequate attention to due process requirements, are not discriminatory (equal protection of the law) and whether they can support criminal prosecution.

In 1974, the Senate Special Committee on National Emergencies issued a comprehensive report on abuses of Executive Orders, particularly abuses relating to the use of Executive Orders in situations of "National emergency." The Committee reported that "although there is no constitutional provision to do so, it has been the practice over the past 40 years that the simple declaration by the President that a national emergency exists is all that is required to obtain extraordinary grants of authority contained in over 470 provisions of law."[289] The Committee's Report detailed other abuses in the use of Executive Orders. The Congress in 1976 ended four Presidentially declared states of National emergency and outlined procedures for the declaration and termination of future National emergencies. But clearly further Congressional action in clarifying the powers of Executive Orders and setting ground rules for their use would be beneficial.

PART FIVE: Can Congress Regain Legislative Power?

A. Rising Storm Over The Presidential Budget

> *"The Office of Management and Budget has become the invisible government of the United States . . . The newspapers are the only source I have to learn where the Presidential ax will fall, and has fallen. The OMB is delivering the blows of that ax . . . I and my staff cannot keep up with what Congressional programs are being abolished daily."*—Congressman J.J. (Jake) Pickle, 1973

> *"The budget is the culmination of a year-long struggle in shadowy bureaucratic bear pits"*—Norman Kempster, 1975

Money talks. And Spending it occupies most of the President's and Congress' time. Thus the budget has become a major battleground in the fight between recent Presidents and the Congress over who controls legislation.

Like the President's other powers the budget power doesn't end with legislation; it just begins there. The Federal budget is vital, it is nothing less than the annual work plan of the whole Federal government. Budgetary tricks are legendary. They have been developed to a fine art by a succession of recent Presidents—so much so that Congress, in the wake of a furious battle over Presidential impoundment (blockage) of funds, reasserted its power over the purse by passing the Budget and Impoundment Control Act of 1974.

Let's look at the development of the President's budgetary powers in recent years, review the rising storm of protest that led to the passage of the 1974 Act, and attempt to predict the future of the President's legislative power over the budget.

Under the Constitution, there is no question that the Congress has full and exclusive power to pay the government's bills. In the words of Article I, section VIII of the Constitution:

> "The Congress shall have power to lay and collect taxes, duties, imposts and excises, to pay the debts and provide for the common defense and general welfare of the United States . . ."

And Article I, section ix, states clearly that:

> "No money shall be drawn from the Treasury but in consequence of appropriations made by law . . . "

As for the President's role, he simply is charged under Article II with taking care that the laws be "faithfully executed." Yet due to the vacuum created by congressional indifference to spending in the Executive Branch, the Executive has amassed a number of potent budgetary tools. These powers include transfer authority, disposition of excess stocks, covert fundings, "pipeline" powers, reprogramming, and—the most notorious of all—the impoundment power.

Indeed, a first look at some of these powers makes us wonder what power the Congress still maintains over the budget. Through secrecy and transfer powers Presidents have hired mercenaries, discouraged a rump insurrection in Ceylon, promised the South Koreans some $3.5 billion, and turned over an unknown amount of military aid and bases to South Vietnam and other nations. Through a budget gimmick called reprogramming, the President authorized the Navy to continue the development of the F-14 fighter even after the Congress ordered its production deferred. And through the use of the "pipeline"—unexpended funds left over from prior budgets—the Pentagon and other agencies have spent far over the limit of their appropriations for any one year.

Budgeting is a black art practiced by bureaucratic magicians. According to a 1971 memorandum from the Joint Chiefs of Staff to former Defense Secretary Melvin Laird, there were many ways of simply bypassing the Congress' limited military aid appropriations to generate $52 million in additional funds to increase the strength of the Cambodian army.[290] In the first place, millions of dollars appropriated for economic aid could be transferred to the military aid program. Secondly, economic aid money could be used to buy all so-called common-use items—that is, those items which have both a civilian and a military purpose, such as trucks and jeeps. Thus, other funds could be freed for military use. Third, procurement for the U.S. Army could bc increased and the material could be given to the Cambodians with repayment to come "later." Or, the Defense Department supply regulations could be amended to declare certain equipment "in excess" so that it could be given to the Cambodians. In addition, the Joint Chiefs' memorandum provided for clandestine programs which would be funded out of the State Department's Agency for International Development (AID) funds, such as a paramilitary force, which would number more than 500,000 by 1977. The secret CIA budget could be used to train and direct Cambodian units—as the CIA was then doing in Laos—and could provide airlift support through its subsidized airline, Air America. These proposals in effect, provided a formula for an end-run around Congress.[291]

Just as interesting as the existence of such powers is the fact that they are used almost daily with consistent success for the Executive. Let's look at a few of these powers in action.

1. *Transfer Authority*

Transfer authority allows a department head to shift funds from one appropriation account to another. As we will see, it is different from reprogramming, which involves the shifting of funds within one account. While transfer authority is usually based on statutes, and can be found there with some searching, reprogramming authority (which is discussed below) is usually non-statutory. Thus, it can only be located, if at all, "in committee reports, committee hearings, agency directives, correspondence between subcommittee chairmen and agency officials, and also 'gentlemen's agreements' and understandings that are not part of the public record."[292]

There's nothing new about transfer authority. Alexander Hamilton once offered an example in which the condition of public roads, which was worse then had been expected, resulted in the exhaustion of the fund which had been appropriated for wagon repairs. Simultaneously, the consumption of forage for animals turned out to be less than expected. What would be more reasonable, asked Hamilton, than to transfer the surplus in the forage fund to the wagon repair fund? If this were not allowed, "the motions of the army might, in this way, be suspended, and in the event, famine and ruin produced."[293] Using transfer authority, the Secretary of Defense can make huge changes in actual use of the budget. In one year alone he used this power to make 836 transfers totalling $590 million. Obviously military transfers in certain circumstances are a necessary administrative tool. But sometimes, particularly in the foreign aid field, a vast slush fund can be created with little opportunity for Congress to review such actions. Under current law, the President can convince the Congress of the need for foreign aid to one country, and then turn around and give it to another. He can even shuffle funds from economic aid to military aid or vice versa. Section 614 of the Foreign Assistance Act, for instance, allows the President to waive all requirements of that Act whenever such action is "important to the security of the United States."[294] According to one account, there were seventeen such waivers between July 1970 and October 1971, and in no case was the Congress notified before the waiver occurred.[295]

> "One of these pumped $110 million of military aid into Cambodia following the 1970 invasion by siphoning money originally intended for Taiwan, Greece, Turkey, and Vietnam. Nixon didn't inform Congress until later that year when he asked it to replace the funds ex post facto. Another waiver was for $3 million in military aid to Ceylon, given on an oral authorization by the U.S. Ambassador . . . to help Ceylon put down a leftist insurrection begun five days earlier which had cap-

tured large sections of the country. Helicopters were supplied, and within a month government forces were again in control."[296]

Military aid to Cambodia developed into a potential article of impeachment against President Nixon. Congressional hearings in 1973 by the Senate Armed Services Committee developed information that secret bombings of Cambodia had been conducted by the Administration between 1969 and 1970. These were concealed from the Congress until 1973.

The Department of Defense had created a system of false reporting to hide these bombings. Bombings were made to appear as if they had taken place in South Vietnam rather than in Cambodia. B-52 bombers strikes on targets in South Vietnam were ordered through usual channels. Then using a highly classified channel, a strike on Cambodian targets near South Vietnam would be requested. The planes would fly their missions in such a way that they would pass near the Vietnam target before releasing their bombs in Cambodia. Reports then would reflect only that Vietnam targets had been hit.

In 1974, the House Judiciary Committee considered a proposed article of impeachment dealing with this program of unauthorized bombing of another nation, and the concealment of it from Congress. This article stated that the President had violated his oath to preserve, protect and defend the Constitution and to faithfully executive the laws by ordering such bombing, and that he concealed the facts of it from the Congress in "derogation of the power of the Congress to declare war, to make appropriations and to raise and support armies . . . ."[297]

The funds the President used for this bombing operation had already been transferred from other programs. When Nixon asked for money to replace these funds, Senator J. William Fulbright remarked:

> "Now the administration has well underway a vast program of aid to Cambodia, without having sought any approval by the Congress for such a policy. I have no doubt that the leaders of Cambodia's Government feel confident that the United States is now committed to their survival. And Congress' approval of this bill, as written, will be taken as a ratification of that commitment, both by Cambodia and in the eyes of the world. Once again Congress is faced with a proposal to endorse a policy ex post facto."[298]

2. *"Excess" Stocks*

One of the President's most potent budgetary powers is the use of excess stocks of surplus war goods. Grants of such surplus goods don't have to be listed as current outlays for military aid. Thus the departments of Defense and State were able to keep Chiang Kai-shek's Nationalist Chinese forces on Taiwan well-stocked with "excess" aircraft, tanks, howitzers and the new M-14 rifles, even though the Congress was in theory engaged in reducing Taiwan's regular military assistance. In fact, one commentator concluded:

> "When one looks at the budget documents of 1966-1971, there is an almost dollar-for-dollar increase in handouts of excess war articles as congressional appropriations for all military aid programs were being decreased. To conceal the trajectory of this rise, the Pentagon suddenly switched from listing the acquisition cost of excess armaments to something called "utility value," a rough approximation of market value which averaged out at about one-fourth to one-third the equipment's original cost."[299]

There is no clear estimate of the total value of the present amount of "obsolete weapons and supplies" available to the Department of Defense for distribution as "excess."

One source has suggested that in one recent year the amount might have been as high as $9 billion.[300] Because there are no clear guidelines as to what might become "excess," theoretically it is possible to declare virtually all military equipment "excess" when the Pentagon wishes to give it away as military aid.

The largest such gift of military equipment—hundreds of millions of dollars worth—went to Vietnam. No one today knows the total value of the military bases, artillery, ammunition, helicopters, airplanes and other supplies given to the government of Vietnam. Obviously, much of the equipment was given through regular channel appropriations, but an unknown amount of "surplus" material was also given away. When asked about this situation, one representative of the Comptroller's Office in the Pentagon was quoted as saying, "Hell, man, that's my job: to lose track of it."[302]

3. Covert Funding

In a democratic society, government expenditures are expected to be made public so that those spending the funds may be accountable to the people. This need for accountability was recognized by the Founding Fathers with specific language in Article I, section ix of the Constitution: "A regular statement and account of the receipts and expenditures shall be published from time to time."[302] Numerous statutes buttress this requirement. The Budget and Accounting Procedures Act of 1950 requires that the Federal Government shall provide "full disclosure of the results of financial operations . . .",[303] and the Secretary of the Treasury is required to prepare reports on the results of financial operations "for the information of the President, the Congress, and the public . . . ."[304] Despite these provisions however, the funding of many agencies and uncounted programs is still hidden from the public and even most members of Congress. The published budget is extremely vague and sometimes internally contradictory, or inaccurate.

For many years a mighty weapon in the President's struggle with Congress has been the power to withhold information under the label of "secret." In an atmosphere in which, until recently, the switchboard operator of the CIA would not even identify the agency when you called (a practice still followed by some non-secret government agencies), it is not surprising that the classified stamp is frequently used to foil congressional investigation of the funds which the Congress should knowingly be appropriating. Senator Stuart Symington once told *The Atlantic,* "They don't tell the truth. What is driving me up the wall is what on earth are they doing with the money I am turning over. If they won't put that on the record, we might as well stay home and just send in a batch of proxies."[305]

Executive secrecy in the budget prevents congressional control at both ends. The budget is both initiated and spent without effective congressional oversight. Oversight must therefore be limited to the brief exposure time during the appropriations process. This is largely the fault of the Congress, but the Executive hasn't made Congress' job any easier. No one really knows just how much foreign assistance is given, nor even in how many different ways. In 1971, the only items in the budget clearly marked as military aid totaled around $400 million. But in that same year hearings before the Joint Economic Committee indicated that more than $6.9 billion in military assistance and sales were budgeted for fiscal year 1972. While one Defense Department official put the total cost at $4.9 billion, another pegged it at $6.3 billion. In Senator Proxmire's words, military assistance is an example of "a giant discount supermarket with no checkout counters, no cash registers, no store manager."[306] Asked about the President's free hand in making military agreements calling for substantial military aid, former Senator Allen Ellender, while Chairman of the Senate Appropriations stated:

> "What can you do? It's out of our hands. I believe in having one, strong Commander-in-Chief. Once war material is ordered, no member of Congress—no one—is supposed to follow through to see how it's used. It's to be used by the Commander-in-Chief as he sees best. I wouldn't want Congress to do a damned thing about it. If I were President, I wouldn't want all these 'arm-chair generals' around me."[307]

Even Senator Clifford P. Case of New Jersey, a member of both the Appropriations Committee and the Foreign Relations Committee, didn't know that the Administration had agreed to finance Thai troops in Laos until he read about it in the newspaper.[308]

4. The Pipeline

Each year, the Treasury Department has an enormous balance of funds which is carried over into the following year. This unexpended authority is called the "pipeline." Many have expressed concern that this pipeline might be tapped for purposes never intended, and has become a hidden river of money, beyond the control of Congress. During floor debate over the Vietnam-war era ceiling on funds for Laos proposed by Senator Symington, Senator Fulbright expressed his suspicions about this pipeline:

> "I never have figured out how (Defense Department managers) are able to spend money that has neither been authorized nor appropriated. They have ways of drawing on unexpended funds. I imagine there is at least $50 billion of unexpended funds in the pipeline as reserve for the Pentagon. So I would not be sure that even with a prohibition against appropriation of any money, they could not find some in a very short time."[309]

These pipeline funds come from a budgetary device known as "full funding." Traditionally, appropriations are annual, and revert to the Treasury Department if they are unspent at the end of the fiscal year. However, full funding, which is primarily used for long-term procurement and construction, may authorize multiple-year funds which carry over for a specified period until spent. Funding for an aircraft carrier, for example, may be on the books for some six or seven years. Full funding theoretically lets the Congress know the total price tag for big items, and is supposed to help hold down cost overruns—through its success in this is doubtful. The problem is that once a long-term program falls through, or negotiations are terminated, carry-over funds continue and accumulate. Depending on the flexibility of the original appropriation language, an agency has a built-in reservoir of funds. In one recent year the Department of Defense was carrying some $43 billion worth of unspent authority, which was more than three-fifths the size of the $71 billion annual Defense budget.[310]

This pipeline complicates effective budget accountability. While the Congress often focuses on yearly appropriations (rather than outlays) the Pentagon has been spending more than its annual appropriation for years. In 1971, the Senate voted down the foreign aid bill, only to find that $4.7 billion (one and one half times the amount of the defeated bill) was still in the aid pipeline.[311]

5. Reprogramming

Reprogramming is a little known budgetary technique which can completely circumvent the usual legislative process of authorizing and appropriating funds. It is the power of an agency to shift funds from one program to another within an appropriation account. Reprogramming has developed into a shell-game deferral of approved projects and the substitution of new ones. An agency can request money for a popular program and then shift it into one which the Congress would never have funded. On the other hand, Congress can mandate that funds be spent on one program and find that the agency has reprogrammed them for use directly contrary to Congress' intent. Reprogramming has often been used to start programs of which the Congress wasn't even aware. In 1966, the Pentagon began building the "McNamara Line", an electronic battlefield in South Vietnam. Senator Stuart Symington, a high-ranking member of the Senate Armed Services Committee, learned about the project one day while reading a magazine.

Reprogramming is a closed game, played only by senior committee members in Congress and a few people in the agency. Different congressional committees handle reprogramming in different ways. In the past, all that was required for an agency to shift funds from one program to another was for four men on the Hill to give their informal approval: the two chairmen of the appropriate subcommittees of the House and Senate Appropriations Committees and the two chairmen of the authorizing committees. Occasionally, reprogramming is handled at the staff level by the subcommittee clerks. At other times, congressmen are polled on the proposed changes, but often only a closed hearing is held.

Sometimes Congress isn't informed at all. A 1973 Government Accounting Office (GAO) Report concluded that the Internal Revenue Service had reprogrammed $43 million over three years without approval by the appropriations committees, a clear violation of prior understandings made between the Treasury Department and the Congress.

One interesting variety of reprogramming called "deob-reob," is practiced by the Agency for International Development (AID). Under this procedure, AID administrators de-obligate funds from one program and then re-obligate them to another. This practice has become so widespread that at one point, Congressman O.H. Passman (chairman of the appropriations subcommittee handling foreign aid matters) said, "it may very well be that perhaps half, or more, of the projects now funded were never approved in the beginning, by any committee of the Congress."[312]

Sometimes, reprogramming is nipped in the bud, such as when Congress refused to provide the Pentagon with funds for a third Nimitz-class aircraft carrier because the Administration had not submitted a formal budget request. Later, however, Senators Walter Mondale and Clifford Case learned that the Navy planned to finance construction of a third carrier by reprogramming $139 million in shipbuilding funds already approved for an oil tanker and three salvage submarines. After sending warnings to Chairman Ellender of the Appropriations Committee that reprogramming wouldn't wash for such a major project, Defense Secretary Packard announced that the Department would abandon the reprogramming and indefinitely postpone any formal budget request for the carrier.

No one really knows how much reprogramming takes place in any fiscal year. In the words of one House Appropriations Committee report on Pentagon spending:

> "The volume of reprogramming is a strong indication that much defense planning is superficial and without firm foundation."[313]

Many budget experts on the Hill and in the agencies feel that some reprogramming is necessary, given the great time-lag between drawing up program requests, passage of authorization and appropriation acts by the Congress, and the quarterly allocation of funds to agencies. The problem is that no one can be sure just what is happening when funds are reprogrammed. One classic example is the F-14 case.

In 1969, the House Appropriations Committee reported that the Navy was moving "too fast" in authorizing production of the F-14 fighter plane before structural tests were completed. Mindful of earlier problems with the C-5A and the F-111, the Committee slashed the requested $275 million for purchase of the first six F-24's, and ordered in the clearest language that "none of the funds provided are to be utilized for tooling beyond that needed for fabrication of the test aircraft." Committee members breathed a sigh of relief, only to find out some nine months later at a Navy briefing that the plane was in production. The Navy had gone back to Chairman Mahon's Defense Appropriations Subcommittee and gained some $517 million for the construction of 26 production models. Apparently no notification was given to anyone outside the subcommittee.[314]

The Congress has begun to take notice of reprogramming. At first, the Appropriations Committees merely required the Department of Defense to keep them posted on major reprogramming. Later the Department was required to submit semiannual reports. Finally, the Committees required prior approval before taking certain reprogramming actions. Then, in 1961, the Armed Services Committees were included in this prior approval system.[315]

The Congress can prevent reprogramming abuses. The first step is to require that all reprogramming be reported to the public. It can be highlighted in committee reports or published in the *Congressional Record.* Over the past few years some actions have made reprogramming more visible. The Defense Subcommittee of the House Appropriations Committee has begun to open up its hearings on reprogramming actions. Most reprogramming actions are now printed as a part of committee hearings. And the Congress has taken steps to reduce funds that agencies are allowed to carry over from year to year. One way this has been done is to change "no year funds," which are available until expended, to "single year" or "multiyear" appropriations which must be reviewed periodically by the Congress.

6. Other Budgetary Tricks

In addition to the budgetary tricks outlined above, there are an endless number of other tricks that can be used from time to time by Presidents or agencies to make an end run around Congress. The Federal Reserve System, for instance, spends almost half a billion dollars per year, but its funds are neither appropriated by the Congress nor reviewed by the Office of Management and Budget. The "Fed" gets its income from the profit made by buying and selling government securities. And the Fed is only one example of the lack of accountability which permeates the government's spending process despite the clear constitutional requirement that funds be disclosed. "For more than 40 years, the Treasury Department has had its own private $4 billion kitty to spend for almost whatever it pleases." The Exchange Stabilization Fund, established to stabilize the international value of the dollar, has been used by Treasury to pay CIA agents, provide travel funds for Treasury personnel and other expenses. Expenditures from this fund are reported annually to the Congress, but apparently are outside of the usual detailed appropriations process.[316] Estimates of the total amount of money beyond the control of the Congress run from $10 to $15 billion annually. These funds are hidden from the usual Congressional reviews because of secrecy, confidentiality or other similiar reasons. Even the Government Accounting Office is unable to properly audit these funds.

One of the more obscure examples of budgetary hocus pocus is the Feed and Forage law.[317] This law provides extraordinary power to the Pentagon. Generally, Pentagon officials must come to the Congress hat in hand to justify their budget requests, obtain authorization and appropriations for each of these requests, and wait for full action by the Congress before they may obligate funds. With the Feed and Forage law however, the process is just the opposite. The Pentagon can enter into obligations without limit, and then come to the Congress for the money. By the time the Congress is notified, contracts have been signed and the Congress has no honorable choice but to fund them.

This legislation allows the military departments to contract for clothing, subsistance, forage, fuel, quarters, transportation, or medical and hospital supplies before receiving appropriations. The only limit on it is that the obligations incurred, "shall not exceed the necessities of the current year." It is a blank check—always signed by the Congress when presented.

Although this legislation is unknown to many members of Congress and their staffs, the Pentagon hasn't forgotten about it. From 1960 to 1972 the Pentagon used it to obligate $1.7 billion. Indeed, it is a wonder that more money hasn't been spent this way.[318]

In 1973, when Defense Secretary Elliot Richardson appeared before the Senate Appropriations Committee, he blatantly said that the Defense Department could continue to bomb Cambodia even if the Congress denied the Administration's request for $500 million in transfer authority. In Richardson's words:

> "We will consider that we have the authority to do it anyway. We can find the money to do it anyway . . . We could invoke section 3732 authority [the feed and forage law]."[319]

B. The Impoundment Crisis

> *"Impoundment amounts to government by decree, and if the practice is permitted, the collective voice of 535 members of Congress could be overridden by one man. That would be government without law."* —Senator Sam Ervin.

> *"The constitutional right for the President of the United States to impound funds and that is not to spend money, when the spending of money would mean either increasing prices or increasing taxes for all the people, that right is absolutely clear."*—President Richard M. Nixon.

Senator Lawton Chiles of Florida once received complaints from Jacksonville that despite the demands of poor people, the city had been unable to obtain Food Stamps. The Department of Agriculture had told the city that the funds simply were not available. This puzzled Chiles because he knew that adequate funds had been appropriated. On inquiring, Chiles learned that not only Jacksonville, but some 40 counties across Florida and several hundred areas nationwide had been denied Food Stamp money. The roadblock was that the Office of Management and Budget was impounding, or refusing to release, $200 million in funds specifically earmarked for these stamps.

The Senator took to the Senate Floor, castigated the practice of impounding, and warned that the President, in hatcheting a legislative program because he considered it inefficient, was twisting constitutional principles and usurping the Congress' appropriation power. In Chiles' view, impoundment was an unconstitutional item veto over programs the President had signed into law without the danger of being overridden by a two-thirds vote of the Congress. Of course, Senator Chiles was not alone.[320]

Congressman Olsen of Montana once received a one-line telegram from an Indian tribal chairman asking what had happened to Indian health money. It turned out that $2 million in Indian health funds had been frozen, thus cancelling immunization, contract care programs and other Indian medical benefits. The Congressman's staff spent the next two weeks gathering the signatures of 90 congressmen and senators to force release of the money. Congressman Olsen, too, had learned about impounding.[321] It is often only in this way, by accident, that a member of Congress learns that money has been impounded. OMB has had a history of jealously guarding its figures on impounded funds.

In 1970, Senator Sam Ervin's Subcommittee on the Separation of Powers held hearings on the impoundment question. These hearings provided the first time in anyone's memory that a breakdown on impounded funds had been released. One of the Subcommittee staff was quoted as saying:

> "We had a hell of a time. We had been after the budget bureau for three and half years before the information was finally released."[322]

Impoundment presents a strange picture: members of Congress with hat in hand asking the President to spend money they already have authorized and appropriated. The typical congressman's complaint runs, "I thought that once the Congress passed the appropriation bill and the President approved it and signed it and said to the country, 'This has my approval,' that the money would be used, instead of sacked up and put down in the basement somewhere."[323] Those were the words of a frustrated Senator Lyndon Johnson when he was on the Hill. After assuming the Presidency, Johnson played the impoundment game himself.

Impoundment took a decidedly different turn under President Nixon. In the recent past there had been a liberal, Democratic administration trying to push programs which the more conservative Congress would not fund. Under Nixon, however, the Democratic Congress often pushed liberal programs which the President didn't want funded. In addition, the intensity of the impoundment debate in the Nixon Administration may be traced to two other factors: first, the use of impoundment as an instrument of broad fiscal policy and political philosophy rather than, as in the past, a more narrowly targeted tactic. Senator Hubert Humphrey called this "policy impoundment," and said that "Policy impoundment is executive arrogance."[324] The second factor that made Nixon's impoundments different was the level of the impoundments—in excess of $8 billion—according to OMB, with some congressional opponents of the practice charging that more than $12 billion had been placed in reserve.[325]

Under the Nixon Administration, Congress steadily became more restive over impoundment. In 1970, Congress added language to a hospital construction bill that ordered the entire appropriation to be spent. Nixon vetoed it because it constituted an "assault on presidential options," but the veto was overridden and that spending language remains as a precedent.[326]

In 1972, the Federal Impoundment and Information Act was passed. This legislation required that impoundment actions be reported to Congress together with citations of legal authority and the reasons for each instance of impoundment. But this Act merely required information. It didn't limit the President's impoundment powers.

The classic congressional tactic in opposing impoundment has been old-fashioned political blackmail: The 1971 Senate version of the foreign aid bill, for instance, forbade any expenditures abroad until the President released urban development funds. But it was not until the Congressional Budget and Impoundment Control Act of 1974 (discussed below) that the President's free-wheeling use of impoundments was significantly restrained.

The impoundment issue has been marked by great heat and little light. A brief look at some basic budgetary mechanics might be helpful.

1. Impoundment in the Budgetary Cycle: What Is It?

There are even uncertainties as to what impoundment really is. But we can perhaps come closest to defining it by looking at some basic steps in the budget process.

Until the Budget and Impoundment Control Act of 1974, the Executive budgetary cycle was a six-step process. First, basic authorizing legislation is enacted. Both House and Senate rules require that appropriation bills can't be reported unless the expenditure is first authorized by law. There are some exceptions to this rule, the major one being that a statute may provide simultaneously for both authorization of programs and appropriation of funds for those programs.

Once the authorization has been enacted, the second step is the President's request for funds. This request really begins in the spring of each year, when the Office of Management and Budget (OMB) starts planning for the fiscal year that is more than a year away. During this "spring review," each major department and agency submits information to OMB which is reviewed by the President. Agencies then receive general spending guidelines called their "mark." Throughout the summer and fall agencies use these guidelines to develop detailed budget requests which are reviewed by OMB in winter. The result goes to the President for review, final decision and the President's budget is born. This budget is transmitted to the Congress each January.

But the budget process is not even half-way over at this point. The third step is the enactment of appropriations, which must come before any moneys may be withdrawn from the Treasury. This step is mandated by the Constitution. Once funds are appropriated, control over the budget shifts back to the Executive and it is at this point that Congress is itching to get back into the game.

In the fourth budget step, the new obligational authority (new power to contract or spend money) granted to the agencies by Congress is apportioned to the agencies on a quarterly basis by OMB. This allocation of funds prevents agencies from spending their appropriations in the first few months and then having to return later for more. Apportionment according to the fiscal quarter-year, which is authorized by statute, doesn't simply divide the appropriations pie into four equal parts. It adjusts each slice of the pie depending upon inflation, spending rates and other factors. In recent years, such adjustments have been used to keep total amounts below those set by Congress. The fifth step is the incurring of obligations by agencies, through placing of orders, awarding contracts, hiring personnel and so on. Finally, the Treasury Department makes payment.

If impoundment occurs at all, it is likely to occur as part of the fourth step, the apportionment and reservation of funds. After the Congress has appropriated funds, but before the agencies can incur any obligations, the Executive steps in and puts the funds into reserve. In other words they are frozen. After a time, some of these funds in reserve may "lapse" under the legislation involved, and impoundment has done its job—permanently.[328]

But when is a budgetary reserve an impoundment? Basically, any reservation which, when viewed objectively, is in accord with a congressional purpose, is not an impoundment. It's simply a matter of congressional intent. If the Congress has already given the President discretion to reserve funds, the President's action would merely be an exercise of this permissible discretion. One example of this is the 1968 Revenue and Expenditure Control Act. In this

Act, Congress provided a spending ceiling and made about half of the spending cuts provided by the Act. It directed the President to make the other half.[329] In addition, if the President reserves funds under the Antideficiency Act of 1950, which provides that money may be reserved "to provide for contingencies" or "to effect savings whenever savings are possible through changes in requirements," there is no impoundment.[330] This is just a sound, legislatively mandated management practice. But when the President cuts back a program solely because he disagrees with the Congress over its merits, that is clearly impoundment.

Some people don't agree. They say that any management actions that reserve funds, such as those under the Antideficiency Act, are impoundments. And that any time the President doesn't spend all of an appropriation, even though his action is based on a statute, that this is impoundment, too.

2. The History of Impoundment

The Nixon Administration claimed that its impoundment practices were similar to those of previous administrations, and thus supposedly they were legal. While there is some support for the argument that what has been "gotten away with" is legal, the Supreme Court in the landmark case of *Youngstown Sheet and Tube Co. v. Sawyer,*[331] made it clear that the powers of Congress cannot be usurped merely by prior assertions of executive power.

What has been the past practice in the use of impoundments? There is quite a long history of budgetary reserves. Longer, in fact, than the Budget Bureau has been in existence. An early example, frequently cited, occurred during the administration of Thomas Jefferson. In 1803, Jefferson declined to spend an appropriation of $50,000 for gunboats:

> "The favorable and peaceful turn of affairs on the Mississippi rendered an immediate execution of that law unnecessary, and time was desirable in order that the institution of that branch of our force might begin on models the most approved by experience."[332]

In short, when the United States purchased the Louisiana Territory, the threat of war that made the gunboats necessary abated, so the money was impounded. Senator Humphrey has cited this as an example of an impoundment which is legal because it saves money.[333]

Years later, the Nixon Administration cited this case as an example that impoundment was a tried and true custom. But a closer examination of the facts reveals otherwise. Jefferson didn't really refuse to spend the money the Congress had voted for gunboats. He wanted more gunboats but he wanted the latest models. Just one year later Jefferson reported to the Congress that the money was being fully spent. This was just a temporary deferral of spending, not a refusal to spend the money.[334]

Again, in 1840, the Supreme Court upheld the exercise of a Presidential impoundment based on good management practices. In that case the Secretary of the Navy witheld a payment from a widow whose claim was based on a congressional resolution. If the Secretary had paid her the money, the widow would have gotten two pensions. The Court agreed that the Congress never intended to provide her with double benefits.[335] This is more a case of statutory construction however, than impoundment.

The first Director of the Budget Bureau, Charles Dawes, believed in budgetary reserves and worked with President Harding to create machinery to reserve any funds that agencies saved. Because the Congress apparently never saw this practice as anything more than a savings program, this practice doesn't fit the most widely accepted definition of impoundment.[336]

In 1921 Bureau of the Budget Circular implemented the Dawes program by requiring each agency to estimate: (1) indispensable expenditures, and (2) the balance which might be saved under each appropriation. These estimates were sent to the Budget Director and submitted by him to the President for approval. If approved, the estimated savings were locked up in the Treasury as a general reserve.

In the 1930s the concept of savings took a flying leap. President Herbert Hoover, in the midst of the Depression, ordered departments to cut proposed expenditures by 10 per cent and then froze the money in reserve so that it couldn't be spend without Presidential approval. Because these steps appear to have met with uncritical acceptance by everyone including the Congress, they may not have constituted impoundment. In addition, it appears that most of the programs affected were authorized by legislation which left room for less than full and immediate execution.[337]

In the 1940s President Franklin D. Roosevelt expanded the concept of reserving funds. Now reserves were used to control programs. In January of 1941, shortly before the Japanese attack on Pearl Harbor, the President's budget message expressed his intention to cut certain types of spending, principally public building funds, to offset military expenditures. The following year similar program reductions were announced, including reduced spending for highway construction. Neither of these two reservations produced great outcry, but Administration action late in 1941 to reserve funds appropriated for the National Youth Administration and the Civilian Conservation Corps aroused major controversy.[338] In 1942 Roosevelt developed a rationale for such cuts. He stated that to mandate that all funds be spent "would take from the Chief Executive every incentive for good management and the practice of common-sense economy."[339] These cuts were undertaken under a threat of imminent war to marshal the nation's reserves toward programs relating to national defense. There is no question that such policies had an aura of impoundment—on the theory that substantial program reductions were contrary to the intent of Congress which had not expressly authorized them. But the war atmosphere provided an apparent cover of legitimacy to Roosevelt's practices.

In fact, because the country was facing war, it may have been the implied intent of the Congress that such program changes be made. But implying intent from silence is dangerous business. Although Roosevelt did encounter criticism for his actions, he saw the reservations not as a test of wills with the Congress, but as savings legitimately made from permissive legislation. In addition, he publicly disavowed any notion that the practice could be used to circumvent the veto power or "nullify the expressed will of Congress . . . ."[340]

At the close of World War II the Budget Bureau pulled in its horns on reserving funds, perhaps because it was unsure of its powers. In 1950, the Administration sought legislative authority for what had become a custom of reserving funds. The Congress responded by passing the Anti-Deficiency Act of 1950, which authorized reserves for the purpose of effecting savings. This Act went no further on its face than merely legitimatizing some past practices by legislation.

Although the Anti-Deficiency Act was narrow in scope, during the 1950s it was used as the basis to reserve more funds. In the mid-to late-1950s, the Budget Bureau placed in reserve several hundred million dollars appropriated for military purposes, and in the 1960s the Bureau increasingly reserved domestic funds. Throughout the present decade reserved funds have been hoarded at multibillion levels each year. On an individual basis some of these reservations certainly amounted to impoundments. But viewed in the context of legislative intent, it should be noted that these reserves usually were not made in the face of a hostile Congress. Rather Congress showed—if only by its inaction—a willingness to subordinate the funding of specific projects to a policy of government economy. Indeed, on those few occasions when Congress asserted itself in clear and mandatory terms, the Executive typically retreated.[341] Although there had been Executive impoundments before the Nixon years, there had never been a notorious case involving a clearly expressed clash of wills between the President and Congress.

This is not to say there weren't skirmishes. In the Truman Administration, Congress appropriated funds for a 58-Group Air Force over the opposition of the President, who sought a 48-Group Force. Truman signed the legislation, but directed the Secretary of Defense to place $735 million dollars in reserve. Although the House apparently intended the legislation to be mandatory, the Senate had intended it to be permissive. Thus, there were no clearly drawn lines of confrontation.[342] Again, in 1950, the Truman Administration cancelled construction of the aircraft carrier Forrestal after funds already had been appropriated. But no confrontation with Congress followed. On the contrary, the House Appropriations Committee stated that economy "neither begins nor ends in the Halls of Congress."[343] The Committee went on to say that an appropriation only fixed a ceiling for any category of spending and the officials responsible for the program had a duty to render all necessary service while spending the smallest amount possible.[344]

In the Eisenhower Administration, the President reserved funds for Nike-Zeus missile development. In addition, the Senate Armed Services Committee's Preparedness Investigating Subcommittee held hearings inquiring into the failure of the Administration to use funds appropriated for such purposes as the support of the Marine Corps at a given strength, and construction of Polaris submarines. But again no major confrontations developed.

In the Kennedy Administration, the House Armed Services Committee recommended that a 1963 bill to authorize armed forces appropriations include mandatory language directing the Secretary of the Air Force to spend not less than $491 million for an RS-70 weapons system. The President, through an exchange of letters with the Chairman, convinced the Committee to delete the mandatory provisions, and a showdown was averted. Until the Nixon Administration, Presidential impoundment remained within the framework of the give-and-take of the political process. If the Congress screamed loudly enough, the funds were released. More important, such impoundment was always rooted either in statutes or in the President's constitutional authority as commander-in-chief. In 1963, when the Civil Rights Commission proposed that federal aid be cut off to Mississippi because of a violation of desegregation orders, Kennedy replied:

> "I don't have the power to cut off the aid in a general way. What they were suggesting ... was ... a blanket withdrawal of Federal expenditures ... I said that I didn't have the power to do so, because it could be used in other ways differently." [345]

C. Legislative Justifications for Impoundment

It is generally conceded that when funds are authorized and appropriated their full expenditure is not mandatory. This presumption has two bases: First, the language of most programs is not in mandatory terms. Second, efficient management demands some power to trim costs when possible as long as the congressional policy is carried out.

Efficient management covers three types of situations. First, the witholding of funds to effect savings. Second, changing events which make an expenditure unnecessary. In Harry S Truman's words, "What looks like a good program one day may be completely unnecessary six months later."[346] And third: to carry out managerial responsibilities.

The presumption that funds need not be spent in full means that great weight must be given to the specific language used in appropriations acts. If these acts used words like "mandate," "require," and "shall," they are often deemed mandatory. Otherwise they leave discretion to spend or not to spend the funds in the President's hands.

Others have felt that no such flexible policy could pass a constitutional test. One of President Nixon's own appointees to the Supreme Court took this view. In a 1969 memorandum dealing with the impoundment of impacted school funds, then-Assistant Attorney General Rehnquist said:

> "With respect to the suggestion that the President has a constitutional power to decline to spend appropriated funds, we must conclude that existence of such a broad power is supported by neither reason nor precedent...

> It may be argued that the spending of money is inherently an executive function, and it seems an anomalous proposition that because the Executive branch is bound to execute the laws, it is free to decline to execute them."[347]

Not surprisingly, the Nixon Administration disavowed this memorandum.

If permission to impound cannot be found within the four corners of the appropriation itself, then the Executive is forced to find other legal sources for its impoundment authority. These sources fall into two categories: the Constitution and other laws. The Nixon Administration turned to the Employment Act of 1946 as one law justifying impoundment.

1.Employment Act of 1946

This Act states in part:

> "... it is the continuing policy and responsibility of the Federal Government to use all practicable means ... for the purpose of maintaining ... conditions under which there will be afforded useful employment ...."[348]

Nixon's position was that this Act required the Administration to take all necessary steps to stop inflation so that purchasing power could be increased. This position was soft-peddled, however, when it met with substantial disbelief and some derision. The Act appears to provide only the most tenuous support for withholding funds. Indeed, it says absolutely nothing about withholding funds. While it does require the President to submit an annual economic report it confers no special powers on him. Moreover, increasing employment and purchasing power may be conflicting policies. While inflation might promote increased employment, it might also reduce purchasing power. In addition, the Act doesn't refer to the Executive Branch at all, but to the whole federal government. Finally, any act of Congress coming afterwards and specifically mandating full spending would implicitly repeal such language.

2. Antideficiency Act Amendments

The second legislation the Nixon Administration used as justification for impoundment was the 1951 amendment to the Anti-Deficiency Act. That amendment states that:

> "... reserves may be established to provide for contingencies, or to effect savings whenever savings are made possible by or through changes in requirements, greater efficiency of operations, or other developments subsequent to the date on which such appropriation was made available."[349]

As we saw, this amendment was enacted merely to provide a legal stamp of approval to past practices. And only when reserves were made consistent with the will of Congress. Indeed the Act itself states that any reservations were only to be made as they carried out the purpose of the appropriation concerned—not as they might nullify its purposes.[350] In addition, the intent of the Antideficiency Act came through loud and clear in the BOB Budget Examiner's Handbook which stated, "Reserves must not be used to nullify the intent of Congress with respect to specific projects or level of programs."[351]

But there was some question as to what kind of "other developments" would justify "savings" under the Act. Would a general rise in inflation be such a development or only a more particular development in any given program, such as the discovery that a weapons system would not work? OMB Director Roy Ash argued that inflation was a "development" which justified placing funds in reserve. But there was no authority for such a proposition. And indeed the "other development" clause was later deleted by the Congress to prevent such an interpretation.

3. Economic Stabilization Act

Deputy Attorney General Joseph T. Sneed once argued that the President had substantial latitude to refuse to spend money for general fiscal reasons. Senator Thomas Eagleton became concerned that there might be support for this position in the Economic Stabilization Act Amendments of 1971, and immediately introduced legislation to provide that "nothing in the Stabilization Act may be construed to authorize" impounding.[352] The Eagelton amendment became law two months later and cut off this argument at the roots.

4. Harmonizing Various Laws: Budget Ceilings, Debt Limits, Economy and Reorganization Acts

The need to harmonize various laws was also used by the Nixon Administration to justify impoundments. For example, the passage of a *budget ceiling* directing that expenditures be held below a certain limit may directly conflict with the total spending level already enacted in appropriation bills. This gives the Executive an argument that Congress has given it discretion to impound in order to get total funding below the ceiling Congress itself has mandated. The counter-argument is that budget ceilings are "rubber ceilings" which are raised by implication every time the Congress later adds to appropriations.

But even if this counter-argument is accepted, the budget ceiling may still present the Executive with a real conflict. This is because the ceiling, which controls total outlays, may not apply to so-called "uncontrolables" at all. Uncontrollables are such items as trust funds, social insurance programs, and interest payments not subject to the usual appropriations process. Ceilings usually contain only estimates regarding these uncontrollables. Thus, if uncontrollables exceed estimates, the President might be forced to cut controllables in order to limit the total budget. Thus, even with a "rubber ceiling" the Executive may have to place funds in reserve. Limiting total expenditures may mean cutting popular programs. Congress sometimes would rather pass the task to the President by making him cut the budget through impounding. This takes the heat off of the Congress, and then gives congressmen a chance to hypocritically complain that the President is exceeding his powers by impounding.

A similar situation to that of budget ceilings exists when a *debt limit* bill is passed. The Executive may argue that an expenditure at appropriated levels will exceed the allowed federal debt limit, and that the existence of such a conflict demands that the President have the power to reduce expeditures. But the debt limit dilemma is probably more illusory than real. As a matter of practice, the Executive has routinely gone to the Congress to raise the debt limit whenever necessary.[353]

Economy and reorganization acts have also been used by Presidents as authority to reserve funds. In 1932, Congress gave President Herbert Hoover authority to make layoffs, cut salaries and consolidate agencies to save money. Although the Congress later disagreed with his actions, they turned right around in 1933 and granted Franklin D. Roosevelt's request for authority to reduce Veterans' payments by several hundred million dollars.[354] In 1950, in a one-shot grant of authority, the Congress directed President Harry S Truman to cut the budget by not less than $550 million dollars "without impairing national defense."[355]

5. *Miscellaneous Statutory Provisions*

Finally, there are a host of miscellaneous statutory provisions which give the President discretion to withold funds. He can withold economic assistance from underdeveloped countries which obtain sophisticated weapons;[356] cut off economic aid to a country overthrown by "communist" forces;[357] and, under the Hickenlooper Amendment, he must suspend aid to any country seizing U.S. property without compensation.[358] Another law empowers the President to cut off funds to domestic programs in which there is racial discrimination,[359] and states have been threatened by the President with a suspension of highway aid for noncompliance with Federal anti-billboard laws.[360]

The fact that there is a conflict in outstanding spending legislation does not automatically give the President an excuse to impound. He has two clear alternatives. First, he may ask Congress for legislation to guide him. For example, he might ask the Congress to authorize proportionalized budget cuts. Second, he can limit his reserves to programs authorized by statutes where discretion has been specifically granted by the Congress.

D. Constitutional Authority for Impoundment

1. Appropriation Powers

In addition to legislative rationalizations for impoundments, the Executive also has used constitutional ones. The Nixon Administration made two basic constitutional arguments to justify impoundments. First was the argument that Article I, section ix of the Constitution only means that no money can be spent without an appropriation—and that it does not mandate that appropriated funds be spent. Article I, section ix, paragraph 7 reads:

> "No money shall be drawn from the treasury, but in consequence of appropriations made by law . . . ."

Therefore, by implication (it was claimed) moneys which are appropriated need not be spent. The obvious counterargument is that there is simply no such implication here. This argument claiming the implication, was first floated by OMB Director Weinberger in 1971, but was soon dropped.

2. Spending Requirements

The second Constitutional argument, advanced in 1973, was that the Constitution nowhere explicitly directs the Executive to spend appropriated funds. In the absence of a clear constitutional provision, any assertion must stand or fall depending on what evidence can be summoned to fill the gap. In this case there are two gap-fillers. First, there is the constitutional provision that the Executive must take care that the laws be faithfully executed. The Executive has a duty to carry out an act of Congress where its provisions are clear unless there is some supervening executive power. The Supreme Court endorsed this principle in the *Kendall* case.[361] In that 1838 decision, the Court totally rejected the argument that the take care clause gave the President exclusive control over officers in the Executive Branch. The Court then described the argument that faithful execution might somehow include the power not to execute as "a novel construction of the Constitution and entirely inadmissible."[362] This interpretation of the faithful execution clause has been endorsed by commentators as well. Alexander Bickel has stated that the "distinct duty of the President to execute the law is just as distinct as the prohibition against spending unappropriated money" and is the "only foundation for saying that the President can't impound."[363]

A third constitutional argument against impoundment is that it would give the President an item veto to nullify laws with no opportunity for the Congress to override them. Indeed, the veto clause itself would be meaningless. Why would the Constitution spell out the veto and the Congress' right to override when the President could merely refuse to enforce appropriations bills at will to accomplish the same thing? In addition, the Constitution states "All legislative powers herein granted shall be vested in a Congress of the United States. . . ." [Article I, section i] Power to nullify a law is a legislative power. Thus the President appears to violate this provision by impounding.

Constitutional scholars have pointed out a further constitutional problem with impoundment authority. The Constitution grants the Congress power not only to pass all laws necessary and proper for carrying out its own powers, but also for carrying out all other powers vested by the Constitution in the government of the United States. If the Executive can disapprove laws by inaction, then the Congressional power to affect the other branches is contingent on the President's approval.[364] Of course an answer to this argument is that the President makes most laws contingent anyway, by his veto power. Countering this is the reply that the veto power is the *only* means for the President to disapprove of a proposed law, and that even this is subject to an override and therefore is not absolute.

3. Inherent and Implied Powers

Some day the President may claim that under the Constitution he has either inherent or implied powers to impound. Implied powers are those that aren't specifically enumerated but are necessary to carry out those that are enumerated. Inherent powers are those believed to be necessary to the function of the Executive Branch which are neither enumerated in the Constitution nor implied by the enumerated powers.

Theodore Roosevelt, a great believer in inherent powers, argued that the President was limited only by specific restrictions in the Constitution or mandated by Congress.[365] That doctrine however, has been stopped pretty much in its tracks. In the *Youngstown* case,[366] for instance, Harry Truman argued that because of the Korean war he could use inherent war powers to seize the steel mills. The Court split right down the middle on this assertion, with four Justices recognizing such powers, four not, and one refusing to take a position. Even among those supporting such inherent powers, however, there was a consensus that exercise of such powers should be limited to situations involving serious national danger. Such a view would be consistent with Justice Brandeis' caution in the *Meyers* case that any inherent Presidential power should be limited to "the least possible power adequate to the end proposed."[367]

The doctrine of implied Presidential power has had even less success. The primary source of the doctrine was once thought to be the opening words of Article II: "The executive power shall be vested in a President of the United States of America." Chief Justice Taft, in *Meyers* argued that this phrasing amounted to a grant of a general executive power, strengthened and limited by the Constitution as necessary.[368] In view of later Supreme Court cases, however, and Justice Jackson's attack in the *Youngstown* case on the Taft position, it is doubtful that this view carries much weight today.

Some hold that because the President's powers in Article II are enumerated without particularity, the executive power should be construed expansively and not "niggardly."[369] But offsetting this is the fact that there is no "necessary and proper" clause for the Executive as there is for the Legislative Branch in Article I, section viii, paragraph 18. Thus although the Constitution was deliberately vague about the outer limits of Congress' power in some respects, it did not specifically provide for any such additional powers for the President.

4. Military and Foreign Affairs Powers

The President may also attempt to justify impoundment under his general military and foreign affairs powers. Such an approach immediately runs into the problem of who has the military and foreign affairs power in question. The Constitution has split these responsibilities between the President and Congress. Another problem is that domestic programs would appear to have absolutely nothing to do with military or foreign affairs. But the Nixon Administration came up with a linkage argument that attempts to get around that obstacle. Under the linkage theory, galloping domestic inflation dilutes the dollar, which in turn may aggravate a host of foreign relations and national security problems. The next step was then to claim that impounding was necessary to control inflation to keep foreign affairs under control.

The more the Congress heard of these legal and other justifications for impoundment, the angrier it became.

Ironically, President Nixon himself proved to be the greatest catalyst for Congressional reaction and reform. In a 1973 news conference, he waved a red cape at Congress.

> "[The] constitutional right for the President of the United States to impound funds . . . is absolutely clear."[370]

Finally, after such statements, hundreds of bills affected, and years of debate, the Congress finally acted against what it clearly regarded as an Executive grab for the legislative's most important power—the power of the purse. The Congressional Budget and Impoundment Control Act of 1974 was born.

E. Reform—the Congressional Budget and Impoundment Control Act of 1974

"You can retire that word impoundment from your type. We may even forget how to spell it."—OMB Director Roy Ash[371]

"To my mind, this is the most important piece of legislation I've worked on in my 20 years in the Senate."—Senator Sam J. Ervin Jr. commenting on the Congressional Budget and Impoundment Control Act of 1974.

The Congressional Budget and Impoundment Control Act of 1974 was revolutionary legislation. It established House and Senate budget committees, revamped the Congressional budget process, established a Congressional Budget Office, and (as the opening lines of the Act stated) took other steps "to assure effective congressional control over the budgetary process."[372] In short, the Act took what steps differing Congressional interests could agree upon to wrest legislative power over the budget back from the President. Whether it succeeded, however, is another question. To help answer that question we must first look at what the Act provided.

1. Contents of the Act

(a) The Budget Process

To provide more expertise on budgetary matters, the Act established House and Senate Budget Committees to play the key role in a new budget process. Because the slow-moving Congress had trouble completing appropriation bills by the July 1 fiscal year date, continuing resolutions and other devices were often used to fund agencies each year. These produced budgetary chaos. The Act, therefore, changed the fiscal year to begin on October 1. Each November 10, Executive Branch agencies are required to submit a "current services" budget for the following fiscal year. This estimates the spending levels required without policy changes. Next, the Joint Economic Committee reviews that budget and reports its general economic projections by December 31. When the President sends his budget to Congress on January 20, he includes certain new information, including five-year spending projections, and a new list of revenue losses caused by tax loopholes.

The Act creates a Congressional Budget Office (CBO) to analyze the information in the President's budget and give staff support to the budget committees. CBO's role is parallel to OMB's role in the Executive Branch. Once the Budget Office reviews the President's budget, the budget committees report out an initial budget resolution which Congress must approve by May 15. This resolution is a comprehensive tentative federal budget. Thus for the first time, the Act requires that Congress must look at the whole budget and be responsible for it.

In the past, the Congress has appropriated piecemeal, with each committee being responsible only for its share—the right hand of Congress didn't know what the left hand was doing. The committees setting the level of federal tax and other receipts (the Ways and Means Committee in the House and the Finance Committee in the Senate) never before put their estimates together with the appropriations committees which spent the money. Under the Budget Act, however, the budget resolution now sets target levels for taxes and spending and then sets levels for the federal debt or surplus. In addition, spending is broken down by the same categories used in the President's budget: defense, welfare, general government programs and so forth. This budget resolution must be adopted before any tax, debt or appropriations bills can be passed; and to insure prompt action on appropriations bills, authorizing legislation must clear the Congress by May 15, the deadline for enacting the budget resolution.

After the budget resolution is passed, the appropriation bills must be completed by September. At that time, the Congress must get down to brass tacks. It either has to affirm or revise the budget targets set by the budget resolution. If the appropriations bills total more than provided for in the budget resolution, appropriations have to be cut, or the budget resolution has to be modified.

(b) Impoundment controls

The Act also tried to control impoundments. Two types of impoundment controls were included. One for impoundments which only delayed spending of funds, and another for impoundments which cut total spending or attempted to terminate programs. For impoundments that defer spending, either the Senate or House can pass a simple resolution ordering their expenditure, and it thus becomes mandatory. No time limit is set for action. For impoundments that terminate or cut programs, the President automatically is thus ordered to spend the money unless both the House and Senate pass a recission bill within 45 days recinding the appropriation.

In addition, to squelch any presidential justification for impoundment based on the Anti-Deficiency Act of 1950 (which allowed the Executive to withhold funds because of "other developments," etc.), Congress repealed these portions of the 1950 Act. To keep Congress informed on impoundments, the President is required to report all deferrals. If the President refuses to comply with a congressional action overruling an impoundment, the Comptroller General of the United States is authorized to seek a court order requiring spending of the funds.[373]

Whether the Act will effectively stop impoundments (and without producing paperwork chaos) is anyone's guess. By 1975, about one half of the $27 billion that President Ford sought to withhold had been released. Some of this was let go as a result of court action, some voluntarily, and the rest was released as a result of the Act.

(c) Other Controls

The Act did little, if anything, to reduce the President's other budgetary powers such as transfer authority, excess stocks, using covert funding, turning on the "pipeline," and reprogramming. These powers continue undiminished.

2. Outlook for Success

"To make it work, Congress and its individual members will have to act a hell of a lot differently than they do now."[374] —Samuel M. Cohn, former assistant director, Office of Management and Budget.

Just because the 1974 Act is on the books doesn't mean it will work. Nearly 25 years earlier, the Congress passed the Legislative Reorganization Act, which had some similar provisions. That Act crumbled to dust over the next three years as Congress abandoned its procedures. The reorganization Act also required that Congress set a maximum amount to be appropriated each year and live within it. But in 1947, Congress couldn't agree on how to spend a surplus and in 1948 its appropriations exceeded the maximum amount it had set by $6 billion. The 1949 legislative budget was never produced, and the process broke down completely.[375]

To put the new budget procedures to work, Congress clearly will have to discipline itself. It will need "to overcome a lack of budgetary expertise, some committee jurisdictional jealousies, the temptation to waive budget-making deadlines, and some of the personal political interests of 100 Senators and 435 House members."[376] Senator Edmund Muskie, the first Chairman of the Senate Budget Committee, predicted that whether the whole process will work depends on how closely members and the Committee can sublimate themselves to the budget timetable. "If they ask for an extension here and an extension there, we could end up with the whole timetable collapsing." Sam Cohen, former assistant director of OMB, sees things another way. Congress may be sincere about budget control, but, he says,

> "I've worked with presidents and budget directors and secretaries of the Treasury who were sincere but couldn't do anything about it. There's always pressure to somehow shove in more money . . . the politics are such that they'd rather be for things than against them."[377]

If it appears that if the differences between the budget resolution and appropriations aren't too great, then the process may work. In Cohen's view, if the amounts are not too large, "they could find a gadget or gimmick" to adjust the figures. "But," he continued, "if they are large, God help us."[378]

The budgetary timetable is a strict taskmaster for Congress. Senator Muskie has pointed out:

> "What we've got here is a kind of timetable that nobody's ever lived by before, the kind of process that was never created before, and an attempt to impose this on an institution that's almost 200 years old that's generated considerable momentum and habits over those years."[379]

One forecaster put it more glumly:

> "Congress has an almost bizarre fear of failure, so it may display at least the mechanics of success. They'll try to cut spending, look into tax loopholes, cheat a little, lie about forecasts, like the executive branch." [380]

There is no question that the Congress needs to play a greater role in the budget. Unfortunately, although the public may be willing to express great outrage over the level of taxation, they rarely object to how the money is spent by the President.

> "A student of English history has noted that numerous revolts have been triggered by high or unauthorized taxation, and yet there is only one known instance of a revolt against 'extravagant or unauthorized expenditure'—that of Robin of Redesdale in 1469 . . . ."[381]

The Founding Fathers, however, had no doubts about where the spending power should lie. Alexander Hamilton said that the Constitution was designed so that "the purpose, the limit and the fund of every expenditure should be ascertained by a previous law."[382] In Madison's words, "the legislative department alone has access to the pockets of the people."[383]

What can be done, then, to insure the budgetary abuses we have seen are prevented? First, we can't strip all discretionary powers from the Executive. Some need to remain.

As was stated by budget expert Louis Fisher:

> "Take away the power to make transfers and agency officials pad their budgets. Eliminate discretionary authority altogether and agencies incur deficiencies. Give the President the power to apportion funds—as a means of preventing deficiencies—and he uses that power to impound funds and further his own policies."[384]

Although the Congress needs to redress the balance of power with the Executive over the power of the purse, it should not go too fast or too far. Reform movements have a way of getting out of hand. As one political commentator stated:

> "American reform movements had a tendency to deal with the institution they wish to cure much as Charles II's physicians threated his last illness. They bled him. They blistered him from head to foot with hot metal. They gave him purge after purge, using, among other medicaments, a salt extracted from human skulls. They made him inhale powders to induce sneezing. While this was going on, they fed him broth laced with cream of tartar and a light ale brewed without hops. When he complained of his discomforts (mildy, for he was a polite and considerate man), the doctors strictly bade him be silent . . . After a few days, mercifully, Charles died."[385]

Second, the remaining Presidential discretion must be controlled systematically and regularly by the Congress through effective oversight. Third, the Congress must distinguish in its oversight duties between important items and minutia. Fourth, any substantial budgetary moves by the Administration taken outside of the regular appropriation and authorization process should be reported to the Congress as a whole and made public, unless overriding matters of national security are involved. In the words of one commentator:

> "Just what happens behind the doors of a budget hearing is sometimes clouded in as much mystery as the deliberations of the monks of the Spanish Inquisition."[386]

The President took the power of the purse, and the power of Congress vanished. The big question is whether the Congress wants its Constitutional power of the purse enough to fight for it.

FOOTNOTES

1. 118 *Congressional Record* 36709 (1972), remarks of Rep. Moorhead citing an unnamed member of Congress.

2. DAWES, Charles G., *The First Year of the Budget of the United States,* G.P.O. 1923 at xi.

3. Haremann, Joel, "White House Report—OMB's Legislative Role Is Growing More Powerful and More Political," *National Journel Reports,* Oct. 27, 1973 at 1589.

4. Office of Management and Budget, "Circular A-19, Revised, Legislative Coordination and Clearance," July 31, 1972 at 1.

5. Letter from Velma N. Baldwin, OMB, to David J. Muchow, Dec. 17, 1975.

6. Will, George F., "The Tradition of Mediocrity," *Washington Post,* Oct. 17, 1975 at A6.

7. Fialka, John J., "Capitol Lobby, Flim Flam or Technician, To Big-Timers, It's An Art," *Washington Star,* Dec. 16, 1975 at A1.

8. Ibid.

9. Id.

10. 2 U.S.C. 261 *et seq.*

11. Stuart, Peter C., "Lobbying Reform: A New Drive to Close the Loopholes," *Christian Science Monitor,* Oct. 14, 1975 at 21.

12. Ibid.

13. *United States v. Harriss*, 347 U.S. 612 (1954).

14. Supra n. 11.

15. Stuart, Peter C., "The New Lobbyists: Persuaders in the Public Interest," *Christian Science Monitor*, Oct. 10, 1975 at 16.

16. Ibid.

17. Stuart, Peter C., "The New Lobbying: Whining Computers, Floods of Mail," *Christian Science Monitor*, Oct. 9, 1975 at 15.

18. Fialka, John J., "Capitol Lobbying: Grass Roots Approach is the Vogue," *Washington Star*, Dec. 18, 1975 at A1.

19. Gilmour, Robert S., "Central Legislative Clearance: A Revised Perspective," *Public Administration Review*, Mar.-Apr. 1971 at 150.

20. Supra n. 4.

21. Op. cit. n. 4 at 6-7.

22. Op. cit. n. 4 at 4.

23. See generally, NEUSTADT, Richard E., *Presidential Power*, New American Library, New York 1964 (originally pub. 1960) at 102ff, and GREEN, Mark) et al, *Who Runs Congress*, Bantam Books, New York 1972 at 95ff.

24. "Circular A-19" at 3; 31 U.S.C. 11(a)(12).

25. The Legislative Reference Division's history is given elsewhere in this volume.

26. For a detailed discussion of these procedures see Fisher, Joseph, "How Our Laws Are Made," H.R. Doc. No. 144, 92d Cong., 1st Sess. (1971) at 9.

27. Gilmour, Robert S., "Central Legislative Clearance: A Revised Perspective," *Public Administration Review* (Mar.Apr. 1971) at 153.

28. Supra n. 3.

29. Ibid.

30. Op. cit. n. 23 at 1597.

31. This story was whispered in OMB at the time.

32. "Circular A-19" at 8-9.

33. Op. cit. n. 23 at 1593.

34. Houston, Paul, "Rep. Hays Threatened USIA Fund," *The Washington Post*, March 4, 1976 at A2.

35. Pipe, G. Russell, "Congressional Liaison: The Executive Branch Consolidates its Relations with Congress," *Public Administration Review*, Vol. xxvi (Mar., 1966) 14.

36. Anderson, Jack, "The Washington Merry-Go-Round: 600 Lobbying for U.S. Government," *Washington Post*, Dec. 12, 1974 at G11.

37. Letter from Col. C.W. Hammond, Special Asst., Office of Asst. Secretary of Defense, Legislative Affairs, to David J. Muchow, Sept. 12, 1973.

38. Supra n. 36.

39. Op. cit. n. 35 at 15.

40. Levine, Richard J., "Capitol Hill Soldier," *Wall Street Journal*, Jan. 21, 1976 at 1, 26.

41. Ibid. at 26.

42. Id.

43. 2 U.S.C. 266.

44. Op. cit. n. 40 at 1.

45. Supra n. 36.

46. Op. cit. n. 35 at 17.

47. Op. cit. n. 35 at 19.

48. Op. cit. n. 35 at 22.

49. For criticism see op. cit. n. 36.

50. Supra n. 36.

51. "New Life for White House Liaison With Congress," *Congressional Quarterly* (Feb. 1, 1975) at 226.

52. Op. cit. n. 28 at 1598.

53. Op. cit. n. 28 at 1590.

54. Op. cit. n. 28 at 1592.

55. Ibid.

56. Id.

57. Maass, Arthur A., "In Accord With the Program of the President?" *Public Policy,* ed. by C.J. Freidrick and J.K. Galbraith, Harvard Univ. Press, Cambridge, Mass., 1953 Vol. iv. at 79.

58. Ibid. at 80.

59. Op. cit. n. 57 at 81.

60. Op. cit. n. 27 at 156.

61. Ibid.

62. Supra n. 28.

63. Ibid.

64. Op. cit. n. 28 at 1590.

65. Op. cit. n. 28 at 1591.

66. Ibid.

67. Id.

68. NEUSTADT, Richard E., *Presidential Power: The Politics of Leadership,* John Wiley and Sons, New York 1960 at 34.

69. Ibid. at 39.

70. ECCLES, Marriner S., *Beckoning Frontiers,* Alfred A. Knopf, New York 1951 at 336.

71. CORNWELL, Elmer E., Jr., *Presidential Leadership of Public Opinion,* Univ. of Indiana Press, Bloomington, Ind., 1964, and KOENIG, Louis W. *The Chief Executive,* rev. ed., Harcourt, Brace and World, New York 1968, ch. 8.

72. POLLAND, James E., *The Presidents and the Press,* New York 1974 at 37; Koenig, op. cit. n. 71 at 183.

73. Koenig, op. cit. n. 71 at 185-87; Polland, op. cit. n. 72 at 557, 796; HILLMAN, William, *Mr. President,* New York 1952 at 141.

74. Koenig, op. cit. n. 71 at 187.

75. Cornwell, op. cit. n. 71 at 261.

76. VINYARD, Dale, *Congress,* Scribners, New York 1968 at 108ff.

77. Op. cit. n. 76 at 112.

78. See e.g., BLAU, Peter, *Exchange and Power in Social Life,* John Wiley and Sons, New York 1964 and CURRY, R.L. and WADE, L.L., *A Theory of Political Exchange,* Prentice-Hall, Englewood Cliffs, N.J. 1968.

79. TAFT, William Howard, *Our Chief Magistrate and His Powers,* Columbia Univ. Press, New York 1925 at 138-39 |quote in SICKLES, Robert J., *Presidential Transactions,* Prentice-Hall, Englewood Cliffs, Nov. 1944 at 116.

80. ROOSEVELT, Theodore, *An Autobiography, Macmillan,* New York 1914 at 372.

81. Sickles, op. cit. n. 79 at 116.

82. HARRIS, Richard, *Decision,* Ballantine, New York 1972 at 105, 106, 154, 161, 210, 211 |cited in Sickles, op. cit. n. 79 at 117-18|.

83. Quoted in Sickles, op. cit. n. 79 at 138.

84. Koenig, op. cit. n. 71 at 89.

85. Koenig, op. cit. n. 71 at 90.

86. See generally, RIPLEY, Randall B., *Majority Party Leadership in Congress,* Little Brown, Boston 1969.

87. EVANS, Rowland and NOVAK, Robert, *Lyndon Johnson: The Exercise of Power,* New American Library, New York 1966 at 514-15: see also op. cit. n. 76 at 104-05.

88. FARLEY, James A., *Behind the Ballots,* New York 1938 at 293.

89. Koenig, op. cit. n. 71 at 92.

90. Rossiter, Clinton, "Let's Not Lose the Losing Candidate," *New York Times Magazine,* Nov. 6, 1960 at 24. See also KALLENBACH, Joseph E., *The American Chief Executive,* Harper and Row, New York at 286, f.n.3.

91. ROSSITER, Clinton, *The American Presidency,* New American Library, New York 1962 at 26 et. seq.

92. RICHARDSON, *Messages and Papers of the Presidents,* v.1, 218-219 |cited in Kallenbach, op. cit. n. 90 at 288|.

93. BUTT, Archie, *Taft and Roosevelt,* Doubleday, Garden City, N.Y. 1930, v. II, 645 [quoted in TOURTELLOT, Arthur, *The Presidents on the Presidency,* Doubleday 1964 at 387|.

94. Koenig, op. cit. n. 71 at 98.

95. ROSEBOOM, Eugene H., *A Short History of Presidential Elections,* Collier, New York 1967 at 2.

96. Ibid. at 4.

97. Id. 98. Richardson, op. cit. n. 92 at 218-219.

99. SCHACHNER, Nathan, *Thomas Jefferson: a Biography,* New York 1951 at 703 |cited by Koenig, op. cit. n. 71 at 99|.

100. Richardson, op. cit. n. 92 at 322.

101. BRUCE, William Cabell, *John Randolph of Roanoke,* New York 1922 at 265 |cited by Koenig, op. cit. n. 71 at 100|.

102. Roseboom, op. cit. n. 95 at 37.

103. CLARK, Bennett Champ, *John Quincy Adams,* Boston 1932 at 242-46 |cited by Koenig, op. cit. n. 71 at 101|.

104. Kallenbach, op. cit. n. 90 at 291.

105. CHITWOOD, Oliver Perry, *John Tyler: Champion of the Old South,* New York 1939 at 317 |cited by Koenig, op. cit. n. 71 at 103|.

106. Ibid.

107. WILSON, Woodrow, *Congressional Government,* World Pub. Cleveland 1884 at 253. See also Wann, A.J., "The Development of Woodrow Wilson's Theory of the Presidency: Continuity and Change," in LATHAM, Earl, ed., *The Philosophy and Politics of Woodrow Wilson,* Univ. of Chicago Press, Chicago 1958 at 46.

108. Kallenbach, op. cit. n. 90 at 293.

109. See generally Wilson, op. cit. n. 107.

110. FARLEY, James A., *Jim Farley's Story,* New York 1948 at 231.

111. Ibid. at 59-62.

112. Koenig, op. cit. n. 71 at 107.

113. SCHLESINGER, Arthur M., Jr., *The Politics of Upheaval,* v.3 of *The Age of Roosevelt,* Boston 1960 at 419.

114. Ibid. at 409-23.

115. Ibid. at 25-26.

116. Koenig, op. cit. n. 71 at 110.

117. ADAMS, Sherman, *First-Hand Report,* New York 1961 at 187.

118. Ibid. at 25-26.

119. Koenig, op. cit. n. 71 at 112.

120. *New York Times,* Jan. 30, 1961; Koenig, op. cit. n. 71 at 114-115.

121. *New York Times,* April 3, 1966; Koenig, op. cit. n. 71 at 119.

122. Koenig, op. cit. n. 71 at 119.

123. Black, Charles L., "The Presidency and Congress," 32 Washington and Lee Law Review 842 (1975.

124. Ibid. at 849.

125. Gelb, Leslie H., "Tug of War on Shaping U.S. Policy," *The Washington Star,* April 19, 1976 at A3.

126. Op. cit. n. 91 at 70.

127. Ibid.

128. JEFFERSON, Thomas, *Notes on Virginia,* quoted in op. cit. n. 91 at 71.

129. *The Federalist,* quoted in op. cit. n. 91 at 74.

130. Op. cit. n. 91 at 75.

131. Zinn, Charles J., "The Veto Power of the President," House Judiciary Committee Print, 1952 at 1.

132. Ibid. at 2.

133. BAGEHOT, *The English Constitution,* 2d. Ed. 1873, at 122 |cited in op. cit. n. 131 at 3|.

134. Op. cit. n. 131 at 8.

135. Kallenbach, op. cit. n. 90 at 350.

136. Op. cit. n. 131 at 8, citing FARRAND, *The Records of the Federal Convention,* rev. ed., 1937 v.II at 301, 582.

137. Op. cit. n. 90 at 345-6.

138."The Congress shall have the power . . . To make all laws which shall be necessary and proper for carrying into execution the foregoing powers, and all other powers vested by this Constitution in the Government of the United States, or in any department or officer thereof."—Article I, Sec. viii, paragraph 18 of the Constitution.

139. CORWIN, Edward S., *The President, Office and Powers,* 3rd ed., New York Univ. Press, New York 1948 at 341, 503.

140. Op. cit. n. 131 at 352.

141. Op. cit. n. 131 at 16.

142. Op. cit. n. 131 at 19.

143. Op. cit. n. 131 at 20.

144. 32 Opinions of the Attorney General 225 |cited in op. cit. n. 131 at 20|.

145. 286 U.S. 482.

146. SCHLESINGER, Arthur M., Jr., *The Imperial Presidency,* Houghton Mifflin, Boston 1973 at 242.

147. *Okanogan Indians v. U.S.,* 279 U.S. 655 (1929).

148. 302 U.S. 583 (1938).

149. Op. Cit. n. 146 at 244.

150. 511 F.2d 430 (1974). For a full list of intrasession pocket andadjournment vetoes, see pp. 442-445.

151. 511 F.2d 444, n. 36. The U.S. Attorney is quoted at 436 in a note as arguing that there was no legally recognizable injury because: "(1) If disapproval is anticipated, Congress may delay the presentation of a bill until after the recess in order to preserve its right to override; (2) Congress may re-enact a pocket-vetoed bill and present it to the President a second time. Appellants' Br. at 44-45. While both of these procedures might be effective, they would not change the fact that the pocket veto power will have been used as an obstacle—however temporary—to the implementation of the will of Congress. Moreover, such delays may for practical purposes become permanent. As appellee points out in his brief at 54:

" 'It is no answer to say that if Congress wishes, it can simply pass a pocket-vetoed bill again and present it to the President at a time when the pocket veto cannot be used. At best, the legislative route is arduous and time-consuming, involving numerous subcommittee, full committee, and other proceedings in both the Senate and the House. At worst, if delay has dimmed the constellation of public and private interests that facilitated the original passage of the bill, if the unique alchemy that enabled the legislative process to function successfully the previous time around has disappeared, the result may be that the bill cannot be passed at all.

" 'It is significant, too, that the utilization of a broadly construed pocket veto power is likely to grow with the increasing frequency of brief, intrasession adjournments."

152. *Kennedy v. Jones,* civil action 74-194 (D.D.C. April 21, 1976). See also remarks of Sen. Edward Kennedy in the *Congressional Record,* (daily ed.), April 26, 1976 at S 5912.

153. Keeffe, Arthur John, and Jorgenson, John Henry, "Solicitor General Pocket Vetoes the Pocket Veto," 61 *American Bar Assn. Journal,* 755, June 1975.

154. Article I, Section vii of the Constitution.

155. Op. cit. n. 131 at 21, f.n. 1, citing WATSON, *Constitution of the United States,* 1910, v.1 at 377-8.

156. 3 Wall. 378 (1798).

157. 55 stat. 31, Ch. 11 [cited in op. cit. n. 131 at 27].

158. Ibid., Section 3(c).

159. 50 U.S.C. 2297.

160. Op. cit. n. 131 at 22, f.n. 7, citing HINDS, *Precedents of the House of Representatives,* 1907, Sec. 3483.

161. Cotter, Cornelius P., "Legislative Oversight," in DeGRAZIA, Alfred, *Congress: The first Branch of Government,* American Enterprise Institute for Public Policy Research, Washington 1966 at 59ff.

162. WASHINGTON, George, *Writings of George Washington,* 1940, v. 33 at 96 [cited in op. cit. n. 131 at 22, f.n. 9].

163. Op. cit. n. 90 at 354.

164. Eisenhower, Dwight D., "Press Conference Transcript," June 17, 1959, in *Public Papers of the Presidents: Dwight D. Eisenhower,* G.P.O. Washington, D.C. 1959 at 468.

165. Article I, section vii of the Constitution.

166. Op. cit. n. 131 at 33.

167. Douglas: *Cong. Globe,* 36th Cong., 2d Sess., at 1179 (1861) cited in FISHER, Louis, *Presidential Spending Power,* Princeton Univ. Press, Princeton, N.J., 1975 at 1659.

168. 480 F.2d 1159 (1973).

169. Supra n. 146.

170. "Mr. President, We're in Trouble," *Time* (Feb. 9, 1976) at 16.

171. BARBER, Sotiras A., *The Constitution and the Delegation of Congressional Power,* Univ. of Chicago Press, Chicago 1975 at 112ff.

172. DAVIS, Kenneth Culp, *Administrative Law Treatise,* West Publ., St. Paul, Minn., 1958, 1970 Supplement at 204; HARRIS, Joseph P., *Congressional Control of Administration,* Brookings Institution, Washington, D.C., 1964 at 8-11.

173. Cooper, Joseph and Ann, "The Legislative Veto and the Constitution," 30 *George Washington University Law Review* 467 (1964).

174. ELLIOT, Jonathan, ed., *Debates of the Adoptation of the Federal Constitution,* Washington, D.C., 1861 at 5:431.

175. Op. cit. n. 131.

176. WILSON, Woodrow, *Constitutional Government in the United States,* New York 1908 at 138 [cited in op. cit. n. 146 at 79].

177. CORWIN, Edward S., *The President: Office and Powers, 1787-1957,* 4th rev. ed., New York Univer. Press, New York 1957 at 109-10.

178. For relevant court decisions and a brief discussion of the treaty power, see CORWIN, Edward S., *The Constitution and What It Means Today,* Athenium, New York 1963 at 107ff.

179. WILSON, Woodrow, *Congressional Government,* 15th ed., Boston 1901 at 49-50 and 233-34 [cited in op. cit. n. 146 at 80].

180. Supra. n. 178.

181. This applies also to technical and commercial agreements.

182. Op. cit. n. 146 at 49.

183. For additional examples, see op. cit. n. 178 at 115.

184. Op. cit. n. 146 at 88.

185. *Congressional Record* (daily ed.) [remarks of Senator Sparkman] S. 20102 Department of State Legal Advisor's Reply to Senate Office of Legislative Counsel Memorandum on Certain Middle East Agreements.

186. *United States v. Belmont,* 301 U.S. 324 (1937); see also *United States v. Pink,* 315 U.S. 203 (1942).

187. Supra n. 185. See also, Berger, Raoul, "Executive Privilege v. Congressional Inquiry," 12 *UCLA Law Review,* 1077 (1965).

188. James Madison to Thomas Jefferson, May 13, 1798, from WHITE, L.D., *The Federalists,* New York 1948 at 65 [cited in op. cit. n. 146 at 15].

189. From the diary of Thomas Jefferson, quoted in PADOVER, Saul K., ed., *The Complete Jefferson,* New York 1943 at 1222-23.

190. Op. cit. n. 187.

191. Op. cit. n. 187 at 1085, 1088.

192. Thomas Jefferson's Message to Congress of January 22, 1807, from RICHARDSON, J.D., ed., *Messages and Papers of the Presidents,* New York 1897, v. I at 400.

193. Op. cit. n. 146 at 45.

194. From Richardson, op. cit. n. 192 at v. III, 1255 and 1351-52 [cited in op. cit. n. 146 at 46].

195. 100 *Congressional Record* 6621 (1954); cited in Ervin, Sam J., Jr., "Executive Privilege: The Need for Congressional Action," *Case and Comment,* (Jan.-Feb., 1974) at 42.

196. Ibid.

197. TREWHITT, H.L., *McNamara: His Ordeal in the Pentagon,* New York, 1971 at 92-93.

199. See Library of Congress study, "The Present Limits of Executive Privilege," *Congressional Record,* March 28, 1973, H2242-H2246.

200. U.S. Congress, Hearings on The Witholding of Information by the Executive, before the Subcommittee on Separation of Powers of the Senate Judiciary Committee, 92d Cong., 1st Session (1971) at 220 [cited in op. cit. n. 146 at 248].

201. *Congressional Record,* (daily edition) April 10, 1973, S6692-S6695.

202. Letter of April 20, 1972, Jeremy J. Stone, Director of the Federation of American Scientists, *Washington Post,* March 26, 1973.

203. Op. cit. n. 146 at 251.

204. Ibid.

205. *In re Neagle,* 135 U.S. 1 (1890); see also op. cit. n. 177 at 119.

206. *United States v. Nixon,* 418 U.S. 683 (1973).

207. 418 U.S. 683 at 713 (1973).

208. Syllabus, 7, 418 U.S. 683, at 685; see 418 U.S. 707 et. seq.

209. *New York Times,* June 28, 1973.

210. Statement of Antonin Scalia, Assistant Attorney General, Office of Legal Counsel, before the Subcommittee on Separation of Powers, Senate Judiciary Committee, March 12, 1976, p. 4.

211.

212. Neustadt, Richard E., "The Presidency and Legislation: Planning the President's Program," *American Political Science Review,* 1955 at 1014.

213. "The Constitution of the United States of American, Analysis and Interpretation," S. Doc. No. 92-82, 92d Cong., 2d Session, 473 (1973); citing FERRAND, M. *The Records of the Federal Convention of 1787,* (New Haven) rev. ed., 1937 at 70ff.

214. Op. cit. n. 178 at 537.

215. Act of April 3, 1794, 1 Stat. 353.

216. Other parts of the Constitution also touch on the President's legislative powers, such as the President's power as Commander in Chief. These will not be dealt with, however, because they are outside the main scope of this book.

217. *In re* Neagle, 135 U.S. 1 (1890).

218. 135 U.S. 64.

219. 31 U.S.C. 1 et. seq.

220. 3 U.S.C. 106; 31 U.S.C. 2.

221. 31 U.S.C. 665, 1400 et. seq.

222. BRUNDAGE, Percival, *The Bureau of the Budget,* Praeger, New York 1970 at 5.

223. Act of May 10, 1800; see ibid. at 6.

224. Act of July 7, 1884; see op. cit. n. 221 at 6.

225. Op. cit. n. 222 at 6.

226. Ibid.

227. WILMERDING, Lucius, Jr., *The Spending Power*, Yale Univer. Press, New Haven, Conn. 1943 [cited in op. cit. n. 222 at 7].

228. Op. cit. n. 222 at 8.

229. House Committee Report No. 362, 66 Cong. 1st Session (1919) at 7.

230. Op. cit. n. 222 at 15.

231. See op. cit. n. 222 for the text of this report.

232. Executive Order No. 8248 (1939).

233. *The Christian Science Monitor*, Dec. 6, 1972; *Congressional Quarterly*, Jan. 13, 1973, at 38-39; [cited in DAVIS, James W. and RINGQUIST, Delbert *The President and Congress*, Barron's Educational Series, New York, 1975 at 36].

234. GROSS, Betram M., *The Legislative Struggle*, New York, 1953 at 169 [cited in op. cit. n. 237 at 642].

235. Letter from House Appropriations Committee Chairman Madden to Budget Bureau Director Dawes, Nov. 17, 1921 (central files) [cited in op. cit. n. 237 at 643].

236. OMB Circular 49, Dec. 19, 1921.

237. Neustadt, Richard E., "The Presidency and Legislation: The Growth of Central Clearance," 48 *American Political Science Review*, 645 (Sept. 1954).

238. Ibid.

239. National Emergency Council, "Proceedings of the Nineteenth Meeting," December 17, 1934 at 7 [cited in op. cit. n. 237 at 649].

241. Ibid.

242. Op. cit. n. 237 at 651.

243. Ibid.

244. Witte, Edwin E., "The Preparation of Proposed Legislative Measures by Administrative Departments," *Studies on Administrative Management in the Government of the United States for the President's Committee on Administrative Management*, G.P.O., Washington, D.C. 1937 at 56.

245. National Emergency Council, "Proceedings of the Twenty-eighth Meeting," December 17, 1935 at 17 [cited in op. cit. n. 237 at 656].

246. Budget Bureau central files, 1921-38: *Enrolled Bills No. 1*, undated memorandum from Rudolph Forster to F.J. Bailey [cited in op. cit. n. 237 at 656, 657].

247. Op. cit. n. 23 at 656.

248. Op. cit. n. 237 at 658.

249. Op. cit. n. 237 at 661.

250. Op. cit. n. 237 at 667.

251. Op. cit. n. 212 at 1015.

252. Op. cit. n. 212 at 988-89.

253. Op. cit. n. 212 at 991-92.

254. Op. cit. n. 212 at 991-994.

255. Op. cit. n. 212 at 994.

256. Op. cit. n. 68 at 171.

257. Op. cit. n. 68 at 670.

258. Bureau of the Budget, "Legislative Coordination and Clearance Functions," June, 1961 at 2-11.

259. Ibid at 5.

260. See section on impoundment infra.

261. Report of the Subcommittee on National Policy Machinery, Senate Committee on Government Operations, Oct. 16, 1961 |cited in op. cit. n. 222 at 44-45|.

262. Carey, William D., "The Budget Bureau Staff Member," Remarks at staff orientation conference, Sept. 17, 1954.

263. Jones, Roger W., "The Budget Bureau Staff Member," Remarks at Bureau of the Budget staff orientation conference, Sept. 15, 1955.

264. Executive orders were first numbered in 1907. From that time until 1971 there were 11,615 numbered Executive Orders, but knowledgeable estimates of unnumbered ones range as high as 50,000. See FISHER, Louis, *President and Congress: Power and Policy,* The Free Press, Glencoe, N.Y. 1972 at 105 |cited in DAVIS, James W., and RINGQUIST, Delbert, *The President and Congress,* Barron's Educational Series, New York 1975 at 1129.|.

265. In the previous year (1862) Lincoln had severely rebuked General John C. Fremont for issuing a similar proclamation aimed at freeing slaves in Missouri. See HEFFNER, Richard D., *A Documentary History of the United States,* New American Library, New York 1952 (rev. ed. 1956) at 148; see also excerpts from the text of the Proclamation at 150-51.

266. U.S. Congress, *Executive Orders in Times of War and National Emergency,* Report of the Special Committee on National Emergencies and Delegated Emergency Powers, Senate Document 93d Cong. 2d Sess. (1974) at 2. See also, Johnson, Mark, "How Little-known Presidential Orders Affect Your Life," *Parade Magazine,* Jan. 27, 1974 at 11.

267. Ibid. *Parade* at 12.

268. Id.

269. For a discussion of the power of Executive Orders, see SCHUBERT, Glendon A., Jr., *The Presidency In the Courts,* Univ. of Minnisota Press, Minneapolis, Minn. 1957 at 283ff.

270. *Hirabayashi v. United States,* 320 U.S. 81 (1943).

271. *Korematsu v. United States,* 323 U.S. 214 (1944).

272. *Ex Parte Endo,* 323 U.S. 283 (1944). For a discussion of these several cases, see KELLY, Alfred H., and HARBISON, Winfred A., *The American Constitution,* W. W. Norton, New York 1948 at 814-21.

273. 42 A.B.A. Rep. 232, 238 (1917), |cited in op. cit. n. 169 at 286|.

274. Op. cit. n. 269 at 286.

275. U.S. Congress, *Executive Orders and Proclamations: A Study of A Use of Presidential Powers,* Comm. Print, House Committee on Government Operations, 85th Cong. 1st Sess. (1957) at 15.

276. *Youngstown,* 343 U.S. 579 (1952), at 635, 637.

277. 12 Stat. 326. See also Sec. 4, Act of March 3, 1863, 12 Stat. 820 and Sec. 1, Act of May 11, 1866, 14 Stat. 46. The Constitutionality of those statutes was upheld in *United States v. Hosmer,* 9 Wall. 432, 434 (1870) and *Hamilton v. Dillin,* 21 Wall. 73, 96 (1875). See Schubert, op. cit. n. 169 at 290, n. 38.

278. Op. cit. n. 169 at 291, citing *United States v. Hodges,* 218 F. 87, 88 (D. Mont. 1914; *United States v. Midwest Oil Co.,* 236 U.S. 459 (1915); *Norwegian Nitrogen Producers Co. v. United States, 288 U.S. 294 (1933).*

279. Op. cit. n.119-28. *Ex parte Vallandigham,* 1 Wall 243 (1863); *Ex parte Milligan,* 4 Wall 2 (1866); *Ex parte Merryman,* CCA Dist. Md. (1861); Habeas Corpus Act of March 3, 1863.

280. 48 Stat. 1; see op. cit. n. 169 at 291, n. 496. See also *Maryland Casualty Co. v. United States,* 251 U.S. 342, 349 (1919) [cited in U.S. Congress op. cit. n. 265 at 8].

281. *United States v. Smith,* 27 Fed. Cas. 1192, 1230 (C.Ct.N.Y., 1806) No. 16, 342. Schubert notes however that the "President does have the power to dispense in the sense that he may direct non-enforcement of the laws . . . " [op. cit. n. 269 at 293, n. 48].

282. *United States v. Klein,* 13 Wall. 128 (1871); see also *Armstrong v. United States,* 13 Wall. 156 (1872); *Knote v. United States,* 10 Ct. Cl. 397, 407;

aff'd. 95 U.S. 149 (1877) [cited in op. cit. n. 269 at 293, 294, n. 50].

283. *Werner v. United States,* 119 F. Supp. 894, 896 (S.D. Cal, C.D., 1954).

284. Op. cit. n. 169 at 302.

285. *Panama Refining Co. v. Ryan,* 293 U.S. 388, 412 (1935). See also Jaffe, Louis, "An Essay on Delegation of Legislative Power," 41 *Columbia Law Review,* 359, 561 (1947).

286. Act of July 26, 1935, 49 Stat. 502.

287. See *Executive Order of June 19, 1962* (President John F. Kennedy), "Preparation, Presentation, Filing and Publication of Executive Orders and Proclamations."

288. *Sugar v. United States,* 252 F. 74, 77-78 (1918), cert. denied, 248 U.S. 578 (1918). Kempster, Norman, "How the Budget is Made," *Washington Star,* Jan. 29, 1975 at A1.

290. Ingram, Timothy H., "The Billions in the White House Basement," *Washington Monthly,* Jan., 1972) Vol. 3, No. 11, p. 37.

291. Ibid. at 38. For an editorial view, see "The Impoundment Battle," *Washington Post,* Feb. 6, 1973 at A18.

292. FISHER, Louis, *Presidential Spending Power,* Princeton Univ. Press, Princeton, N.J., 1975 at 76.

293. HAMILTON, Alexander, *The Works of Alexander Hamilton,* Henry Cabot Lodge, ed., G.P. Putnams, New York, 1904, Vol. 7, 158-59 [cited in Fisher, op. cit. n. 292 at 99].

294. Act of Sept. 4, 1961, 75 Stat. 444, 22 U.S.C. 2364.

295. Op. cit. n. 290 at 38. For a list of $10 billion in 1972 impoundments, see *Congressional Record* (daily ed. Aug. 16, 1972), remarks of Sen. Metcalf, at S13667.

296. Ibid. at 38.

297. U.S. CONGRESS, *Impeachment of Richard M. Nixon, President of the United States,* House Report No. 1305, 93d Cong., 2d Sess. 217 (1974) [cited in Fisher, op. cit. n. 292 at 120].

298. U.S. CONGRESS, *Supplemental Foreign Assistance Authorizations, 1970,* Hearings before the Senate Comm. on Foreign Relations, 91st Cong., 2d Sess. (1970), 2, 87-88 [cited in op. cit. n. 191 at 108].

299. Op. cit. n. 190 at 38.

300. Op. cit. n. 290 at 40. For a short history of Presidential budget making, see remarks of Sen. Hubert Humphrey, *Congressional Record,* (Sept. 17, 1975-daily ed.) at S16104.

301. Ibid.

302. Article I, Section ix, the Constitution.

303. 31 U.S.C. 65 (1970).

304. 31 U.S.C. 66b(a) (1970); see also Fisher, op. cit. n. 292 at 202.

305. Op. cit. n. 190 at 40.

306. Ibid.

307. Op. cit. n. 290 at 41.

308. 117 *Congressional Record* S7503 (daily ed. May 20, 1971) [cited in op. cit. n. 191 at 217].

309. Op. cit. n. 290 at 41.

310. Op. cit. n. 290 at 42.

311. Ibid.

312. 106 *Congressional Record* 13127 (1960).

313. Op. cit. n. 290 at 43.

314. Op. cit. n. 290 at 44.

315. Op. cit. n. 292 at 81.

316. Anderson, Jack, "Treasury's $4 Billion Kitty," *Washington Post*, May 24, 1976 at B9.

317. 41 U.S.C. 11.

318. For an excellent discussion of the Feed and Forage law see Fisher, op. cit. n. 191 at 238 et seq.

319. U.S. CONGRESS, *Second Supplemental Appropriations for Fiscal Year 1973* (Part 2), Hearings before the Senate Committee on Appropriations, 93d Cong., 1st Sess., (1973) at 2025. See also Fisher, op. cit. n. 292 at 247.

320. Op. cit. n. 290 at 44.

321. Op. cit. n. 290 at 44-45.

322. Op. cit. n. 290 at 45.

323. Ibid.

324. Humphrey, Hubert H., "Is the Impoundment of Appropriated Funds a Valid Exercise of the Executive Power?" *Congressional Digest*, vol. 52, No. 4, (Apr. 1973) at 119.

325. "Controversy Over the Presidential Impoundment of Appropriated Funds," *Congressional Digest*, vol. 52, No. 4. (Apr. 1973) at 99.

326. Op. cit. n. 290 at 46.

327. The term "impoundment" has been used to describe a variety of financial decisions affecting spending. Fisher (in "Funds Impounded by the President: the Constitutional Issue," 38 *George Washington Law Review* 124 (1969)) believes "... impoundment occurs whenever the President spends less than Congress appropriated for a given period." Church, however (in "Impounding of Appropriated Funds," 22 *Stanford Law Review* 1240, 1245 (1970)) would limit use of this term, and distinguishes it from "apportioning" and "reserving." In S.373 (1973) [see infra n. 336], impoundment was defined as "any type of executive action which effectively precludes the obligation of expenditure of the appropriated funds" of such obligation on expenditure.

328. See Church, ibid.

329. 31 U.S.C. 665(c)(2) (1970).

330. Supra n. 324.

331. 343 U.S. 579 (1952).

332. Quoted in op. cit. n. 325 at 100.

333. Supra n. 324.

334. Op. cit. n. 146 at 235.

335. *Decatur v. Paulding*. 39 U.S. (19 Peters) 497 (1840). See also " Funds Impounded by the President:The Constitutional Issue," 38 Geo. Wash. L. Rev. 124, 126-28 (1969), and ref. court battles over impoundment, *Congressional Record* (daily ed. Oct. 18, 1973), remarks of Joe L. Evins at E6633.

336. U.S. CONGRESS, *Joint Hearings on Impoundment and S. 373*, Before the Ad Hoc Subcommittee on Impoundment of Funds of the Committee on Government Operations and the Subcommittee on the Judiciary, 93rd Cong. 1st Sess., 181, 182 (1973).

337. "Likely Law of Impoundment," 59 Iowa Law Review 50 (1973) at 58, 59.

338. Ibid. at 59.

339. *Hearings on First Supplemental National Defense Appropriation Bill for 1944*, Before the Senate Committee on Appropriations, 78th Cong. 1st Sess., 739 (1943) (letter from President Franklin D. Roosevelt to Senator Richard Russell, Aug. 18, 1942).

340. Williams, "The Impounding of Funds by the Bureau of the Budget," Inter-University Case Program—Cases in Public Administration and Policy Formation (No. 25) (1955), in *Hearings of Executive Impoundment of Appropriated Funds*, Before the Subcommittee on Separation of Powers of the Senate Committee on the Judiciary, 92d Cong., 1st Sess. (1971) at p. 385, cited op. cit. n. 337 at 59.

341. Op. cit. n. 336 at 189.

342. Op. cit. n. 337 at 60-61.

343. H.R. Rep. No. 1797, 81st Cong., 2d Sess. 9 (1950).

344. Ibid.

345. KENNEDY, John F., *Public Papers*, G.P.O., Washington 1963 at 333, 347 [cited in op. cit. n. 334 at 237]. Compare Weaver, Warren Jr., "White House Expected to Cite Legal Backing for President's [Nixon's] Refusal to Spend Funds Congress Voted," *New York Times*, Feb. 6, 1973 at A16.

346. 89 *Congressional Record* 10362 (1943) [cited in Fisher, op. cit. n. 292 at 150].

347. Rehnquist, William H., "Memorandum re Presidential Authority to Impound Funds Appropriated for Assistance to Federally Impacted Schools," *Hearings on Executive Impoundment of Appropriated Funds*, Before the Subcommittee on Separation of Powers of the Senate Committee on the Judiciary, 92d Cong. 1st Sess. (1971) at 279-84, see also 285-91.

348. 15 U.S.C. 1021 (1970). For a discussion of the inflationary aspects of impoundment, see Naughton, James N., "No Benefit Found In Impoundment," *The New York Times*, July 8, 1973 at A24.

349. General Appropriations Act of 1951, sec. 1211, 64 Stat. 765 (1950), as amended, 31 U.S.C. 665(c)(2) (1970).

350. Act of Sept. 6, 1950, Ch. 896, sec. 1211, 64 Stat. 765.

351. Supra n. 340. See also *Congressional Record* (daily ed.) Feb. 4, 1974 S1164 n. 46.

352. Act of April 30, 1973, Pub. L. No. 93-28, Sec. 4, 87 Stat. 28.

353. Op. cit. 337 at 70.

354. Act of March 20, 1933, Ch. 3, 48 Stat. 8; see op. cit. n. 292 at 163 n. 19.

355. Act of Sept. 6, 1950, Ch. 896, 1214, 64 Stat. 768; see op. cit. n. 292 at 163 n. 25.

356. Act of Feb. 9, 1970, Pub. L. 91-194, sec. 119, 84 Stat. 10; 22 U.S.C. 2370(3) (1970).

357. Act of Feb. 9, 1970, Pub. L. No. 91-194, sec. 109(b), 84 Stat. 9; 22 U.S.C. 2370(f) (1970).

358. 22 U.S.C. 2370(c) (1970).

359. 42 U.S.C. 2000(d)(1) (1970).

360. Fisher, op. cit. n. 292 at 1165, n. 73, citing *The Washington Evening Star*, Feb. 27, 1971, at A2.

361. *Kendall v. United States ex rel. Stokes,* 37 U.S. (12 Pet.) 524 (1838).

362. 37 U.S. 613.

363. Op. cit. n. 347 at 283.

364. Article I, section viii; see also op. cit. n. 337 at 72-73.

365. Goostree, "The Power of the President to Impound Appropriated Funds: With Special Reference to Grants-In-Aid to Segregated Activities," 11 American Univ. Law Review 32 (1962) at 40.

366. *Youngstown Sheet and Tube Co. v. Sawyer,* 343 U.S. 579 (1952).

367. *Meyers v. United States,* 171 U.S. 52, 183 at 246, 247 (1926).

368. 272 U.S. at 118.

369. 343 U.S. 641.

370. *Weekly Compilation of Presidential Documents* 110 (1973).

371. Remarks of Sen. Hubert H. Humphrey on introducting S. 1030, quoted in the *New York Times,* Jan. 20, 1974, A1. For predecessor bills, see *Congressional Record* (daily ed.) Feb. 27, 1973 at S3435, and for a summary of earlier bills, Hopkins, Bruce R., "Congressional Reform Advances in the Ninety Third Congress," 60 *American Bar Assn. Journal* 47 (Jan. 1974).

372. Ibid.

373. "Conferees Approve Budget Procedures Reform," *Congressional Quarterly,* June 15, 1974 at 1590.

374. "Congressional Budget Reform: Will it Work?" *Congressional Quarterly* Sept. 7, 1974 at 2416; *Congressional Record* (daily ed.) Dec. 4, 1974, remarks of Sen. Humphrey, at S10487. Rich, Spencer, "Congress Tackles Budget Job . . . ," *The Washington Post,* Jan. 12, 1975 at K3.

375. Op. cit. n. 290 at 49.

376. "Congressional Budget . . . " supra n. 374.

377. Ibid at 2418. See also "The Budget and Congress," *The Washington Post,* April 16, 1975, A14.

378. Ibid.

379. "Budget Control: Making Haste Carefully," *Congressional Quarterly,* March 22, 1975 at 594.

380. Ibid. at 590. Congress may also try hard to make the system work. See *Congressional Record* (daily ed.) Jan. 29, 1974, remarks of Sen. Humphrey at S662; "Impoundment Issue Still Troubles Capitol Hill," *The Christian Science Monitor* May 8, 1975 at 13; Millius, Peter "New Congressional Budget System Presents a Challenge," *The Washington Post,* Apr. 28, 1975 at A2.

381. EINZIG, Paul, *The Control of the Purse* (1959), 71- 72; cited in op. cit. n. 292 at 258-9.

382. Op. cit. n. 293, v. XIX at 405.

383. MADISON, James, *Federalist* No. 48.

384. Op. cit. n. 292 at 261.

385. Ways, Max, "Congress Should be a Stronger Partner in National Policy," *Fortune,* vol. LXXXVII No. 1 Jan., 1973 at 65.

386. Kempster, Norman, "How the Budget is Made," *The Washington Star* Jan. 29, 1975, A1.

APPENDIX: SELECTED PORTIONS OF

The Constitution of the United States of America

PREAMBLE

We, the people of the United States, in order to form a more perfect Union, establish justice, insure domestic tranquility, provide for the common defense, promote the general welfare, and secure the blessings of liberty to ourselves and our posterity, do ordain and establish this CONSTITUTION for the United States of America.

ARTICLE I

LEGISLATIVE POWERS

Section I

All legislative powers herein granted shall be vested in a Congress of the United States, which shall consist of a Senate and House of Representatives.

HOUSE OF REPRESENTATIVES

Section II

HOW COMPOSED

1. The House of Representatives shall be composed of members chosen every second year by the people of the several States, and the electors in each State shall have the qualifications requisite for electors of the most numerous branch of the State Legislature.

MEMBERS' QUALIFICATIONS

2. No person shall be a Representative who shall not have attained to the age of twenty-five years, and been seven years a citizen of the United States, and who shall not, when elected, be an inhabitant of that State in which he shall be chosen.

APPORTIONMENT OF REPRESENTATIVES AND DIRECT TAXES

3. Representatives and direct taxes shall be apportioned among the several States which may be included within this Union according to their respective numbers, which shall be determined by adding to the whole number of free persons, including those bound to service for a term of years, and excluding Indians not taxed, three-fifths of all other persons. The

actual enumeration shall be made within three years after the first meeting of the Congress of the United States, and within every subsequent term of ten years, in such manner as they shall by law direct. The number of Representatives shall not exceed one for every thirty thousand, but each State shall have at least one Representative; and until sucn enumeration shall be made the State of New Hampshire shall be entitled to choose three; Massachusetts, eight; Rhode Island and Providence Plantations, One; Connecticut, five; New York, six; New Jersey, four; Pennsylvania, eight; Delaware, one; Maryland, six; Virginia, ten; North Carolina, five; South Carolina, five; and Georgia, three.

FILLING OF VACANCIES

4. When vacancies happen in the representation from any State, the Executive Authority thereof shall issue writs of election to fill such vacancies.

OFFICERS—IMPEACHMENT

5. The House of Representatives shall choose their Speaker and other officers, and shall have the sole power of impeachment.

SENATE

Section III

HOW COMPOSED

1. The Senate of the United States shall be composed of two Senators from each State, chosen by the Legislature thereof, for six years; and each Senator shall have one vote.

ROTATION OF SENATORS

2. Immediately after they shall be assembled in consequence of the first election, they shall be divided as equally as may be into three classes. The seats of the Senators of the first class shall be vacated at the expiration of the second year, of the second class at the expiration of the fourth year, and of the third class at the expiration of the sixth year, so that one-third may be chosen every second year; and if vacancies happen by resignation, or otherwise, during the recess of the Legislature of any State, the Executive thereof may make temporary appointments until the next meeting of the Legislature, which shall then fill such vacancies.

QUALIFICATIONS OF SENATORS

3. No person shall be a Senator who shall not have attained to the age of thirty years, and been nine years a citizen of the United States, and who shall not, when elected, be an inhabitant of that State for which he shall be chosen.

PRESIDENT OF THE SENATE

4. The Vice-President of the United States shall be President of the Senate, but shall have no vote unless they be equally divided.

SENATE OFFICERS

5. The Senate shall choose their other officers, and also a President pro tempore, in the absence of the Vice-President, or when he shall exercise the office of President of the United States.

THE SENATE'S POWERS

6. The Senate shall have the sole power to try all impeachments. When sitting for that purpose, they shall be on oath or affirmation. When the President of the United States is tried, the Chief Justice shall preside; and no person shall be convicted without the concurrence of two-thirds of the members present.

7. Judgment in cases of impeachment shall not extend further than to removal from office, and disqualification to hold and enjoy any office of honor, trust, or profit under the United States; but the party convicted shall nevertheless be liable and subject to indictment, trial, judgment, and punishment, according to law.

MEMBERS OF CONGRESS

Section IV

HOW ELECTED

1. The times, places, and manner of holding elections for Senators and Representatives shall be prescribed in each State by the Legislature thereof; but the Congress may at any time by law make or alter such regulations, except as to places of choosing Senators.

WHEN CONGRESS SHALL MEET

2. The Congress shall assemble at least once in every year and such meeting shall be on the first Monday in December unless they shall by law appoint a different day.

POWERS AND DUTIES OF EACH HOUSE

Section V

1. Each House shall be the judge of the elections, returns and qualifications of its own members, and a majority of each shall constitute a quorum to do business; but a smaller number may adjourn from day to day, and may be authorized to compel the attendance of absent members in such manner and under such penalties as each House may provide.

RULES, ETC.

2. Each House may determine the rules of its proceedings, punish its members for disorderly behavior, and with the concurrence of two-thirds expel a member.

JOURNALS OF EACH HOUSE

3. Each House shall keep a journal of its proceedings, and from time to time publish the same, excepting such parts as may in their judgment require secrecy; and the yeas and nays of the members of either House on any question shall, at the desire of one-fifth of those present, be entered on the journal.

ADJOURNMENT

4. Neither House, during the session of Congress, shall, without the consent of the other, adjourn for more than three days, nor to any other place than that in which the two Houses shall be sitting.

PAY, PRIVILEGES AND INCAPACITIES

Section VI

1. The Senators and Representatives shall receive a compensation for their services, to be ascertained by law, and paid out of the Treasury of the United States. They shall in all cases, except treason, felony, and breach of the peace, be privileged from arrest during their attendance at the session of their respective Houses, and in going to and returning from the same; and for any speech or debate in either House they shall not be questioned in any other place.

OTHER OFFICES PROHIBITED

2. No Senator or Representative shall, during the time for which he was elected, be appointed to any civil office under the authority of the United States which shall have been created, or the emoluments whereof shall have been increased during such time; and no person holding any office under the United States shall be a member of either House during his continuance in office.

REVENUE BILLS

Section VII

1. All bills for raising revenue shall originate in the House of Representatives, but the Senate may propose or concur with amendments, as on other bills.

HOW BILLS BECOME LAWS

2. Every bill which shall have passed the House of Representatives and the Senate shall, before it becomes a law, be presented to the President of the United States; if he approves, he shall sign it, but if not, he shall return it, with his objections, to that House in which it shall have originated, who shall enter the objections at large on their journal, and proceed to reconsider it. If after such reconsideration two-thirds of that House shall agree to pass the bill, it shall be sent, together with the objections, to the other House, by which it shall likewise be reconsidered; and if approved by two-thirds of that House it shall become a law. But in all such cases the votes of both Houses shall be determined by yeas and nays and the names of the persons voting for and against the bill shall be entered on the journal of each House respectively. If any bill shall not be returned by the President within ten days (Sundays excepted) after it shall have been presented to him, the same shall be a law, in like manner as if he had signed it, unless the Congress by their adjournment prevent its return; in which case it shall not be a law.

ORDERS AND RESOLUTIONS

3. Every order, resolution or vote, to which the concurrence of the Senate and House of Representatives may be necessary (except on the question of adjournment), shall be presented to the President of the United States, and before the same shall take effect, shall be approved by him, or, being disapproved by him, shall be repassed by two-thirds of the Senate and House of Representatives, according to the rules and limitations prescribed in the case of a bill.

POWERS OF CONGRESS

Section VIII

The Congress shall have power:

1. To lay and collect taxes, duties, imposts and excises, to pay the debts and provide for the common defense, and general welfare of the United States; but all duties, imposts and excises shall be uniform throughout the United States;

2. To borrow money on the credit of the United States;

3. To regulate commerce with foreign nations, and among the several States, and with the Indian tribes;

4. To establish an uniform rule of naturalization, and uniform laws on the subject of bankruptcies, throughout the United States;

5. To coin money, regulate the value thereof, and of foreign coins, and fix the standard of weights and measures;

6. To provide for the punishment of counterfeiting the securities and current coin of the United States;

7. To establish post offices and post roads;

8. To promote the progress of science and useful arts, by securing, for limited times, to authors and inventors, the exclusive right to their respective writings and discoveries;

9. To constitute tribunals inferior to the Supreme Court;

10. To define and punish piracies and felonies committed on the high seas, and offenses against the law of nations;

11. To declare war, grant letters of marque and reprisal, and make rules concerning captures on land and water;

12. To raise and support armies; but no appropriation of money to that use shall be for a longer term than two years;

13. To provide and maintain a navy;

14. To make rules for the government and regulation of the land and naval forces;

15. To provide for calling forth the militia to execute the laws of the Union, suppress insurrections and repel invasions;

16. To provide for organizing, arming and disciplining the militia, and for governing such part of them as may be employed in the service of the United States, reserving to the States, respectively, the appointment of the officers, and the authority of training the militia according to the discipline prescribed by Congress;

17. To exercise exclusive legislation, in all cases whatsoever, over such district (not exceeding ten miles square), as may, by cession of particular States, and the acceptance of Congress, become the seat of government of the United States; and to exercise like authority over all places purchased by the consent of the legislature of the State in which the same shall be, for the erection of forts, magazines, arsenals, dock-yards and other needful buildings; and—

18. To make all laws which shall be necessary and proper, for carrying into execution the foregoing powers and all other powers vested by this Constitution in the government of the United States, or in any department or officer thereof.

LIMITATIONS OF THE POWERS OF CONGRESS

Section IX

1. The migration or importation of such persons as any of the States now existing shall think proper to admit, shall not be prohibited by the Congress, prior to the year one thousand eight hundred and eight, but a tax or duty may be imposed on such importation, not exceeding ten dollars for each person.

2. The privilege of the writ of habeas corpus shall not be suspended, unless, when in cases of rebellion or invasion, the public safety may require it.

3. No bill of attainder, or ex post facto law shall be passed.

4. No capitation or other direct tax shall be laid, unless in proportion to the census or enumeration hereinbefore directed to be taken.

5. No tax or duty shall be laid on articles exported from any State.

6. No preference shall be given, by any regulation of commerce or revenue, to the ports of one State over those of another; nor shall vessels bound to or from one State be obliged to enter, clear or pay duties in another.

7. No money shall be drawn from the treasury, but in consequence of appropriations made by law; and a regular statement and account of the receipts and expenditures of all public money shall be published from time to time.

8. No title of nobility shall be granted by the United States; and no person holding any office of profit or trust under them, shall, without the consent of the Congress, accept of any present, emolument, office or title of any kind whatever, from any king, prince or foreign State.

LIMITATIONS OF THE POWERS OF INDIVIDUAL STATES

Section X

1. No State shall enter into any treaty, alliance or confederation, grant letters of marque and reprisal; coin money; emit bills of credit; make anything but gold and silver coin a tender in payment of debts; pass any bill of attainder, ex post facto law, or law impairing the obligation of contracts; or grant any title of nobility.

2. No State shall, without the consent of the Congress, lay any imposts or duties on imports or exports, except what may be absolutely necessary for executing its inspection laws; and the net produce of all duties and imposts laid by any State on imports or exports, shall be for the use of the treasury of the

United States; and all such laws shall be subject to the revision and control of the Congress.

3. No State shall, without the consent of Congress, lay any duty of tonnage, keep troops or ships of war in time of peace, enter into any agreement or compact with another State, or with a foreign power, or engage in war, unless actually invaded, or in such imminent danger as will not admit delay.

ARTICLE II

THE EXECUTIVE POWER

Section I

1. The executive power shall be vested in a President of the United States of America. He shall hold his office during the term of four years, and, together with the Vice-President, chosen for the same term, be elected as follows:

HOW ELECTED

2. Each State shall appoint, in such manner as the legislature thereof may direct, a number of electors equal to the whole number of senators and representatives to which the State may be entitled in Congress; but no senator or representative, or person holding an office of trust or profit under the United States shall be appointed an elector.

ELECTORAL COLLEGES

3. The electors shall meet in their respective States, and vote by ballot, for two persons, of whom one, at least, shall not be an inhabitant of the same State with themselves. And they shall make a list of all the persons voted for, and of the number of votes for each; which list they shall sign and certify, and transmit, sealed, to the seat of the government of the United States, directed to the President of the Senate. The President of the Senate shall, in the presence of the Senate and House of Representatives, open all the certificates, and the votes shall then be counted. The person having the greatest number of votes shall be the President, if such number be a majority of the whole number of electors appointed; and if there be more than one who have such majority, and have an equal number of votes then the House of Representatives shall immediately choose by ballot, one of them for President; and if no person have a majority, then from the five highest on the list, the said House shall in like manner choose the President. But in choosing the President, the votes shall be taken by States, the representation from each State having one vote; a quorum for this purpose shall consist

of a member or members from two-thirds of the States, and a majority of the States shall be necessary to a choice. In every case, after the choice of the President, the person having the greatest number of votes of the electors, shall be the Vice-President. But if there should remain two or more who have equal votes, the Senate shall choose from them, by ballot, the Vice-President. (See XIIth amendmcnt.)

4. The Congress may determine the time of choosing the electors, and the day on which they shall give their votes, which day shall be the same throughout the United States.

WHO MAY BE ELECTED PRESIDENT

5. No person except a natural born citizen, or a citizen of the United States at the time of the adoption of this Constitution, shall be eligible to the office of President; neither shall any person be eligible to that office who shall not have attained to the age of thirty-five years, and been fourteen years a resident within the United States. (See XIIth amendment.)

ON THE DEATH, REMOVAL, ETC., OF THE PRESIDENT, THE POWERS AND DUTIES DEVOLVE UPON THE VICE-PRESIDENT

6. In case of the removal of the President from office, or of his death, resignation or inability to discharge the powers and duties of the said office, the same shall devolve on the Vice-President; and the Congress may, by law, provide for the case of removal, death, resignation or inability, both of the President and Vice-President, declaring what officer shall then act as President, and such officer shall act accordingly, until the disability be removed, or a President shall be elected.

COMPENSATION OF THE PRESIDENT

7. The President shall, at stated times, receive for his services a compensation which shall neither be increased nor diminished during the period for which he shall have been elected; and he shall not receive, within that period, any other emolument from the United States or any of them.

8. Before he enters on the execution of his office, he shall take the following oath or affirmation:

THE OATH

"I do solemnly swear (or affirm) that I will faithfully execute the office of President of the United States, and will, to the best of my ability, preserve, protect and defend the Constitution of the United States."

POWERS, ETC., OF THE PRESIDENT

Section II

1. The President shall be commander-in-chief of the army and navy of the United States, and of the militia of the several States, when called into actual service of the United States; he may require the opinion, in writing, of the principal officer in each of the executive departments, upon any subject relating to the duties of their respective offices, and he shall have power to grant reprieves and pardons for offenses against the United States, except in cases of impeachment.

TREATIES, AMBASSADORS, ETC.

2. He shall have power, by and with the advice and consent of the Senate, to make treaties, provided two-thirds of the Senators present concur; and he shall nominate, and by and with the advice and consent of the Senate shall appoint, ambassadors, other public ministers and consuls, judges of the Supreme Court, and all other officers of the United States whose appointments are not herein otherwise provided for, and which shall be established by law. But the Congress may, by law, vest the appointment of such inferior officers as they may think proper in the President alone, in the courts of law, or in the heads of departments.

APPOINTING POWER

3. The President shall have power to fill up all vacancies that may happen during the recess of the Senate, by granting commissions, which shall expire at the end of their next session.

DUTIES OF THE PRESIDENT

Section III

He shall, from time to time, give to the Congress information of the state of the Union, and recommend to their consideration such measures as he shall judge necessary and expedient; he may, on extraordinary occasions, convene both Houses, or either of them; and in case of disagreement between them with respect to the time of adjournment, he may adjourn them to such time as he shall think proper; he shall receive ambassadors and other public ministers; he shall take care that the laws be faithfully executed and shall commission all the officers of the United States.

IMPEACHMENT, ETC.

Section IV

The President, Vice-President and all civil officers of the United States shall be removed from office on impeachment for, and conviction of, treason, bribery or other high crimes and misdemeanors.

ARTICLE III

THE JUDICIAL POWER

ARTICLE IV

ACTS, RECORDS, ETC., OF EACH STATE

ARTICLE V

AMENDMENTS TO THE CONSTITUTION—HOW MADE

The Congress, whenever two-thirds of both Houses shall deem it necessary, shall propose amendments to this Constitution; or, on the application of the Legislatures of two-thirds of the several States, shall call a convention for proposing amendments, which in either case shall be valid, to all intents and purposes, as part of this Constitution, when ratified by the Legislatures of three-fourths of the several States, or by conventions in three-fourths thereof, as the one or the other mode of ratification may be proposed by the Congress; provided, that no amendment which may be made prior to the year eighteen hundred and eight shall in any manner affect the first and fourth clauses in the ninth section of the first article, and that no State, without its consent, shall be deprived of its equal suffrage in the Senate.

ARTICLE VI

FORMER DEBTS VALID

ARTICLE VII

WHEN THE CONSTITUTION TO TAKE EFFECT

AMENDMENTS

To the Constitution of the United States, Ratified According to the Provisions of the Fifth Article of the Foregoing Constitution.

ARTICLE I

RIGHT OF CONSCIENCE, FREEDOM OF THE PRESS, ETC.

Congress shall make no law respecting an establishment of religion, or prohibiting the free exercise thereof; or abridging the freedom of speech, or of the press; or the right of the people peaceably to assemble, and to petition the government for a redress of grievances.

ARTICLE II

OF THE MILITIA

A well-regulated milita being necessary to the security of a free State, the right of the people to keep and bear arms shall not be infringed.

ARTICLE III

OF QUARTERING SOLDIERS

No soldier shall in time of peace be quartered in any house without the consent of the owner; nor in time of war, but in a manner to be prescribed by law.

ARTICLE IV

OF UNREASONABLE SEARCHES AND SEIZURES

The right of the people to be secure in their persons, houses, papers, and effects, against unreasonable searches and seizures, shall not be violated; and no warrant shall issue but upon probable cause, supported by oath or affirmation, and particularly describing the place to be searched, and the persons or things to be seized.

ARTICLE V

OF CRIME AND INDICTMENTS

No person shall be held to answer for a capital, or otherwise infamous crime, unless on a presentment or indictment of a grand jury, except in cases arising in the land or naval forces, or in the militia, when in actual service in time of war or public danger, nor shall any person be subject, for the same offense to be twice put in jeopardy of life and limb; nor shall be compelled in any criminal case to be witness against himself; nor to be deprived of life, liberty or property, without due process of law, nor shall private property be taken for public use without just compensation.

ARTICLE VI

OF CRIMINAL PROSECUTIONS

In all criminal prosecutions, the accused shall enjoy the right to a speedy and public trial, by an impartial jury of the State and district wherein the crime shall have been committed, which district shall have been previously ascertained by law, and to be informed of the nature and cause of the accusation; to be confronted with the witnesses against him; to have compulsory process for obtaining witnesses in his favor, and to have the assistance of counsel for his defense.

ARTICLE VII

OF TRIAL BY JURY IN CIVIL CASES

In suits at common law, where the value in controversy shall exceed twenty dollars, the right of trial by jury shall be preserved; and no fact tried by a jury shall be otherwise re-examined in any court of the United States, than according to the rules of the common law.

ARTICLE VIII

OF BAILS, FINES AND PUNISHMENTS

Excessive bail shall not be required, nor excessive fines imposed, nor cruel and unusual punishments inflicted.

ARTICLE IX

RESERVED RIGHTS

The enumeration in the Constitution, of certain rights, shall not be construed to deny or disparage others, retained by the people.

ARTICLE X

POWERS NOT DELEGATED RESERVED

The powers not delegated to the United States by the Constitution, nor prohibited by it to the States, are reserved to the States respectively, or to the people.

ARTICLE XXII

LIMITATION ON PRESIDENTIAL TERM

Section I

No person shall be elected to the office of the President more than twice, and no person who has held the office of President, or acted as President, for more than two years of a term to which some other person was elected President shall be elected to the office of the President more than once. But this article shall not apply to any person holding the office of President when this article was proposed by the Congress, and shall not prevent any person who may be holding the office of President, or acting as President, during the term within which this article becomes operative from holding the office of President or acting as President during the remainder of such term.

ARTICLE XIV

CITIZENS AND THEIR RIGHTS

Section I

All persons born or naturalized in the United States, and subject to the jurisdiction thereof, are citizens of the United States, and of the State wherein they reside. No State shall make or enforce any law which shall abridge the privileges or immunities of citizens of the United States. Nor shall any State deprive any person of life, liberty or property without due process of law, nor deny to any person within its jurisdiction the equal protection of the laws.

NOTES

THE SIGN OF THE SLEEPING MAN

A NORTH AMERICAN INTERNATIONAL BOOK

NOTE TO READERS: Additional copies of this book may be obtained, while the supply lasts, directly from the publisher, postpaid.

North American International is a small firm with a name much too big for its present size. It was founded in 1971, and is dedicated to publishing quality books from around the world. If you would like information on other carefully designed, hand-crafted books as they are published, please drop us a letter or postcard. Have patience, however: we work quite slowly, doing all of the design work in our own shops, and publish only a very few books each year. Orders from dealers are welcome. Bulk discounts (available to anyone) begin at five copies of any one title.

NORTH AMERICAN INTERNATIONAL
Publishers of Quality Books from Around the World